Fighting Poverty Together

Fighting Poverty Together

Rethinking Strategies for Business, Governments, and Civil Society to Reduce Poverty

Aneel Karnani

palgrave
macmillan

FIGHTING POVERTY TOGETHER
Copyright © Aneel Karnani, 2011.

First published in 2011 by
PALGRAVE MACMILLAN®
in the United States—a division of St. Martin's Press LLC,
175 Fifth Avenue, New York, NY 10010.

Where this book is distributed in the UK, Europe and the rest of the world,
this is by Palgrave Macmillan, a division of Macmillan Publishers Limited,
registered in England, company number 785998, of Houndmills,
Basingstoke, Hampshire RG21 6XS.

Palgrave Macmillan is the global academic imprint of the above companies
and has companies and representatives throughout the world.

Palgrave® and Macmillan® are registered trademarks in the United States,
the United Kingdom, Europe and other countries.

ISBN: 978–0–230–10587–4

Library of Congress Cataloging-in-Publication Data

Karnani, Aneel.
    Fighting poverty together: rethinking strategies for business,
governments, and civil society to reduce poverty/ Aneel Karnani.
        p. cm.
    ISBN 978–0–230–10587–4
        1. Poverty—Government policy—Developing countries. 2. Job
creation—Developing countries. I. Title.

HC59.72.P6K37 2011
362.5'84091724—dc22   2010043760

A catalogue record of the book is available from the British Library.

Design by Newgen Imaging Systems (P) Ltd., Chennai, India.

First edition: April 2011

10 9 8 7 6 5 4 3 2 1

Printed in the United States of America.

Contents

CHAPTER 1

Fighting Poverty

Despite the tremendous economic growth around the world in the last thirty years, the number of people living in poverty has gone up, except in China. Thus, it seems clear that, while economic growth is necessary for poverty reduction, it is not enough: Prosperity has not "trickled down" to the poor. About two-fifths of the world population can be classified as poor, living on less than $2.00 per day, and about a fifth is considered extremely poor, living on less than $1.25 per day. UNICEF reports that 24,000 children die each day due to poverty, that is about 9 million children a year. The impact of poverty on children is heartbreaking.

Sidebar 1.1   Global Poverty

- 2.6 billion people live on less than $2 per day.
- The poorest 39% of the world's population accounts for 2% of global consumption.
- 1.2 billion people are hungry.
- 1 billon people are illiterate.
- 884 million people have inadequate access to clean water.
- 2.6 billion people lack basic sanitation.
- 1.6 billion people live without electricity.

Sidebar 1.2   The Impact of Poverty on Children

- About half the children in the world live in poverty.
- 9 million children die every year before their fifth birthday due to poverty.
- 4 million newborns die in the first month of life.
- 22 million infants do not get routine immunization.
- 101 million children (more girls than boys) are not attending primary school.
- 148 million children under the age of five are underweight.
- 1.8 million children die of diarrhea every year.
- 2 million children under the age of 15 are living with HIV.
- 150 million children under the age of 14 are engaged in child labor.

Policies and actions directed at reducing global poverty have not been effective, despite the considerable attention and resources such efforts have garnered. Developed countries, international institutions such as the World Bank and United Nations, various aid agencies, and civil society have all contributed trillions of dollars to the fight against poverty. Local governments in less developed countries have contributed even more resources. Academics, consultants, government officials, and many experts have brought intellectual energy to the fight. In September 2000, building upon a decade of major United Nations conferences and summits, world leaders came together at UN headquarters in New York City to adopt the United Nations Millennium Declaration, committing their nations to a new global partnership to reduce extreme poverty and setting out a series of time-bound targets—with a deadline of 2015— that have become known as the Millennium Development Goals (MDGs). While the agreement has galvanized unprecedented efforts, poverty persists on a large scale. Some progress has been achieved, but not enough.

Sidebar 1.3   Millennium Development Goals

Goal 1: Eradicate extreme poverty and hunger
- Halve, between 1990 and 2015, the proportion of people whose income is less than $1 a day.
- Achieve full and productive employment and decent work for all, including women and young people.
- Halve, between 1990 and 2015, the proportion of people who suffer from hunger.

Goal 2: Achieve universal primary education
- Ensure that, by 2015, children everywhere, boys and girls alike, will be able to complete a full course of primary schooling.

Goal 3: Promote gender equality and empower women
- Eliminate gender disparity in primary and secondary education, preferably by 2005, and in all levels of education no later than 2015.

Goal 4: Reduce child mortality
- Reduce by two thirds, between 1990 and 2015, the under-five mortality rate.

Goal 5: Improve maternal health
- Reduce by three quarters the maternal mortality ratio.
- Achieve universal access to reproductive health.

Goal 6: Combat HIV/AIDS, malaria, and other diseases
- Have halted and begun to reverse the spread of HIV/AIDS by 2015.
- Achieve, by 2010, universal access to treatment for HIV/AIDS for all those who need it.
- Have halted and begun to reverse the incidence of malaria and other major diseases by 2015.

Goal 7: Ensure environmental sustainability
- Integrate the principles of sustainable development into country policies and programs, and reverse the loss of environmental resources,
- Reduce biodiversity loss, achieving, by 2010, a significant reduction in the rate of loss.

- Halve, by 2015, the proportion of the population without sustainable access to safe drinking water and basic sanitation.
- By 2020, to have achieved a significant improvement in the lives of at least 100 million slum dwellers.

Goal 8: Develop a global partnership for development

- Address the special needs of least developed countries, landlocked countries and small island developing states.
- Further develop an open, rule-based, predictable, nondiscriminatory trading and financial system.
- Deal comprehensively with developing countries' debt.
- In cooperation with pharmaceutical companies, provide access to affordable essential drugs in developing countries.
- In cooperation with the private sector, make available benefits of new technologies, especially information and communications.

Defining Poverty

Nobel Prize–winning economist Amartya Sen has eloquently argued that development can be seen as a "process of expanding the real freedoms that people enjoy."[1] Conversely, poverty is the lack of those freedoms. Reducing poverty implies expanding the "capabilities of persons to lead the kind of lives they value—and have reason to value." Poverty is a multifaceted phenomenon having three main dimensions. First, poverty is the lack of income and assets needed to attain basic necessities, such as food, shelter, clothing, and fuel. Second, poverty means the lack of access to basic services that directly affect the material welfare of the poor, such as public health, education, safe drinking water, sanitation, infrastructure, and security. Third, poverty means the social, cultural, and political exclusion of its victims, and includes such issues as gender, racial and ethnic discrimination, and a lack of civil rights. These multiple aspects of poverty are intertwined. Sen believes that "economic unfreedom can breed social unfreedom, just as social or political unfreedom can also foster economic unfreedom." He emphasizes that these multiple freedoms are important on their own and do not have to be justified by their effects on the economy or individual income.

Ultimately, poverty cannot be measured only in monetary terms. Nonetheless, it is easy to argue that income is a very important, perhaps the single most important, measure of poverty. In a modern market economy, income enables people to fulfill their basic needs. With improved material conditions, poor people might eventually become less powerless and less vulnerable in their relations with their families, the community, and the state. Moreover, income is relatively easy to measure quantitatively and is thus the starting point for public debate and political action. It is not surprising that income statistics attract the greatest interest and commentary within the development community.

Poverty is therefore most often measured in monetary terms and defined as consumption below a certain benchmark, but such measures are, of course, matters of degree and involve subjective judgments, and there are intense debates about where to draw the poverty line. Richer countries tend to place it at higher consumption levels than do poorer countries. Since 1990, the World Bank has measured poverty by the standards commonly used in low-income countries, which generated the widely accepted "$1 a day" definition of poverty.

To measure global poverty, it is necessary to compare incomes across countries. It is well known that income comparisons based on market exchange rates tend to understate real incomes (or, real purchasing power) in developing countries. Market exchange rates can be expected to eventually equate purchasing power only over internationally traded goods. But there are also nontraded goods, such as services, which are cheaper in countries with lower wages. Purchasing power parity (PPP) rates adjust for this difference, allowing more valid income comparisons, and are therefore used instead of market exchange rates in measuring global poverty.

The poverty line is then converted to local currency using the PPP rates, and the local consumer price indices are then used to adjust for inflation.

People below the "extreme poverty" line of "$1 per day" cannot meet basic needs for survival: nutrition, health care, safe drinking water, sanitation, education, adequate shelter, and clothing.[2] Yet, this definition of extreme poverty is probably too conservative. Another commonly used standard, which is more representative of middle-income countries, is "$2 per day." At this level, basic survival needs are met, though just barely. Both of these measures are widely used in the development economics and public policy fields. The World Bank uses both $1/day and $2/day lines. Virtually all research on poverty uses either one of these two poverty lines or something in between. The MDGs use the $1/day standard.

In 2008, the World Bank significantly revised its poverty measurement, largely because of biases detected in the previous estimates of PPP exchange rates. The old data had underestimated the cost of living in poor countries, and therefore, the extent of poverty. The new global estimates of the numbers of people living in poverty are significantly higher, for some countries dramatically higher, than the previous estimates. The estimated number of people living on less than $1/day in 2005 was revised upward, from 931.3 million to 1,376.7 million worldwide; for China, the estimate was revised from 73.1 million to 207.7 million.

In 2008, the World Bank also updated the international poverty line to $1.25 per day in 2005 prices; this is quite consistent with the definition of poverty underlying the prior $1/day standard. The new line is the average of the poverty lines for the poorest 15 countries in terms of per capita consumption. By way of comparison, India's official poverty line for 2005 was $1.03/day. However, it seems too harsh to base *global* poverty on a standard representative of the 15 poorest countries. Another commonly used poverty line is $2/day, which is the median poverty line found among all developing countries. Many researchers agree that the $2/day criterion is the more realistic one because the $1.25/day standard is too low and results in poverty reduction goals that are not ambitious enough. In a world where many people spend $3 for a cup of coffee, it is unacceptable to set the poverty line at $1.25/day. Many researchers prefer the less harsh $2/day standard.

The Numbers

If we use the $2/day criterion, the number of poor people in the world has remained fairly constant at about 2.5 billion for the last 30 years. Regional trends over the same period, shown in figure 1.1, are even more distressing.[3] The number of poor people has gone up since 1981 in every region of the world except East Asia. The three big pockets of poverty are China, India, and sub-Saharan Africa, which together account for about 75 percent of total global poverty figures. Figure 1.2 shows the poverty trends in these three places over the same time period. Poverty declined dramatically in China, increased significantly in India, and increased dramatically in sub-Saharan Africa. When China is excluded, the number of poor people in the rest of the world increased from 1.6 billion in 1981 to 2.1 billion in 2005.[4] This is unacceptable.

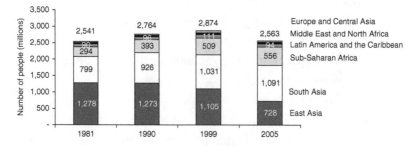

Figure 1.1   Regional trends in poverty
Number of people living on less than $2.00 per day
Source: *PovcalNet* database of the World Bank.

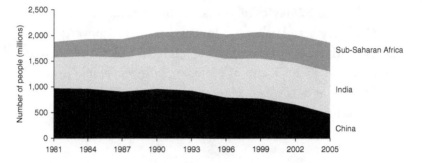

Figure 1.2 Trends in poverty: China, India, and sub-Saharan Africa
Number of people living on less than $2.00 per day
Source: *PovcalNet* database of the World Bank.

The situation is even more deplorable when the definition of poverty is expanded to include indicators besides income. Development experts Sabina Alkire and Marina Santos present new data on multidimensional poverty using household surveys for 104 developing countries.[5] Their Multidimensional Poverty Index (MPI), which "reflects deprivations in very rudimentary services and core human functionings for people," takes into account the following:

1. Health
   - Child mortality: If any child in the family has died
   - Nutrition: If any adult or child in the family is malnourished
2. Education
   - Years of schooling: If no household member has completed five years of schooling
   - Child enrollment: If any school-aged child is out of school in years one to eight
3. Standard of living
   - Electricity: If household does not have electricity
   - Drinking water: If quality does not meet MDG definitions or is more than a 30-minute walk away
   - Sanitation: If it does not meet MDG definitions or the toilet is shared

- Flooring: If the floor is dirt, sand, or dung
- Cooking fuel: If cooking is done with wood, charcoal, or dung
- Assets: If a household does not own more than one of: radio, TV, telephone, bike, motorbike

The data show that while income is an important indicator of poverty, having income above the poverty line is "no guarantee of being non-deprived in core aspects of well-being." Particularly in poor countries, income does not imply access to basic services. "In most countries, more persons are MPI poor than income poor." Thus, estimates of poverty based on income alone tend to under-estimate the extent of real poverty. Poverty is not just a problem, it is a global crisis.

The Fight

If poverty is defined using the $1.25/day criterion, then the pic-ture gets rosier because this lowers the bar. The number of people living on less than $1.25/day fell from 1.9 billion to 1.4 billion over the 1981–2005 period. Simply projecting the current trend forward to 2015 puts the developing world as a whole on track to achieve the MDG of halving the 1990 poverty rate by 2015. However, the developing world outside China is not on track to achieve the MDG for poverty reduction. Using the more humane $2/day target, based on current trends, significant poverty reduc-tion will not be achieved in the foreseeable future. Eradicating poverty in the intermediate future is a desirable goal, but the cur-rent strategies will not accomplish it.

The fight against poverty so far has been, at best, a draw. To win, or to at least make substantial progress, it is necessary to rethink strategies, to analyze which approaches do not work well and which are effective. The objective of this book is to contrib-ute to the analysis of the current approaches, as well as to the rethinking and development of strategies for poverty reduction going forward. Given limited resources—financial, human, and political—indiscriminately pursuing all approaches simultaneously is inefficient and wasteful. There is a need to prioritize and to focus on what works. Besides analyzing the poverty reduction strategies that do not work well and why, this book proposes some that have the potential to work much better. More widespread public debate is clearly needed if we are to achieve greater success in the future.

Moral Imperative

It has been argued, especially by political leaders, that eliminating poverty is essential for reducing war, civil conflict, and terrorism. For example, German chancellor Gerhard Schroder stated, in 2001, "Extreme poverty, growing inequality between countries, but also within countries themselves, are great challenges of our times, because they are a breeding ground for instability and conflict." The UN Millennium Project notes that "poor and hungry societies are much more likely than high-income societies to fall into conflict over scarce vital resources, such as watering holes and arable land...Poverty increases the risks of conflict through multiple paths." Laura D'Andrea Tyson, former chairperson of the Council of Economic Advisors during the Clinton administration, wrote that "we live in a world of unprecedented opulence and remarkable deprivation, a world so interconnected that poverty and despair in a remote region can harbor a network of terrorism dedicated to our destruction."[6] After the terrorist attacks of September 11, 2001, politicians and policy experts were quick to draw an intuitive line connecting poverty and terrorism. From this perspective, poverty is seen primarily as a political challenge.

While this argument is plausible, it is also debatable. There are many other causes of violent conflict, including religious fanaticism, sectarian or ethnic strife, alienation, and perceived humiliation. Empirical research by economist Alberto Abadie explores the connection between poverty and terrorism in depth and finds that the risk of terrorism is not significantly higher for poorer countries once other country-specific characteristics are considered.[7] Some of the world's best-known terrorist groups, such as the Irish Republican Army, the ETA in Spain, the Baader-Meinhof Gang in Germany, Hamas in Israel, Hezbollah in Lebanon, the FARC in Colombia, and the Tamil Tigers in Sri Lanka have neither been rooted in poverty nor had poverty reduction as a goal. Moreover, while global poverty has remained constant or in some cases declined in recent years, terrorist attacks have increased. It is possible that the causality between poverty and conflict runs in both directions. In the end, it is unclear whether poverty directly causes violent conflict.

A different reason to reduce poverty is that it will result in greater global prosperity. Market-based approaches, which are much in vogue these days, emphasize the tremendous "opportunities" for business to serve the needs of the poor. The thinking is that billions of poor people, with an aggregate purchasing power of trillions of dollars, can be the engine for the next round of global trade and prosperity. Serving the world's poor can "generate strong revenues, lead to greater operating efficiencies, and uncover new sources of innovation... building businesses aimed at the bottom of the pyramid promises to provide important competitive advantages as the twenty-first century unfolds."[8] While this is a seductively appealing proposition, it is riddled with fallacies. For, in reality, there is no significant potential for profits in selling to the poor.

The strongest argument for reducing poverty is not that it is a political threat or an economic opportunity, but rather, that it is a moral imperative. Poverty is a violation of absolute standards of social justice. Social justice requires that poor people should receive assistance when they lack the means to live lives that affirm their human dignity. In his Message for the World Day of Prayer for Peace in 1993, Pope John Paul II said that poverty "is a problem which the conscience of humanity cannot ignore, since the conditions in which a great number of people are living are an insult to their innate dignity, and as a result are a threat to the authentic and harmonious progress of the world community." In a world of affluence, even opulence, it is ethically and morally unacceptable that poverty claims the lives of 24,000 children each day, that 28 percent of all children in developing countries are malnourished, and that 1.2 billion people suffer from hunger. It is enraging that there are many more similar depressing statistics.

Moreover, poverty is a trap that cuts across generations. Children born to poor parents tend to grow up to be poor adults, making poverty a vicious intergenerational cycle. The undernourished child whose mother did not get proper prenatal care will grow up to be an adult with stunted mental and physical capabilities. The child who did not go to school will not grow up to be a productive member of the labor force or an entrepreneur. The child who dies of diarrhea will not grow up at all. In 2010, Eppig, Fincher, and Thornhill reported a significant negative relationship between a country's disease burden and the average intelligence of its people, which supports the concept of a "poverty trap."[9] This relationship persists even after controlling for other factors such as income, education, industrialization, and climate. A plausible explanation for the underlying cause of this observed relationship is that the brains of newly born children require 87 percent of children's metabolic energy; in five-year-olds, the figure is still 44 percent; even in adults, the brain consumes 25 percent of the body's energy. Disease saps a person's energy, and the body cannot both fight the disease and develop the brain, especially in early childhood. There is also evidence that certain infections and parasites directly affect cognition. A study of children in Kenya who had survived a cerebral version of malaria suggests that an eighth of them suffered long-term cognitive damage. Eppig, Fincher, and Thornhill believe that the biggest threat is diarrhea, which prevents the absorption of food at a time when the brain is developing rapidly, and is linked to lack of access to clean drinking water.

"The greatest of evils and the worst of crimes is poverty," said George Bernard Shaw. Eradicating poverty is not a means to some other end; it is an end in itself. It is the moral responsibility of all people to fight poverty. The world has the economic capacity to ensure that every human being is lifted out of poverty. Here is a simple, rough calculation to illustrate the magnitude of the response required: Among the 2.56 billion people living on less than $2/day, the average consumption per day is $1.21, according to World Bank data. Raising all poor people to the $2/day standard would require $738 billion at PPP per year—compare this to the size of the global economy: $55 trillion at PPP. This is not an extravagant goal when all it would take is a 1.3 percent shift in global income distribution. There is no excuse for persistent global poverty. As Mahatma Gandhi often said, poverty is the worst form of violence.

Paradigm Shifts

The development community is very large and diverse, consisting of experts in the fields of economics, public administration, business management, and various social sciences, affiliated governments, civil society, or organizations such as the World Bank, International Monetary Fund (IMF), United Nations, aid agencies, think tanks, and universities. There is, of course, no consensus within the development community about the appropriate strategies for poverty reduction. At any point in time, there is, however, a kind of center of gravity, a paradigm that captures, even if only broadly, the views of a large part of the development community. Even as it changes over time, it always involves shifting views on the appropriate roles of markets versus the state in the process of development and poverty reduction. For 30 years, from 1950 to 1980, the development paradigm favored central roles for local governments and the Bretton Woods organizations (IMF and the World Bank). Since 1980, the failure of the state-dominated strategies has led to a decisive swing toward libertarian ideology, which emphasizes the role of free markets and envisions a minimal role for the state.

The diagnosis of the problem was that the developing countries had suffered from too much government and too little of markets. The prescription was for developing countries to implement strict financial discipline, globalize by opening up their markets for trade, create internal markets by deregulating and privatizing, and reduce the size and number of state bureaucracies. The post-1980 development paradigm emphasized free internal and external markets and a minimal role for the state. It was believed that markets could even provide services traditionally in the government domain, such as health care, infrastructure, and education. The dominant policies that resulted from this new thinking came to be known as the Washington Consensus.

The Washington Consensus did not work well either, and disillusionment with those policies has led to a political drift to the populist left in several countries in Latin America, such as Venezuela, Bolivia, and Nicaragua. There also has been much criticism of the Washington Consensus by economists such as Joseph Stiglitz and Ha-Joon Chang.[10]

Traditionally, the discussion of the libertarian approach has been at the macroeconomic level: fiscal and monetary policies, international trade, deregulation, and privatization. Since the 1990s, there has been a significant shift within the libertarian paradigm to the micro level. Three different poverty reduction programs have gained tremendous attention and resources. First, microcredit, pioneered by Muhammad Yunus in Bangladesh in 1976, is based on the underlying premise that granting small loans to the poor will unleash their entrepreneurial energies, and they will then grow thriving businesses and climb out of poverty.[11] The second approach, spearheaded by the Peruvian economist Hernando de Soto, calls for granting formal property rights to the poor.[12] De Soto's underlying premise is that property rights will give the poor greater access to credit, which will lead to poverty reduction (there are obvious parallels between this idea and the microcredit movement). The third approach, popularized by the late C.K. Prahalad as the *base of the pyramid* (BOP) strategies, argues that private companies can help eradicate poverty while earning significant profits by selling to poor people.[13] These three are the latest silver bullets for reducing poverty. In Chapters 2, 3, and 4, I will show that, despite their popularity, none of these three approaches effectively reduces poverty.

The libertarian development paradigm has not worked well, at either the macro or micro levels. Poverty has not declined over the last 30 years. It is time for another paradigm shift that emphasizes the appropriate roles for business and government and a more balanced approach. This is not to advocate a return to the old statist policies that stifled economic growth for decades. Contemporary history clearly demonstrates the central role of markets in generating economic growth. It is impossible to conceive of development and poverty reduction without extensive reliance on markets. But that does not preclude a significant role for the state in providing social support, regulation, and public services to promote social justice. Government must play a major development role.

There are three types of actors involved in tackling the challenge of poverty: private businesses, government, and civil society. (The terms *civil society* and *not-for-profit* are used interchangeably here, to be synonymous with non-profit, NGOs, charitable sector, and citizen sector.) Unfortunately, all three have tended to view each other through the lens of negative stereotypes. Businesses are venal and exploitative, governments are corrupt and inefficient, and civil society is naïve and ineffective. Each actor dismisses the contributions of the other players and minimizes their roles. The challenge each faces is to learn to take a more positive view of the others' involvement: Businesses are efficient, motivated, and have many resources; governments have the power and resources to have a large-scale impact; civil society has passion and energy. The approach taken in this book is ideologically eclectic, and examines the appropriate roles for business, government, and civil society within the context of the specific problem at hand.

Effective Strategy

It is ambitious, and perhaps futile, to try to develop a single holistic theoretical framework or a comprehensive action program to reduce poverty. A problem-solving, pragmatic approach is more likely to be effective than a grand program. This book examines specific problems and proposes targeted interventions, whose efficacy can be supported by conceptual logic and empirical evidence. This approach draws on the distinction that economist William Easterly makes between *planners* and *searchers*.[14] Planners set out a predetermined big goal, and come up with a big plan for reaching it. Searchers' ambitions are more modest; they are on the lookout for favorable opportunities to solve problems—no matter how big or small—whose solution will provide some benefit to the poor. Similarly, the eminent philosopher Karl Popper, in his influential book *The Open Society and Its Enemies,* contrasted two modes of social reform: *utopian social engineering* and *piecemeal social engineering.* Utopian social engineering involves a grand blueprint for society: "it pursues its aim consciously and consistently" and "it determines its means according to this end." Piecemeal social engineering, by contrast, involves tinkering with parts of the system, with no overall plan. The utopian approach is "convincing and attractive" because it appeals to rational thought. Popper, however, argued that it was folly, and that the piecemeal approach is ultimately more effective.

Poor people consistently emphasize the centrality of material opportunities. This implies a focus on two dimensions of poverty: income and access to services such as public health, education, sanitation, infrastructure, and security. This book argues that poverty reduction must also emphasize these two dimensions. First, the best way to raise income is to create employment opportunities for the poor. The private sector is clearly the best engine of job creation; the government can play a useful facilitating role. Second, governments are responsible for providing basic public services. The poor bear a disproportionate share of the burden when governments fail in this responsibility.

The secondary emphasis in poverty reduction should be on the following two issues: BOP modification and government regulation. There is some, even if rather limited potential for firms to earn profits by selling beneficial goods to the poor. The challenge is to creatively find new business models that provide truly beneficial products and services to the poor at prices they can afford. Second, markets often fail, and it is the role of the government to implement appropriate regulation to protect vulnerable consumers, especially the poor.

The book also argues for de-emphasizing two approaches that do not work well: microcredit and the BOP proposition.

Business and government occupy center stage for poverty reduction efforts. Civil society does not have the resources to directly provide products and services to the poor on a large scale. However, civil society has an important role as an advocate and a catalyst for change, and as a watchdog to ensure that the private sector and the government fulfill their responsibilities.

Sidebar 1.4 Effective Strategy for Fighting Poverty

Primary emphasis:
- Create employment opportunities suited to the poor.
- Ensure that the poor have adequate access to public services.

Secondary emphasis:
- Market beneficial goods to the poor at affordable prices.
- Implement appropriate regulations to protect vulnerable consumers.

De-emphasize:
- Microcredit
- The base of the pyramid approach

Pathway for the Future

This book is focused at the micro level and includes many case studies drawn from business, government, and civil society.

Strategies that work, along with those that have not worked, are carefully examined using concepts and theories from economics and business. Applying a pragmatic problem-solving approach, the book proposes strategies that have the potential to work much better.

Chapters 2 through 4 analyze the failure of the libertarian approach. Chapter 2 briefly describes the microcredit movement and assesses the empirical evidence, which leads to the conclusion that microcredit does not significantly reduce poverty. The reasons microcredit has not been more beneficial are also discussed. Chapter 3 analyzes the BOP proposition to show that it is empirically false and logically flawed. The BOP market has proved just too small and not all that attractive. Chapter 4 argues that the BOP proposition is also morally problematic. The romanticized view that the poor are, in the words of C.K. Prahalad, "resilient and creative entrepreneurs and value-conscious consumers," not only results in overemphasis on microcredit and underemphasis on providing meaningful employment opportunities for the poor, but also ignores the clear need for protective legal, regulatory, and social mechanisms and the important role of the state in poverty reduction.

Chapters 5 through 8 develop strategies for poverty reduction that are effective, and outline the appropriate roles for business, government, and civil society. Chapter 5 focuses on how business can satisfy the needs of the poor and simultaneously make a profit. While such opportunities are nowhere as pervasive as the BOP proposition suggests, they occasionally do exist. Guidelines are given that would help to increase these win-win opportunities. Chapter 6 discusses the critical role of employment in poverty reduction, including what government policies are needed to facilitate the growth of business and employment. Chapters 5 and 6 both emphasize the important role that business must play in poverty reduction in both providing beneficial products to the poor and creating employment opportunities. Chapter 7 looks at market failures and the way they produce social inequality. It underscores the reasons government needs to take a strong role in regulation and public services to improve the poors' quality of life. Chapter 8 analyzes the distinct characteristics of the three sectors and focuses on the role of civil society in reducing poverty.

Poverty is a big and complex problem, but it is not unsolvable. It is outrageous that poverty is so pervasive and persistent despite the fact that the problem is solvable. Developing effective strategies to fight it requires analysis of current approaches and new ideas. All of us have a moral responsibility to help eliminate poverty. Moral rage should lead to both private and public action.

PART I

Failure of the Libertarian Approach

CHAPTER 2

Microcredit Misses Its Mark

Since Muhammad Yunus pioneered the concept of microcredit in 1976 and founded the Grameen Bank in Bangladesh, microcredit has become a major movement.[1] The Nobel Peace Prize for 2006 was awarded to the Grameen Bank and its founder, and the Nobel Committee affirmed that microcredit must play "a major part" in eliminating poverty, noting that, "from modest beginnings three decades ago, Yunus has, first and foremost through Grameen Bank, developed microcredit into an ever more important instrument in the fight against poverty." The United Nations designated 2005 as the International Year of Microcredit, and it states on its website, "Currently microentrepreneurs use loans as small as $100 to grow thriving business and, in turn, provide [for] their families, leading to strong and flourishing local economies." Kofi Annan, then Secretary-General of the United Nations, declared that providing microloans to help poor people launch small businesses is a recognition that they "are the solution, not the problem. It is a way to build on their ideas, energy, and vision. It is a way to grow productive enterprises, and so allow communities to prosper."[2] C.K. Prahalad, in his popular book *The Fortune at the Bottom of the Pyramid,* argues that we should recognize the poor as "resilient and creative entrepreneurs," and commends commercial banks, such as ICICI in India, for expanding into microcredit. What makes microfinance such an appealing idea is that it offers "hope to many poor people of improving their own situations through their own efforts," says Stanley Fischer, former chief economist of the World Bank.[3] Microcredit is touted as one of the newest silver bullets for alleviating poverty.

In this book, I use the terms *microfinance* and *microcredit* interchangeably. In the literature, microfinance sometimes also includes other financial services, such as microsavings and microinsurance. However, in practice, microcredit accounts for the bulk of the activities of most microfinance organizations, and thus that is my focus. Microcredit has captured the attention of the development community, the foreign aid industry, government policymakers, journalists, academics, and even the general public. Many books on the subject have been published, with optimistic titles like *Banker to the Poor: Micro-Lending and the Battle Against World Poverty; The Miracles of Barefoot Capitalism; Pathways Out of Poverty; Hands Around the Globe; Back Alley Banking; Defying the Odds; Give Us Credit; The Price of a Dream; Small Loans, Big Dreams; Poverty Capital;* and *A Billion Bootstraps,* to name just a few.

All this enthusiasm has attracted billions of dollars into the microcredit arena. Foreign aid organizations and the World Bank have devoted significant financial capital to microcredit. Wealthy philanthropists, such as financier George Soros, eBay co-founder Pierre Omidyar, and venture capitalist Vinod Khosla, have pledged hundreds of millions of dollars. Global commercial banks, such as Citigroup and Deutsche Bank, have established microfinance funds. When Banco Compartamos, a microcredit bank in Mexico, went public in 2007, it was valued at over $1.5 billion, and its initial public offering was 13 times oversubscribed. Even people with just a few dollars to spare are going to microcredit websites, such as Kiva.org, and with a click of the mouse, lending money to rice farmers in Ecuador and auto mechanics in Togo.

Grameen Bank alone disbursed over $5 billion in microloans over the last ten years, and it now has 7.7 million borrowers. In 2006, about 1,000 microcredit organizations and 300 commercial banks lent $1.3 billion to 17.5 million people in India, says Sanjay Sinha, managing director of the rating agency Micro-Credit Ratings International in India.[4] According to the Microfinance Information Exchange, the 1,395 microfinance institutions (MFIs) that voluntarily reported data had lent $44 billion to 86 million borrowers in 2008.[5] And the total loan amount had been growing at the rate of 34 percent annually for the previous five years. Worldwide, 3,552 microcredit institutions provided loans to 155 million clients, finds the *State of the Microcredit Summit Campaign Report 2009*.[6] This implies that the total amount of microloans worldwide significantly exceeds $44 billion.

This fervor may suggest that microcredit significantly helps the poor. And many proponents make grand claims to this effect, including Yunus, who has said, "We aim to eradicate 50 per cent poverty by 2015 and eliminate it by 2030...the first "museum of poverty eradication" will be established in Bangladesh."[7] Yunus claims that poverty rates in Bangladesh are declining by 2 percent a year thanks to the stellar role played by the Grameen Bank, and that 5 percent of the bank's clients exit poverty annually. Somewhat less extravagantly, but still enthusiastically, the *State of the Microcredit Summit Campaign Report 2006* declared that "microcredit is one of the most powerful tools to address global poverty."

Given the intensity of interest in microcredit, the resources devoted to it, and the claims of success, it is reasonable to ask, How much do the poor really benefit from microcredit? There is surprisingly little evidence that microcredit actually reduces poverty. This, combined with doubts about the underlying logic of microcredit, has led to increasing skepticism about its impact. Besides myself, other prominent critics of microcredit include Thomas Dichter, Vijay Mahajan, Robert Pollin, and Milford

Bateman.[8] The skeptics are becoming increasingly vocal. Recent books to question the success of microfinance include *What's Wrong with Microfinance; Why Doesn't Microfinance Work?: The Destructive Rise of Local Neoliberalism*; and *Confronting Microfinance: Undermining Sustainable Development*. On the whole, microcredit has, at best, a minimal impact on poverty reduction, and in some situations actually works to the detriment of the poor.

Microcredit 101

The microfinance movement addresses a basic yet devastating glitch in the formal banking system: The poor cannot access capital through traditional banks because they do not have the collateral to secure their loans, and banks do not want to take on the risks and costs of making small, uncollaterized loans that typify microcredit. The poor can use the microloans to start or grow a small business and earn income, and thus rise out of poverty. The central objective of the Grameen Bank has been to "reverse the age-old vicious circle of "low income, low savings, and low investment," into virtuous circle of "low income, injection of credit, investment, more income, more savings, more investment, more income."[9] "(Microcredit) is based on the premise that the poor have skills which remain unutilized or underutilized. It is definitely not the lack of skills which make poor people poor....charity is not the answer to poverty. It only helps poverty to continue. Unleashing of energy and creativity in each human being is the answer to poverty."[10]

Microfinanciers have created innovative contractual practices and organizational forms that reduce these risks and costs, such as lending to groups of women, called credit groups, rather than just to one person. Some microcredit organizations provide their clients with more than loans, offering education, training, health care, and other social services. Typically, these organizations are not-for-profit or are owned by customers or investors who are more concerned about the economic and social development of the poor than they are with profits. Among the largest of the social purpose MFIs are Opportunity International, FINCA, ACCION, Oikocredit, and Grameen Bank. In contrast, the commercial banks that make microloans typically provide only financial services. Indonesia's Bank Rakyat, Ecuador's Bank Pichincha, and Brazil's Unibanco all directly target poor customers. Some large commercial banks, such as India's ICICI, do not lend directly to individual microcredit clients, but instead work through small microfinance organizations.

Proponents of microcredit often argue that lending to women not only empowers them, but also has a larger impact on family welfare, and therefore many nonprofit microfinance organizations target women as their primary customers. At Grameen Bank, for example, 97 percent of clients are women, because "women have longer vision [and] want to change their lives much more intensively," says Yunus.[11] He notes that women are more likely to spend the money they earn on their children, for school, and for better food, whereas men are more likely to spend it on alcohol and cigarettes: "When men make money they tend to spend it on themselves, but when women make money they bring benefits to the whole family."[12]

Micro Impact

That financially self-sustaining MFIs can make microloans to poor entrepreneurs, who can then invest these monies to start or grow a business and climb out of poverty seems a win-win proposition—a painless way to reduce poverty. Microcredit proponents often cite case studies and heartwarming anecdotes to prove its value.

This evidence is emotionally appealing and no doubt accounts for the glowing media coverage that microcredit receives. Yet, there have been few credible studies on its actual impact on poverty reduction. Much of the empirical support for positive views of microfinance comes from three well-known studies based on field surveys in Bangladesh in the 1990s. A working paper from the Center for Global Development, published in June 2009, revisits the evidence from all three studies and, after going through a replication exercise, comes to doubt the positive results in each case.[13] In a survey on microcredit, *The Economist* magazine concluded that while "heart-warming case studies abound, rigorous empirical analyses are rare."[14] The Center for Global Development came to a similar conclusion, noting that "there are many stories of the transformational effect of microfinance on individual borrowers but until recently there has been surprisingly little rigorous research that attempts to isolate the impact of microfinance from other factors, or to identify how different approaches to microfinance change outcomes."[15] Advocate Jonathan Morduch, coauthor of a major textbook on microfinance, asserts that economic theory suggests microfinance has benefits, but even he admits that the actual evidence that it helps "is pretty dicey."[16]

One of the more comprehensive studies reaches a surprising conclusion: microloans are more beneficial to borrowers living above the poverty line than to borrowers living below the poverty line.[17] This is because clients with higher income are willing to take risks, such as investing in new technologies that will most likely increase income flows. Poor borrowers, on the other hand, tend to take out conservative loans that protect their subsistence and rarely invest in new technology, fixed capital, or adding employees.

Determining the impact of microcredit on poverty reduction has proved a difficult research problem because the borrowers are self-selected: Most early studies simply compared borrowers with nonborrowers. But borrowers are likely to have more drive, ambition, skills, and entrepreneurial abilities than nonborrowers and may have a found a way to improve their situation even without microcredit by tapping other sources of loans, their social network, and business aptitude. These older studies are thus biased toward overestimating the benefits of microcredit.

That situation may be changing, however. In recent years, a few studies have adopted the randomized control trials methodology to solve the self-selection problem. In this approach, one group of people is randomly assigned to receive a microloan, while another group does not get a loan. Two of these studies found that microcredit does not reduce poverty. The first study, conducted by economists from the Poverty Action Lab at Massachusetts Institute of Technology (MIT), examined microcredit in the slums of Hyderabad, India, and found that it had no impact on overall household spending, a critical measure of financial well-being.[18] The study also found that microcredit had "no impact on health, education or women's decision-making [power]" in the family. The second study, conducted in the Philippines, similarly found that microcredit did not result in higher household incomes.[19] It also found that male borrowers were more likely than female borrowers to increase their small business profits as a result of their loan. Men in the Philippines study also tended to spend their profits on their children's education, which is contrary to the usual claims that it is women who care more for the children.

Microcredit proponents question negative findings like these, arguing that, so far, only these two studies have used randomized control trials (more are needed), and that they in any event measured the impact of microcredit over only 18 months. They further argue that they have "seen the difference" microcredit makes based on their personal experience in the field of talking to many poor borrowers.[20] But even this argument does not stand up to scrutiny. In March 2009, the World Bank and the publisher Palgrave Macmillan copublished *Moving Out of Poverty*, which is to date one of the most thorough field studies of the dynamics of poverty—how people fall into and rise out of poverty— based on narratives from 60,000 poor or formerly poor people in 15 countries in Asia, Africa, and Latin America. An "important insight" from this study is that "the tiny loans usually provided under microcredit schemes do not seem to lift large numbers of people out of poverty."

A few studies have even found that microcredit has a negative impact on poverty: Poor households simply become poorer through the additional burden of debt.[21] Some borrowers get stuck in a debt trap if their income declines because of a health problem, an accident, or some external event. The "vast majority" of those starting below the poverty line "end up with less incremental income after getting a microloan," says Vijay Mahajan, the chief executive of Basix, an Indian rural finance institution. He concludes that microcredit "seems to do more harm than good to the poorest."[22]

Even such a stalwart proponent of neoliberal policies as *The Economist* has concluded that "the few studies that have been done suggest that small loans are beneficial, but not dramatically so."[23] The reality of microcredit is much less attractive than the promise.[24] The 2010 *Report on the World Social Situation,* a flagship publication of the United Nations, makes a compelling case for rethinking poverty and poverty reduction efforts, and comes to a similar conclusion about microcredit. Overall, the empirical evidence suggests that microcredit does not have a significant impact on reducing poverty.

Why Microcredit Does Not Work

Microcredit does not significantly reduce poverty for four major reasons: First, the money from most microcredit loans is spent on consumption rather than invested in business ventures, and therefore cannot result in increased income for the poor. Second, most poor people are not entrepreneurs and lack the skills to succeed at running their own business. Third, the microenterprises funded using microcredit lack economies of scale and have low productivity. Thus, microcredit borrowers earn too little to rise out of poverty. Finally, if the interest rates on microcredit are too high, the borrower might even become poorer rather than wealthier.

Consumption Loans

According to the Grameen Bank website, microcredit is "offered for creating self-employment for income-generating activities and for housing for the poor, as opposed to consumption." The empirical evidence, however, does not support this statement. Between 50 percent and 90 percent of microcredit borrowers use the loans for a nonbusiness purpose, such as repaying another loan, purchasing an appliance, or paying for some other consumption activity. The recent book *Portfolios of the Poor* offers a uniquely detailed picture of the financial lives of the poor.[25] Based on a small sample, only about half the loans made by Grameen Bank have been used for business purposes. More interestingly, less than 15 percent of the borrowers accounted for the bulk of these business loans by taking on multiple loans. Thus, the vast majority of borrowers used microcredit to finance personal consumption. The Hyderabad study cited above found that more than half the loans were used to finance personal consumption, and the authors conclude that these borrowers "may eventually become poorer" because they are "borrowing against the future."

Myth of the Microentrepreneur

The United Nations's declaration that all poor people are microentrepreneurs, who will use their loans to grow thriving businesses, is unrealistic, but the UN is not alone in this belief. Muhammad Yunus asserts, "All poor people are entrepreneurs...Human beings are not slaves so we need not work for someone else as a rule."[26] In reality, most people are just not entrepreneurs, whether they are poor or not.

A microcredit borrower who does use the money for investments is an entrepreneur in the literal sense: She raises the capital, manages the business, and is the residual claimant of the earnings. But, true entrepreneurship is more than that. Entrepreneurship is the engine of Joseph Schumpeter's dynamism of *creative destruction*. An entrepreneur is a person of vision and creativity who converts a new idea into a successful innovation, into a new business model. Some microcredit borrowers are certainly true entrepreneurs, and have created thriving businesses—these are the heartwarming anecdotes. But the vast majority of microcredit borrowers are caught in subsistence activities with no possible prospect of a competitive advantage. The self-employed poor usually have no specialized skills and often practice multiple occupations (such as small farming, livestock rearing, and petty trade).[27] Many of these businesses operate at too small a scale. The median business operated by someone who is poor has no paid staff; most of these businesses have very few assets. With low skills, little capital and no economies of scale, these businesses operate in arenas with low entry barriers and a lot of competition. Because their productivity is low, their meager earning cannot lift their owners out of poverty.

Abraham George, founder of the George Foundation (an NGO engaged in poverty alleviation programs in India), observes that, in rural India, a small number of people, mostly village leaders and their family members, operate the few shops and businesses that exist there.[28] They are the only ones who have the support mechanisms, knowledge, and skills to make a business succeed. A great majority of the poor population is struggling to survive, fearful of losing what little they have, and mostly risk-averse. To expect them to succeed in business is unrealistic. In fact, most microenterprises remain small, and they often fail. A study conducted by The George Foundation in 17 villages and over 50 microcredit programs in South India empirically found that less than 2 percent of microenterprises survive for more than three years. The study concludes that the present form of microcredit, as practiced in India, results in little or no sustainable development benefit for the poor.

This outcome should not be too surprising. Even in developed countries with high levels of education and infrastructure, about 90 percent of the labor force consists of employees rather than entrepreneurs. And, although financial services are more abundant in developed countries, only a small fraction of those populations uses credit for entrepreneurial purposes. In poor countries, most clients of microcredit are microentrepreneurs by necessity rather than by choice, and would gladly take a factory or service job at reasonable wages if one was available. The idea that the poor can be entrepreneurs should not be romanticized. The International Labor Organization (ILO) uses a more appropriate term: *own-account workers*. Most poor people are not entrepreneurs; they are simply self-employed.

The poor by definition have low income. Their plight is exacerbated by the volatility of their income, which is both irregular and unpredictable. One cause of this volatility is that too many poor people are own-account workers in microenterprises rather than holding a salaried job. Growth of microcredit can only make this situation worse.

It is also difficult to argue that capital is the primary constraint that the microentrepreneurs face. The microfinance movement suggests the poor do not have access to credit—this, too, is a myth. The recent book *Portfolios of the Poor* demonstrates that the poor are very active money managers and utilize several financial instruments.[29] In Bangladesh, 88 percent of all borrowing deals were from informal sources, such as friends, relatives, moneylenders, and savings and loan clubs. And this is in Bangladesh where most poor families have access to microcredit given the deep penetration by MFIs. Maybe the problem is that the microenterprises suffer from other constraints such as lack of skills, linkages to markets for outputs and inputs, and basic infrastructure. In the absence of these other enabling factors, microcredit by itself will not have a significant impact on the income of the poor.

Bigger Is Better

Microfinance proponents also ignore the crucial role of economies of scale. Abundant research confirms that there is a positive relationship between the size of a company and its productivity. Evidence from India, for example, shows that labor productivity increases significantly with the size of the manufacturing establishment (see table 2.1).[30] This problem is particularly acute for microenterprises, most of which have no paid employees. A study of microenterprises in Kenya found that only 26 percent of these owners earned an income above the minimum wage.[31]

Microfinance is very closely identified with the promotion of enterprises overwhelmingly below a minimum efficient scale, which could lead to long-term problems in economic development.[32] Microfinance produces an oversupply of inefficient microenterprises that undermines the development of more efficient small and medium enterprises (SMEs). For example, microenterprises forced into drastic cost-cutting strategies to survive routinely, but temporarily, take crucial market share away from local SMEs that might otherwise be able to reduce unit costs and register meaningful productivity growth. China, Vietnam, and South Korea have significantly reduced poverty in recent years with very little microfinance activity. On the other hand, Bangladesh, Bolivia, and Indonesia have been havens for microcredit, and have been far less successful at reducing poverty. Bangladesh "has, in fact, made some economic progress in recent years, most notably through the growth of an export-oriented garment industry. Although the few thousand firms in the industry are smaller and less efficient than their Chinese counterparts, they are larger and more productive than individual craftsmen, microfinanced or not."[33]

The ready-made garment industry in Bangladesh has grown significantly in the last couple of decades and has become a prominent part of the economy. Clothing exports from Bangladesh reached $9.2 billion in 2007, accounting for 76 percent of the country's foreign exchange; the industry employed 2.2 million people, 80 percent of whom were women.[34] Although there has been controversy over the working conditions in garment factories, it is clear that the industry has contributed to foreign exchange earnings, employment creation, poverty alleviation, and the empowerment of women.[35] It is midsized entrepreneurial

Table 2.1 Distribution of firms by size in India

	Own–account	Small–size firm	Medium–size firm	Large firm, formal sector
Average of total workers in establishment	1.7	3.2	10.0	63.9
Employment as % of all manufacturing employment	55.9	12.4	14.4	17.3
Average of hired workers in establishment	0	1.8	7.8	60.9
Value added as % of all manufacturing value added	10.3	6.8	8.9	84.3
Labor productivity index (Formal = 100)	4.2	11.3	12.7	100

Source: Dipak Mazumdar. The Employment Problem in India and the Phenomenon of the Missing Middle. Working Paper, University of Toronto, 2010.

companies, not microenterprises, that have led to the growth of this industry. According to a World Bank study, firms with fewer than 100 employees are not considered to be competitive given the market conditions.[36] Manufacturing firms with 200 to 500 workers are considered to be the most suitable size by the owners and account for the majority of the industry output.

Rather than lending two hundred dollars to 500 women so that each can buy a sewing machine and set up a microenterprise manufacturing garments, it is much better to lend $100,000 to a true entrepreneur with managerial capabilities and business acumen and help her establish a garment manufacturing business employing 500 people. This business could exploit economies of scale, deploy specialized assets, and use modern business processes to generate value for both its owners and employees.

Proponents of microcredit often respond to the above argument by asking why not invest in both microenterprises and larger enterprises. The answer is that we should prioritize and make the best use of scarce resources. The limited supply of capital can be better deployed in businesses larger than microenterprises. It is also possible that the hype surrounding microenterprises might distract governments in impoverished countries from undertaking the necessary reforms to foster true entrepreneurship and larger enterprises. "Governments in fragile states have only so much political capital and capacity. So it is crucial to proceed in a disciplined sequence."[37] Governments need to prioritize and focus on development approaches with a higher payoff.

High Interest Rates

Microcredit interest rates are often in the range of 30 percent to 60 percent per year, and can sometimes be as high as 100 percent or even more. Microcredit proponents argue that these rates, although high, are still well below those charged by informal moneylenders. But if poor borrowers do not earn a greater return on their investment than they owe in interest, they will become poorer as a result of microcredit, not wealthier. Jonathan Morduch, an advocate of microfinance, makes an important acknowledgement: "The microfinance movement rests largely on one basic assertion: that poor households have high economic returns to capital."[38] As discussed above, the bulk of microcredit is used to finance personal consumption, and the return to capital is zero, aside from the benefit of instant gratification. Even if we consider only the loans that are used to invest in businesses, the results are not promising.

Unfortunately, not much of the published research focuses on the return to capital for microenterprises. Morduch reports some recent findings of high returns to capital ranging from 20 percent to 33 percent per month, and as high as 70 percent per month for financially constrained businesses. However, as Morduch admits, these findings have their own limitations. First, there is the problem of self-selection noted earlier: Entrepreneurs with better access to capital might be more skilled, more entrepreneurial, and less risk-averse. Second, and more importantly, it is unclear how these studies take into account the imputed cost of labor. It is difficult to separate the return to capital from the wages the borrower could have earned if he/she had a job. If the opportunity cost of labor is accounted for properly, these supposedly high returns to capital will likely vanish.

Most microenterprises just are not that profitable. Most microenterprises are very simple businesses operating in an environment with low entry barriers. This problem is compounded by MFIs financing a constant stream of new entrants leading to market saturation and hyper-competition. This results in very low and declining profitability for all microenterprises to below the cost of borrowing, especially if interest rates are high.

Potential Benefits of Microcredit

If microcredit does not significantly reduce poverty, does it at least have some corollary benefits? Helping the poor better manage their poverty may be one useful function of microcredit. Because of their volatile income, the poor go through frequent cycles of feast and famine. Microcredit helps the poor smooth consumption over periods of cyclical fluctuations and unexpected crisis, and thus reduces their vulnerability.[39]

Even in this regard, there is a problem. Given the high interest rates attached to microcredit loans and vigorous debt collection practices, it is not only a very expensive way to smooth consumption, but it also increases the risk that the poor will fall into a debt trap if monthly payments cannot be met. The poor would be much better off accumulating savings to achieve that goal. Consider a person who borrows $100 at 50 percent annual interest rate to finance consumption, and repays the loan by making equal monthly payments over the next year. If he had put the same monthly payments into a zero interest savings account for 9.3 months, he would receive the same $100. In other words, if he is willing to delay his consumption by 9.3 months, he can save 23 percent (= 2.7/12) of his total payments. Think of 9.3 months as the "break-even period" for a loan at a 50 percent interest rate for one year. Figure 2.1 plots the breakeven period for different interest rates. If the savings account paid an interest rate, then the break-even period would

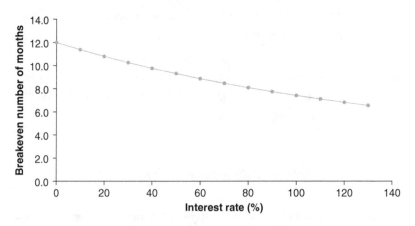

Figure 2.1   Break-even period for a 12-month loan

be even shorter. Not only is microcredit merely a palliative for poverty, it is an expensive palliative.

Empowering Women

Microcredit organizations have primarily targeted women as their clients arguing that it helps to empower women. Research shows that microcredit often yields noneconomic benefits, such as increasing self-esteem and social cohesion, and female empowerment.[40] Microcredit enables women to contribute to the household income, increasing their intrahousehold bargaining power by moving them from positions of marginalization within the household decision-making process and exclusion within the community, to greater centrality, inclusion, and voice. The social processes of microcredit lead to strengthening the personal and social dimensions of women's empowerment. This outcome increases their self-esteem and self-worth and induces a greater sense of awareness of social and political issues, which can increase their mobility and reduce their seclusion.

However, some empirical evidence suggests that microcredit does not necessarily result in increased empowerment for women. As mentioned earlier, the two rigorous empirical studies using the randomized control trials methodology did not find evidence to support the view that microcredit enhances women's empowerment and family welfare. Credit by itself cannot overcome patriarchal systems of control within the household and at the community level. Women's control, or lack of it, over financial resources is probably a key factor in explaining these mixed results. It seems that a significant fraction of women, despite having *access* to credit, do not have *control* over the loan money or the income generated from the microenterprises.[41] Loans made to women often get passed on to the male breadwinners in their families, especially in India and Pakistan, according to Sarita Gupta, vice-president with Women's World Banking, which works with

40 MFIs and banks in 28 countries to bring financial services and information to poor women.[42]

Regulate Microcredit

Microcredit is often cited as a good example of the BOP proposition, and in the past few years, hundreds of for-profit companies have begun financing and marketing loans to the poor in developing countries. In an ironic twist on the BOP proposition, private companies are indeed making a fortune in microcredit—by exploiting the poor! "Now poor people are turning into one of the world's least likely sources of untapped profit, primarily because they will pay interest rates most Americans would consider outrageous, if not usurious."[43] MFTransparency, a new U.S.-based self-monitoring industry association, states that private companies have been attracted to microcredit "by near-monopoly lending environments and misleading pricing systems compounded by borrower's frequent lack of understanding of the financial details of credit transactions."[44]

Whether fair or not, recently a few high profile events have galvanized criticism of the microcredit industry. When Banco Compartamos in Mexico went public in April 2007, the initial investors' stake of $6 million was valued at $1.5 billion—a return of roughly 100 percent a year compounded over eight years. This profitability is due to the fact that Compartamos charges interest rates that exceed 100 percent per year on their loans to the poor. Yunus was particularly critical of Compartamos and said, "Microcredit was created to fight the money lender, not to become the money lender."[45]

A popular debtors' rebellion in Nicaragua—the "No Pago" (I Won't Pay) movement—has spurred mass demonstrations protesting high interest rates and demanding that a legal ceiling be placed on them. Government authorities in the Indian state of Andhra Pradesh closed down 50 branches of two major MFIs and charged them with exploiting the poor by charging usurious interest rates and intimidating them with forced loan recovery practices. The states chief minister, the late Y.S. Rajasekhara Reddy said that "MFIs were turning out to be worse than money-lenders by charging interest rates in excess of 20 per cent."[46] There has been growing criticism of MFIs by government officials and politicians in many countries including Bangladesh, Cambodia, India, Pakistan, and Sri Lanka.[47] Sheikh Hasina Wajed, prime minister of Bangladesh, has said that "[microlenders] are sucking blood from the poor in the name of poverty alleviation."[48]

Based on data from 555 sustainable MFIs (defined as ones that have positive return on assets) in 2006, a paper by Consultative Group to Assist the Poor (CGAP), a consortium of development agencies and private foundations dedicated to promoting micro-credit, shows that the median interest rate is 28 percent per year.[49] Even this number is understated because it does not include the impact of compulsory savings, which increases the effective cost of the loan to the borrower. Muhammad Yunus argues that if the microcredit interest rate is more than 15 percent above the cost of funds, then it is "too high.... You are moving into the loan shark zone."[50] Generously allowing 10 percent for cost of funds implies that more than half of MFIs charge interest rates that Yunus would consider too high. In sub-Saharan Africa and Latin America, 5 percent of MFIs charge interest rates above 70 percent; for the world, 5 percent of MFIs charge interest rates above 50 percent per year. While Compartamos charging interest rates exceeding 100 percent might be exceptional, interest rates exceeding 50 percent are certainly not rare.

Deny the Problem

One response of the microcredit industry to the mounting criticism has been to deny that there is a problem. In an open letter to address their critics, Carlos Danel and Carlos Labarthe, the co-founders of Compartamos, argue that "in an open and free market, we are convinced our clients are in the best position to make the right choices for themselves and their families."[51] The first problem with this assumption is that the marketplace for microcredit organizations is not competitive, turning some MFIs into quasi-monopolies. CGAP states: "In most countries, the microcredit market is still immature, with low penetration of the potential clientele by MFIs and little competition so far."[52] Nimal Fernando, a microfinance specialist working for the Asian Development Bank concurs: "In many countries in the region [Asia], the majority of microcredit is provided by a few leading institutions, and competition among them is mostly on non-price terms."[53]

In their open letter, Danel and Labarthe essentially conceded that microcredit is not a competitive market when they justified the high interest rates and high profitability on the grounds that they "wanted to build an industry,... to draw in investors and competition." The promise is that "competition will make for more and better products at better prices in the future." So, the monopolists exploiting the poor today are doing a service for the consumers of tomorrow! This is a rather disingenuous defense: Exploitation today will draw in competition in the future that will then reduce exploitation. By this logic, we should be grateful to the loan sharks of the last few centuries for charging usurious interest rates that have now attracted microcredit organizations into the market.

An even greater problem with the free-market defense is the assumption that microcredit borrowers are rational economic actors and thus "in the best position to make the right choices." Even in the United States, where there are already many laws to protect consumers of financial services, there is now a strong trend toward increasing consumer protection. The Credit Card Accountability Responsibility and Disclosure Act of 2009 is a recent example of this trend. The Obama administration, in July 2010, created a new independent agency—the Consumer Financial Protection Bureau—with broad authority to protect financial services consumers from abusive, deceptive, and unfair practices. The Obama administration justified regulatory reform on the grounds that "financial products are complex, and it is often difficult for even the most financially astute consumers to recognize the risks financial products can present."[54] Michael Barr, the assistant secretary of the U.S. Department of the Treasury, has said: "It isn't enough to provide consumers with more disclosure and more information, since people often get overwhelmed and make mistakes."[55] And, if financial literacy is a problem in the United States, it is a much bigger problem for microcredit borrowers in poor countries, where the poor are often illiterate and innumerate. The adult illiteracy rate in India is 34 percent, and clearly much higher among the poor, especially among women, who not only are the primary microcredit borrowers but also have an even higher illiteracy rate due to the unfortunate sexist biases that are pervasive throughout the country.[56]

There have been very few empirical studies on financial literacy, especially in developing countries, and those that have been done suggest that levels of financial literacy are low across the world, even in developed countries. A survey of the clients of two microfinance organizations in India finds, not surprisingly, that the great majority of respondents did not know the interest rates on their loans (this is also partly due to lack of transparency).[57] Arithmetic ability is the foundation of financial literacy. The survey also found that only 17 percent of respondents were able to solve the arithmetic problem, "divide 8000 by 10," and only 3 percent got the correct answer when asked to "multiply 4500 by 18." Given such low levels of numeracy, it is difficult to see how microcredit borrowers are able to make good financial choices, such as comparing two loans with different terms.

In a less extreme response than outright denial, the microcredit industry has tried to downplay the problem of consumer exploitation. The CGAP argues: "It is a mistake to assume that Compartamos' interest rates are typical of the industry, or even a substantial part of the industry."[58] Clearly, we should not wait until exploitation has become pervasive before implementing consumer protection regulation. There are laws against stealing, even though most people are not thieves. Similarly, in developed countries, there are laws regulating the loan recovery process, even though abusive practices are not widespread. Moreover, high interest rates are not nearly as rare as the CGAP implies. By their own analysis, 5 percent of microcredit loans worldwide carry interest rates higher than 50 percent per year; and this does not take into account fees and compulsory savings, which would significantly increase the effective interest rates.

The potential for consumer exploitation in the microcredit industry is a direct result of market failure resulting from two underlying causes. First, the lack of significant competition in any given geographic area increases the market power of the MFIs that do operate there, allowing them to charge such exorbitant interest rates. Second, the undereducated, ill-informed poor are a particularly vulnerable market segment. The microcredit industry needs to be regulated to protect the poor borrowers, focusing on three issues: lack of transparency, high interest rates, and abusive loan recovery practices.

Lack of Transparency

At a Microcredit Summit Campaign conference in July 2008, a new self-monitoring organization, MFTransparency, was launched to be the industry's watchdog; since then, 183 industry leaders have endorsed the organization.[59] The MFTransparency website states "due to complications of market conditions and lack of regulation, the true price of our loan products has never been accurately measured or reported." Chuck Waterfield, founder of MFTransparency, says that "this is hard to imagine and even harder to explain."[60] Their viewpoint of the causes of lack of transparency—"complications of market conditions"—seems to be a euphemism for market failure, which is consistent with the argument above.

Complicating things further, the effective interest rate that a borrower pays for microcredit is very different from the interest rate stated in the loan agreement. Microcredit organizations routinely hide the actual interest cost by using "creative" practices; these include (1) calculating interest throughout the repayment period on the original value of the loan rather than on the declining balance; (2) charging the borrower up-front fees, such as a security deposit (which is deducted from the principal of the loan); (3) compulsory savings (collected with loan installments); and (4) charging an insurance premium. These hidden charges commonly bring the effective annual interest rate up over 100 percent even though the stated interest rate is only 15 percent. Finance professor Subrata Mitra has calculated the effective interest rate for an actual product of an Indian MFI when the terms of the loan are the following:[61]

- Loan amount: Rs. 1,000
- Interest rate: 17.5 percent per year, flat
- Repayment in 47 weekly installments
- Interest for one year = 17.5 percent of 1,000 = Rs. 175. Total repayment = 1000+175 = Rs. 1,175. Weekly payment = 1,175/47 = Rs. 25
- Security deposit equaling 10 percent of the total amount of the loan is deducted upfront, and refunded with 5 percent interest at the end of the year.
- Savings: Borrower must deposit Rs. 10 per week and can withdraw after one year with 5 percent interest.
- Insurance premium of 2 percent is charged, and deducted upfront from the loan amount.

Based on these terms, the effective annualized interest rate is 121 percent even though the stated interest rate is only 17.5 percent. Given the low levels of numeracy and literacy in India, let alone financial literacy, it is impossible for microcredit borrowers to compare loan products that may each have a plethora of confusing terms.

Chuck Waterfield cites a similar example from Mexico's Banco Compartamos, which advertises interest rates of 4 percent per month.[62] But the actual effective interest rate on this particular loan was 129 percent per year. So, what explains the difference? Compartamos calculates the interest on the original loan amount rather than on the declining balance, and charges the interest every four weeks rather than every month. And the Compartamos client is required to "save" 10 percent of the loan amount. Of course, the term "save" is a euphemism: The client cannot access these savings until she has fully repaid the loan and receives no interest on these savings. Finally, there is a value-added tax of 15 percent required by Mexican law. Despite all this, Compartamos tells its clients that loans are charged an interest rate of 4 percent per month, which might sound reasonable to a client who does not understand all the terms and conditions.

Portfolios of the Poor applauds MFIs for charging up-front fees as a good way to reduce risk.[63] In fact, although these loans are meant to reduce poverty, they are structured in such a way as to increase the MFI's profits, with provisions that are not good for the poor. For example, the poor clearly need savings options, but bundling savings together with microcredit in a nontransparent manner is not good for the poor. If, in the Indian example above, the security deposit was 20 percent instead of 10 percent, the effective interest rate would jump from 121 percent to 194 percent per year. Either way, such terms exploit the poor.

An essential condition for an open and free market is the ability to compare competing products, which requires pricing transparency. Government regulation is needed that mandates microcredit organizations to explicitly state the effective interest rate calculated using a standard and prescribed approach, and to describe all the loan terms in simple language.

Unreasonable Interest Rates

The CGAP argues: "It is fair to criticize an MFI's interest rates as unreasonable only if its profits or some controllable element of its costs is unreasonable."[64] In fact, many MFIs are very profitable. In the CGAP study, MFIs earned a 2.1 percent return on assets annually, which is well above the 1.4 percent earned by banks in the same countries. MFIs are usually not as highly leveraged as banks, which lowers their return on equity. Despite this, 10 percent of worldwide microcredit loans earned return on equity above 35 percent in 2006. These are high profits by any business criteria. The CGAP study concludes that MFI profits are high because "the microcredit market is still immature, with low penetration of the potential clientele by MFIs and little competition so far." Monopoly rents and vulnerable consumers are the cause of high prices and profits in the microcredit industry.

The industry response is that the high interest rates are not due to high profits, they are due to high costs. Due to fixed costs in servicing a loan, it is proportionally more expensive to service a microloan than a larger loan. Moreover, the poor infrastructure in developing countries leads to high costs as well. However, this argument is not consistent with the empirical evidence. Chuck Waterfield analyzed 22 MFIs in Mexico (thus holding the infrastructure environment constant) and showed "a very wide range of prices (from 38 percent to 90 percent) within a similarly sized loan product."[65] Analysis of 48 MFIs in the Philippines and 31 MFIs in Ecuador yielded similar results. Using data from the Microfinance Information Exchange, figure 2.2 shows the

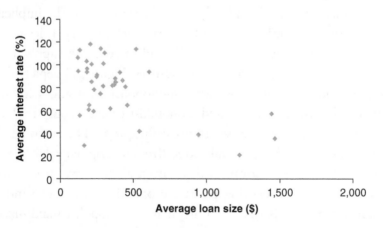

Figure 2.2 Wide range of interest rates
Source: Microfinance Information Exchange.

average interest rate charged and the average loan size for 40 MFIs in Mexico in 2008. For MFIs with an average loan size in the $160-$210 range, the interest rates ranged from 29 percent to 118 percent. Since this analysis holds the loan size and environment constant, the price differential is likely due to local monopoly power which leads to high profits. Costs measured by operating expenses as a percentage of a loan portfolio also vary widely—from 25 percent to 55 percent—for Philippine MFIs with similarly sized loan products. Once again, since the analysis controls for loan size and the environment, the cost differential is likely due to some MFIs having unreasonably high controllable costs. In Bangladesh, the state-backed wholesale funder of microfinance publicly voiced concerns about poor borrowers having to pay high interest rates because of inefficient MFI operations.[66] In a competitive industry, such wide differentials in costs and prices would not persist, and firms with inefficient operations and high prices would be penalized. This is further evidence that microcredit is a monopolistic industry, and supports the position that regulated interest rate caps are needed.

Nimal Fernando of the Asian Development Bank argues that interest-rate ceilings will reduce the availability of microcredit.[67] The CGAP concurs that interest-rate ceilings "often hurt rather than protect the most vulnerable by shrinking poor people's access to financial services."[68] The flaw in this argument is the implicit assumption that microcredit is a competitive industry. Price controls in a competitive industry will lead to reducing supply, but that is not true in a monopolistic industry. Figure 2.3 depicts the supply and demand curves for a monopolist with and without price controls. An unregulated monopolist produces output y^* at price p^*. Regulation imposes a price ceiling at p_0. The outcome of the regulation is that price falls to p_0 (from its original value at p^*) and output increases from y^* to y_0. Even at this lower price, the monopolist is still earning positive economic profits. The intuition behind this is that the unregulated monopolist maximizes profit by restricting output (as compared to a competitive market) and charging high prices. The regulated monopolist increases

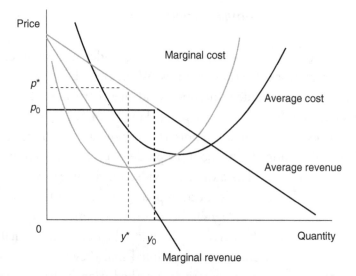

Price

p^*

p_0

Marginal cost

Average cost

Average revenue

0

y^* y_0

Quantity

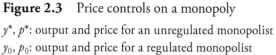

Marginal revenue

Figure 2.3   Price controls on a monopoly

y^*, p^*: output and price for an unregulated monopolist
y_0, p_0: output and price for a regulated monopolist

output (as compared to the unregulated monopolist) and charges the maximum price allowed by regulation (so long as the price is above the marginal cost). Setting an appropriate interest-rate ceiling will actually expand the availability of microcredit given the current monopolistic nature of the industry. This should not be difficult since the gap between the competitive price and the monopoly price prevailing today is so large.

The CGAP paper also argues that interest ceilings can "lead to less transparency about the cost of credit, as lenders cope with interest rate caps by adding confusing fees to their services." This hardly seems possible, since the industry already exhibits no transparency and adds many confusing fees even in the absence of interest rate ceilings. Moreover, as argued above, the industry should also be regulated with regard to pricing transparency.

The microcredit industry is characterized by too little competition and vulnerable consumers. There is enough empirical evidence that a significant fraction of the microcredit industry earns very high profits or has unreasonably high costs to warrant interest rate regulation.

Abusive Loan Recovery

The microcredit industry is also coming under increasing criticism for its debt collection practices. While there is no systematic evidence, there is much anecdotal evidence that some MFIs use coercion to enforce loan repayment. France 24 (an international news television channel) reporters in Bangladesh found that microcredit plunged some poor people deeper into debt. The website for France 24 offers a dramatic video on the negative aspects of Grameen Bank's debt collection practices.[69] In Kalihati, one of the first Bangladeshi villages to benefit from Grameen's low-interest credit scheme, the villagers who had taken loans were unable to reimburse their creditors and claimed that they were harassed by Grameen Bank representatives. Korshed Alom, a former debt collector, was put into early retirement for questioning Grameen Bank's methods: "Their technique is to scare borrowers and insult them. We tell them to sell their clothes, that they have no other choice. I'm not proud of myself, but several times, I had even been obliged to say 'sell your children.'"[70]

Some MFIs in Andhra Pradesh, India were charged with intimidating borrowers with forced loan recovery practices. A 2008 article in the *Wall Street Journal* noted: "As consumer lending soars to record levels, India's banks face mounting criticism and government sanctions for their aggressive loan recovery tactics, which sometimes include using hired thugs."[71] One delinquent borrower was violently beaten by a thug working for a collection agency on behalf of ICICI Bank. The Delhi Consumer Commission fined ICICI Bank for what the judge called "the grossest kind of deficiency in service and unfair trade practice." In Mexico, clients of Azteca who slip behind on repayment "receive frequent visits from motorcycle riding collection agents. Default rates are minimal."[72] Many microcredit practices rely on group liability. Sometimes the coercive practices are undertaken by the group members, not the MFI. Anecdotal evidence includes "group members removing defaulter's nose ring and anklets or damaging her house until the member repaid."[73] There is at least some intimidation in the loan recovery process even though it is not approved by the top management of the MFIs.

Exploitation can occur even when coercive loan recovery practices are not used; all that is needed is for the borrower to believe a priori that coercion will be used. A survey of clients of two microfinance organizations in India found that 53 percent of respondents believed "it is alright" for an MFI to confiscate assets such as cows, house, land, and machinery if the borrower is unable to repay the loan.[74] This is particularly disturbing since the crux of microfinance is uncollateralized lending. The survey results do not imply that assets are in fact confiscated by the MFI in the event of default. But, the borrower's belief, even if mistaken, acts as an effective deterrent to default. The threat of confiscation (or any other threat), even an empty threat, is intimidating and abusive.

This is not to suggest that most MFIs use unethical debt collection practices. Rather, there is potential for exploitation, and some microcredit organizations do exploit the poor. The microcredit borrowers are vulnerable and typically ill informed about their rights as borrowers. There is need for regulation to protect consumers from coercive loan recovery practices and greater transparency on borrowers' rights.

Alternatives to Regulation: Too Little, Too Late

Many industry participants acknowledge the problems of consumer exploitation but do not like regulation as the solution. They plead with microcredit organizations to act more ethically, or argue that the industry should self-regulate. These responses are at best naïvely optimistic and will not work.

Jonathan Lewis, founder of MicroCredit Enterprises, in an article suggestively titled "Microloan Sharks," recognizes "the power of the marketplace to exploit the poor" and focuses on the problems of high interest rates and lack of transparency.[75] Lewis appeals to microcredit organizations to "act ethically and in accordance with our values." However, commercial organizations given opportunities for increasing profits usually act in their own self-interest. In a survey on corporate social responsibility (CSR), *The Economist* magazine concluded that for most public companies, "CSR is little more than a cosmetic treatment."[76] Appeals for self-restraint on the grounds of ethics and values have not been effective in the business world, and there is no reason to believe commercial microcredit organizations will be any different.

An appeal on ethical grounds is complicated by evidence that industry participants do not agree on a common set of values. In April 2008, a group of microfinance leaders signed the Pocantico Declaration in an attempt to develop a common ground and a set of principles.[77] Unfortunately, it is full of vague statements and platitudes with no consensus on specific issues; in fact, it includes an explicit disclaimer, when it states that "we also recognize that we hold diverse views about the appropriate levels and usage of profit."

Self-regulation is a much-discussed topic within the microcredit industry; for example, Alex Counts, CEO of the Grameen Foundation, proposes a third-party certification scheme.[78] The major drawback is that there is no authoritative body to ensure compliance. For example, 37 microfinance organizations have formed the association Microfinance Network and signed the Pro-Consumer Pledge, which includes a clause that "members will price their services at fair rates. Their rates will not provide excessive profits, but will be sufficient to ensure that the businesses can survive and grow to reach more people."[79] Compartamos is a member of this group. Apparently, all rates are "fair" and no profits are "excessive"!

On a larger scale, the American experiment with self-regulation of the financial services industry has been a failure, and the United States is on a path toward greater government regulation. There is little reason to believe that self-regulation will succeed in the context of the microcredit industry in developing countries facing much less competition, less scrutiny, and more vulnerable consumers. In 2004, South Africa switched from the Micro Finance Regulatory Council, which adopted a self-regulatory approach, to the National Credit Regulator, which is a classic public sector regulator.[80]

Government regulation is the best way to protect microcredit borrowers. Muhammad Yunus, the founder of Grameen Bank, agrees with the need for regulation and said: "The Bangladesh government has created a microcredit authority based on our suggestions."[81] In 2009, the Microcredit Regulatory Agency in Bangladesh announced that MFIs will have to limit the interest rate they charge to clients to 30 percent.[82] Similarly, a 2004 presidential decree in Bolivia imposed interest rate ceilings on small loans. And in Nicaragua, the "No Pago" movement scored a major victory in October 2009 when legislators recommended a bill capping interest rates at 12 percent and giving debtors up to five years to repay loans. The government in each country needs to determine the appropriate interest rate ceiling for microcredit such that it is high enough to cover operating costs and reasonable profits, and not so low as to stifle the development of the industry, nor so high as to be exploitative of the poor. About 40 developing countries impose ceilings on interest rates.[83]

While regulating microcredit to protect the borrowers is needed, there is simultaneously a role for other mechanisms to constrain the behavior of MFIs. One example is industry self-regulation as a useful supplement to legal regulation. Another example would be for international donor organizations, such as the World Bank and USAID to pressure their MFI clients to reduce or prevent exploitation of the poor. Large commercial banks that are wholesale lenders to MFIs should exercise their social responsibility and pressure their MFI clients to also behave responsibly. Civil society can also play a large role in shining the light on MFIs that behave inappropriately and in educating microcredit borrowers about their rights. But, none of these mechanisms are sufficiently effective without the foundation of regulation, which is the responsibility of the government in each country. However, international organizations such as the World Bank surely can help governments by drafting appropriate regulations and transferring knowledge of best practices, especially in building up enforcement capacity.

Formal Property Rights

Another popular approach to reducing poverty, which has significant parallels with the microcredit movement, focuses on formalizing property rights. The obvious and strong link between poverty and lack of property has often led to calls for land reforms to transfer land from large landlords to the landless. The most popular advocate of this approach is the Peruvian economist Hernando de Soto, who has argued for granting a land title to the landless laborers and urban slum dwellers.[84] De Soto, the founder and president of the Institute for Liberty and Democracy (ILD), a think tank in Peru, has attracted many supporters and won many awards. De Soto focuses on the huge informal economy that operates outside the legal system in all countries, particularly in the developing world.

In the extralegal economy, the poor accumulate assets in their shanty homes and small businesses, but because they have no legal protections, they cannot access credit against these assets. De Soto advocates unlocking this "dead capital" by giving formal property rights to the poor. Several countries in Latin America and Africa, including Peru, Mexico, Colombia, and South Africa, have attempted to formalize land titles following de Soto's argument. Unfortunately, there have been no positive results.[85]

Instead, there has been much controversy around the problems and mechanisms for granting individual land titles, and the social and cultural issues surrounding property. De Soto has pointed out that his critics mistakenly claim that he advocates that land titling by itself is sufficient for effective development. A brochure from ILD argues for governments to establish the legal identities of all their people, "their assets, their business records and their transactions in such a way they can unleash their economic potential." The assumption is that property rights will lead to access to credit, which in turn will lead to poverty reduction. But, de Soto has offered little empirical evidence that formalizing property rights actually leads to greater credit access. Economists have disputed de Soto's link between titling and the increase in credit to the poor.[86] According to one study by the Peruvian government, out of the 200,000 households in Lima awarded land titles in 1998 and 1999, only 24 percent had received any kind of financing by 2002—and in that group, financing came mostly from the government rather than from private banks. Banks probably do not put much value on the right to repossess shanties in urban slums. Faced with a surge in demand for loans from the poor with legal but tenuous property, the banks probably adjusted their criteria for lending, and cared more about stable employment than property rights.[87]

The bigger problem with de Soto's argument, and one that has not received as much attention in the literature, is the assumption that greater access to credit will automatically lead to poverty reduction. Like the microcredit proponents, the property rights advocates believe that given access to credit, the poor can easily pull themselves up out of poverty. They assume that poor people are all potential entrepreneurs constrained only by their inability to access credit. As argued above, this is a fallacy; all the reasons why microcredit does not work apply to property rights. In addition, the poor are risk-averse and more worried about failing and subsequently losing their asset (land) used as collateral for a loan. "Poverty itself is a barrier to risk-taking and enterprise."[88]

What's Next

Poverty is not a static condition. The poor have low income that is both fluctuating and unpredictable. This makes them vulnerable to economic shocks and personal mishaps. A large number of people on the edge of poverty, just above the poverty line, are economically insecure. These people, while not officially "poor," are at high risk to become poor if their situation changes, such as through loss of job, a bad crop, a major illness, or an accident. People already in poverty are also vulnerable to being pushed deeper into poverty. Affluent people deal with such vulnerability through accumulated savings and buying insurance. That is exactly what the poor need: microsavings accounts and micro-insurance.

A savings account is a much better option than microcredit to achieving the goal of consumption smoothing and dealing with economic insecurity. Unfortunately, the poor do not have access to any savings instrument that provides both safety and a reasonable return. Saving cash at home or elsewhere is neither safe nor protected from inflation. The poor, like everyone else, have problems resisting the temptation to spend money that is easily accessible. And the poor clearly realize the need for a relatively safe savings instrument. Some poor people even pay for a savings service—a negative interest rate! Many MFIs are now starting to emphasize savings accounts. In 2005, the international charity Catholic Relief Services announced it would divest its holdings in microcredit and focus on savings. Kim Wilson, former director of the organization's microfinance unit, says that microcredit was making poor borrowers "poor twice" through high interest rates. In 2010, the Bill and Melinda Gates Foundation announced grants of $38 million to 18 MFIs to spur the development of efficient models and systems for microsavings accounts. The problem, of course, is that providing a savings account is very expensive. The fixed cost of handling a cash transaction is very high, especially in relation to the small size of the transaction. This is even truer for poor people living in remote rural locations with weak infrastructure

Let us do a simple rough calculation to see the magnitude of the problem. Consider a microcredit organization that charges a 40 percent effective annual interest rate, and assume its cost of funds is 10 percent. Therefore, its expenses plus profits equal 30 percent of its loan portfolio. Now, if this organization converts into a savings organization, as a first approximation, it is likely that its cost structure will not change much since it still faces fragmented and dispersed customers who make many small transactions. Generously assume that the organization earns 10 percent on its deposit portfolio. To maintain its profit margin, the MFI will have to impose a negative 20 percent interest rate on its savers—clearly not a desirable policy. There are only two possible solutions. The company could reduce its profit margin, and even incur an economic loss that is then subsidized by charity or the government. That is what some governments have done by requiring rural banks to offer financial services to the poor. Or, a better solution might be that the company creatively finds a new business model that dramatically reduces its cost structure. Hope for a successful business model for savings accounts lies in technology: mobile phones, information technology, and simple ATMs. That is the likely intent of the Gates Foundation grants to MFIs.

Providing microinsurance is an even bigger challenge. A savings account is a relatively simple product. Insurance is a much more complex business involving issues of adverse selection, moral hazard, potential for fraud, and adjudicating claims. All this increases the cost structure, of course. Any form of savings and insurance would have to be subject to the usual financial services regulations, which might further increase costs. To better help the poor, the microfinance industry needs to shift its emphasis from microcredit to microsavings and microinsurance.

In its core microcredit business, the industry should narrow its focus to clients who actually use the loans to start or grow businesses. Besides providing credit, MFIs need to help their clients with other business services, such as training and market access, to ensure the business is profitable and sustainable. In a different context, venture capital firms in the United States do not just provide capital to their entrepreneur clients; they also provide business expertise and support services. Some microcredit organizations, especially the not-for-profit organizations, have already moved in this direction. That would significantly increase the chances of the microcredit borrower rising out of poverty.

In Conclusion

The microcredit industry has received much attention and resources, and has grown rapidly in recent years. It has been hyped as an instrument for development and poverty reduction. But, the empirical evidence does not support such positive assertions. Microcredit has not had a significant impact on alleviating poverty—quite the contrary. The bulk of microcredit loans have been used to finance personal consumption—a pathway that will not lead to future prosperity. The borrowers who actually use their microcredit loans to invest in businesses often lack the entrepreneurial expertise and other skills needed to succeed at running their own business. Microcredit also ignores the critical role of economies of scale in increasing productivity. The high interest rates for microcredit make it difficult for the borrowers to earn enough to rise out of poverty. To better help the poor, the microfinance industry needs to develop creative business models to provide micro-savings and micro-insurance options.

Regardless of the debate about its effectiveness, microcredit has grown significantly and become increasingly commercialized. Microcredit is an attractive industry, with high growth rates, low levels of penetration, minimal competition, vulnerable consumers, high interest rates, and low default rates. It is not surprising that private for-profit companies are playing an ever-larger role in the industry. This has led to some poor people being exploited by microcredit organizations, and, more importantly, the potential for further exploitation. Regulation is needed to protect microcredit borrowers in three areas: transparency, interest rate ceiling, and loan recovery practices.

CHAPTER 3

Mirage at the Base of the Pyramid

F or six decades now, various institutions have been addressing the challenges of reducing poverty: local governments,
developed-country governments, international organizations (such as the World Bank and the United Nations), aid agencies, and civil society.[1] So far, the intellectual discourse on poverty
reduction has been largely in the fields of public policy and development economics. More recently, large companies, management
experts, and business schools have entered this arena, arguing that
business should play the leading role in reducing poverty.

As noted earlier, C.K. Prahalad was one of the pioneers of this
movement, and his 2005 book *The Fortune at the Bottom of the
Pyramid* has received much acclaim.[2] Prahalad was instrumental
in developing a set of ideas often referred to as the "bottom (or
base) of the pyramid" (BOP) proposition, which can be summarized as follows:

1. There is much untapped purchasing power at the bottom of
   the pyramid. Private companies can make significant profits
   by selling to the poor.

2. By selling to the poor, private companies can bring prosperity to the poor, and thus can help eradicate poverty.
3. Large multinational companies (MNCs) should play the leading role in this process of selling to the poor.

Thus, the BOP proposition is that selling to the poor can simultaneously be profitable and eradicate poverty: There is both glory and fortune at the base of the pyramid. This is, of course, a very appealing proposition, and it has attracted the attention of senior managers, large companies, business schools, and the development community.

The United Nations, for example, launched the Growing Inclusive Markets (GIM) initiative in 2006; the tagline on its website is "Business works for development. Development works for business." The GIM is a "global multi-stakeholder research and advocacy initiative that seeks to understand, enable and inspire the development of more inclusive business models around the globe that will help to create new opportunities and better lives for many of the world's poor."[3] The United Nations also hosts the "Business Call to Action," a program designed to challenge companies to adapt their core business models to support poverty eradication. The World Bank promotes "private sector development," as do many other aid agencies. Finally, the think tank World Resources Institute (WRI) emphasizes "development through enterprise."

The international business community seems excited by the BOP proposition and about helping to reduce poverty. Top CEOs have discussed this topic at recent sessions of the World Economic Forum. MNCs Unilever, Hewlett Packard, and SC Johnson have undertaken BOP initiatives. Several business schools, such as IESE Barcelona, University of North Carolina, Cornell University, Harvard University, and University of Michigan, have set up BOP centers and/or offer MBA courses in this area.

Conferences on this topic include Eradicating Poverty through Profit, organized by the WRI (December 2004); Global Poverty: Business Solutions and Approaches, organized by the Harvard

Business School (December 2005); and Business as an Agent of World Benefit, hosted by Case Western Reserve University (October 2006). Many books have been published on the subject, too, including *Alleviating Poverty through Profitable Partnerships; Make Poverty Business; Untapped: Creating Value in Underserved Markets; The Next 4 Billion;* and *Business Solutions for the Global Poor.*

Given the number and diversity of organizations and experts in this domain, there is, of course, no consensus about what the precise role of business in poverty reduction should be. However, there is enough commonality of viewpoints to group them together for the purpose of analysis. Prahalad has certainly been the most visible and prolific writer in this field. Therefore, the analysis here will focus on the BOP proposition as outlined in *The Fortune at the Bottom of the Pyramid,* which Stuart Hart, an early BOP proponent, calls "central to the BOP canon."[4]

The BOP proposition sounds too good to be true, and this chapter argues that it is. It is riddled with unrealistic expectations and false hopes for both businesses and the poor, empirically false, logically flawed, and morally problematic. It is empirically false because the BOP market is just too small, providing only very limited opportunities for firms to make profits. It is logically flawed because the best way to alleviate poverty is to raise the income of the poor by focusing on them not as consumers but as producers. The BOP proposition is morally problematic because it leads to exploitation of the poor, even if unintentionally.

No Fortune

The power of the BOP proposition hinges on the belief that poor people represent a huge and potentially lucrative market. Prahalad claims that the BOP potential market is $13 trillion at purchasing power parity (PPP) exchange rates.[5] An article in the *International Herald Tribune* from July 7, 2006, quotes Allen Hammond, then vice president of WRI and a leading BOP advocate: "The buying power of these poorer markets weighs in at a staggering $15 trillion a year." The report *Next 4 Billion* jointly published by the WRI and the International Finance Corporation (IFC), a member of the World Bank Group, states: "The BOP constitutes a $5 trillion global consumer market."[6] The growing excitement about the BOP is, not surprisingly, fueled by such estimates. The problem is that they grossly overestimate the market size. The true size of the BOP market depends on the number of poor people and their per capita purchasing power, and is only about $0.44 trillion.

The Poverty Line

Determining the actual number of poor people depends on how one measures the poverty line. There is much confusion in the BOP field about where to draw this line. Prahalad and Hart, in their first article on this subject, in 2002, defined poverty as an annual per capita income below $1,500 PPP.[7] Later in 2002, Prahalad and Hammond set the poverty line at $2,000 PPP per year.[8] In his 2005 book, Prahalad uses the $2/day poverty standard. The *Next 4 Billion* report, published in 2007, defines the poor as those with annual incomes below $3,000 PPP. These are, of course, big differences, ranging from $2/day to $8.2/day. To an affluent American or European researcher, a person living on $8/day seems very poor, but to a person living on $2/day, an income of $8/day is a dramatic improvement. There is no discussion in any of the BOP publications of the particular definition of the poverty line. There, of course, is no objective or consensus definition of income poverty either. But, as noted in Chapter 1, virtually all of the development community uses a poverty line in the $1 to $2/day range.

It is difficult, and probably impossible, to prescribe solutions without first defining the nature and scope of the problem. The BOP proposition emphasizes selling to poor people. For example, a household with a per capita consumption of $3,000 per year probably could consider purchasing a motorcycle; a household with a per capita income of $2/day could not even contemplate such a purchase. Whether there is a "fortune" at the base of the pyramid depends on how one defines the "base." Similarly, how to alleviate poverty also depends on the definition of poverty being used. People who subsist on less than $2/day have very different needs and priorities than people who consume more than four times as much.

The BOP argument tends to set the poverty line very high, perhaps in a misguided attempt to increase the estimate of BOP market size and thus its appeal to companies. The BOP proposition also often confuses the emerging middle class in developing countries for the poor. The *Next 4 Billion* report claims that 98.6 percent of the population in India is in the base of the pyramid! According to this report, in most of the developing countries, at least 95 percent of the population falls below the poverty line. Actually, these high percentage numbers include both the poor and the growing middle class. According to World Bank data, 75.6 percent of the population in India is poor if measured by the $2/day standard. Some other BOP proponents equate the BOP with the entire population of a developing country, thus ignoring the sizable and growing middle class in these countries.[9] Indeed, economist Warnholz remarks: "Seen in this light, the BOP argument could simply be restated as a call for big businesses to sell their products in low and middle-income countries. This is neither a novel nor a particularly provocative idea."[10] The *Wall Street Journal* makes the same mistake in a recent article, when it considers selling to the poor to be the same as selling to emerging economy countries—this assumes all the people in emerging economies are poor.[11] In reality, it is the growing middle class in emerging economies that is the attractive target market.

Representing the poor as being more affluent than they really are is harmful to both companies and the poor. Companies following the BOP proposition often fail because they overestimate both the size of the market and the purchasing power of poor people, often setting prices too high, putting their products well out of the reach of their target audience.

More importantly, conflating the emerging middle class and the poor harms the poor because it leads to ineffective poverty alleviation policies. Setting the poverty line too high, as is often done in the BOP literature, in effect marginalizes those usually considered poor.[12] Muhammad Yunus cautions against such overly broad definitions of the poor.[13]

> The inability to reach the poorest of the poor is a problem that plagues most poverty alleviation programs. As Gresham's Law[14] reminds us, if the poor and non-poor are combined within a single program, the non-poor will always drive out the poor. To be effective, the delivery system must be designed and operated exclusively for the poor. That requires a strict definition of who the poor are—there is no room for conceptual vagueness.

Pointing out the problems with the BOP argument in terms of the definition of poverty is not just quibbling about the details. It is also important for defining the nature and scope of the poverty challenge. As discussed earlier, poverty defined by the $2/day criterion has remained the same over the last 30 years. Eradicating $2/day poverty is one of the world's toughest challenges, and it will probably take decades to accomplish, but setting the goal as reducing (or eliminating) the number of people living on less than $8/day is far too ambitious. Eradicating $8/day poverty is pure fantasy; it is impossible to define a program for achieving that.

Counting the Poor

It is interesting that, whereas the articles and books cited above use very different poverty lines, they *all* state that there are 4 billion people below the poverty line. But the World Bank data puts that number at 2.5 billion people living on less than $2 PPP per day.[15] Given that the world population was about 6.5 billion in 2005, the BOP number is wrong by orders of magnitude.[16]

Such ignorance of the facts seems to be contagious. Articles on BOP in both the *Washington Post* and *The Economist*, have similarly exaggerated the number of poor people.[17] Even the highly respected academic journal *Administrative Science Quarterly* has incorrectly quoted the World Bank as saying "four billion people in the world earn less than $2 per day."[18] It seems that much of the subsequent BOP literature has used this 4 billion number without checking the underlying data source. Precision is not critical, but getting the order of magnitude right is necessary for understanding the nature of the problem and size of the profit opportunity.

Sizing the Market

The average consumption of poor people is $1.21/day (according to World Bank data from 2005). Assuming there are 2.56 billion poor people (see figure 1.1), this implies a BOP market size of $1.1 trillion, at PPP in 2005. Yes, the BOP market is huge in terms of number of consumers, but small monetarily. Compared to this, the world's gross national income in 2005 was $55 trillion at PPP. So the bottom 39 percent of the world population accounts for only 2 percent of the total purchasing power.

From the perspective of an MNC, even $1.1 trillion is an overestimate of the BOP market size. To understand the problem of poverty and the consumption patterns of the poor, it is appropriate to convert local currencies into dollars at the PPP rates, as we did above. But, from the perspective of a MNC from a rich country selling to customers in a poor country, profits will be repatriated at the financial exchange rates, not at PPP rates. The ratio of financial exchange rates to PPP rates for poor countries is in the range of 1.5 to 4 (according to World Bank data); for China it is 2.3, and for India it is 3.0. Using a conservative ratio of 2.5, a proxy for the average for all developing countries, the size of the BOP market, from the perspective of a rich-country MNC, is only $0.44 trillion.

In other words, if *all* poor people (living on less than $2/day) in the world spent *all* their income with one hypothetical company, its annual revenues would be $0.44 trillion. Compare this to the $13 trillion economy of the United States; the 2009 revenues of Walmart alone were over $0.4 trillion.

Not So Profitable

Not only is the BOP market much smaller than previously estimated, but the costs of serving this market can be very high. The poor are often geographically dispersed (except for the urban poor concentrated into slums) and culturally heterogeneous. This results in increased distribution and marketing costs and makes it difficult for businesses to exploit economies of scale. Weak infrastructure (transportation, communication, media, and legal system) further increases the cost of doing business. Another factor leading to high costs is the small transaction size. For example, ICICI Bank reckons that providing $1.3 million in loans to microfinance clients currently requires 40 times more manpower than a corporate loan of the same size.[19]

Poor people are, of course, price sensitive. "Companies assume that poor people spend only on basic needs like food and shelter," say Prahalad and Hammond, who disagree, stating that "such assumptions reflect a narrow and largely outdated view of the developing world.... In fact, the poor often do buy "luxury" items."[20] Quite the contrary! Poor people who live on less than $2/day and can barely meet their basic survival needs are unlikely to buy luxury items. Diverting expenditures from these basic needs to luxuries is probably not in their own self-interest. The poor, in fact, do not spend much on luxuries—the BOP misconception is probably based on the $8/day rather than the $2/day standard. The National Sample Survey conducted by the Government of India estimates the consumption pattern for the poor (see table 3.1).[21] Food alone accounts for over 60 percent of the consumption of the poor, which clearly does not leave much room for purchasing luxuries!

Table 3.1 Consumption patterns of the poor in India

	Food	Intoxicants	Clothing	Fuel	Rent	Miscellaneous Services[a]
Urban poor (%)	60	3	8	9	2	19
Rural poor (%)	65	3	8	8	(Included in misc. services)	15

[a]Includes health, communication, entertainment, etc., and rent in the case of the rural poor.

Source: Shubhashis Gangopadhyay and Wilima Wadhwa. Changing Pattern of Household Consumption Expenditure. Society for Economic Research and Financial Analysis, New Delhi, The Planning Commission, Government of India, 2004.

Without an accurate understanding of the income and consumption patterns of their market demographic, companies targeting the BOP often fail. When they overestimate the purchasing power of poor people, they often try to market products/services at too high a price point. Several of the examples that apparently support the BOP proposition involve companies that are profitable by selling to people well above the $2/day poverty line, but who seem poor only in relative terms, especially to a Western researcher.

An extreme example of this confusion is Tata Motors' March 2009 launch of its small (2-cyclinder), fuel-efficient Nano car, which many BOP proponents cited as a BOP venture.[22] But the Nano, which sells for about $2,500 (USD), or about $7,500 at PPP, is way out of reach of the poor living on less than $2 a day. and is actually targeted to India's middle class. The great majority of the poor do not even own a bicycle, and less than 1 percent own any motorized vehicle.[23]

Aside from unrealistic estimates of the BOP market size, many touted BOP success stories are also exaggerated and not credible. When these cases are examined in depth, they actually do not support the BOP proposition (see table 3.2 for an assessment of the nine case studies presented in Prahalad's book). Many examples

Table 3.2 Assessment of case studies presented in Prahalad's 2005 book *The Fortune at the Bottom of the Pyramid*

Case Study	Product/service	Target Market	Profitability	Organization Type
Casas Bahia	Retailer of electronics, appliances, and furniture; provides financial credit to customers.	Above $6/day, and maybe even above $16/day, at PPP	Very profitable	Large Brazilian company
Cemex Patrimonio Hoy	Cement; Patrimonio Hoy program provides credit to customers.	Above US$5/day (equivalent to $7/day at PPP)	"Not as high as for Cemex corporate." "Too early to use profits as measure of success."	Large MNC
Hindustan Unilever, Ltd. (HUL): Annapurna Salt	Iodized salt	Above BOP; sells at a price premium of 275%.	No data. Probably profitable.	Large MNC
HUL: Soap market	Soap	BOP	No data on HUL's profits from this project. Government and civil society scaling back their involvement.	MNC partnering with government and civil society.

Jaipur Foot	Prosthetic foot	BOP	Not profitable by design.	Not-for-profit
Aravind Eye Care System	Eye care and surgery	BOP and more affluent people	Financially self-supporting; affluent customers cross-subsidize the BOP customers.	Not-for-profit
ICICI and microfinance	Microfinance	BOP. But it is debatable whether microcredit helps alleviate poverty.	No data on ICICI's microfinance business.	Large Indian company partnering with NGOs.
e-Choupal	Procurement of soybeans	Mostly middle-income farmers	No data in Prahalad's book. Not yet profitable in 2006, according to CEO of parent company.	Division of a large Indian company
Voxiva	Surveillance of emerging public health crisis.	Clients are government and large public health organizations in both rich and poor countries.	No data. Probably profitable.	Small private company; capital raised about $10 million.

Abbreviations: BOP: base of the pyramid; MNC, multinational corporation; NGO, nongovernment organization.

are of companies that are profitable by selling to people well above the poverty line, which prompted BOP critic Anand Jaiswal to title a 2008 article in the journal *Innovations*, "The Fortune at the Bottom or the Middle of the Pyramid?"[24] Other examples cited are of companies selling to the poor but not making any profit. In fact, some of the examples cited are of not-for-profit organizations, which is contrary to the central claim of the BOP proposition. A few of these examples are examined in more depth below.

Casas Bahia

Prahalad approvingly cites the case of Casas Bahia, which has become a large retailer of household appliances in Brazil by "converting the BOP into consumers.... Casas Bahia carries and sells top-quality brands: Sony, Toshiba, JVC, and Brastemp (Whirlpool). There is a misconception that because customers are poor they do not desire quality products."[25] In his discussion of Casas Bahia, Prahalad defines three economic segments that are considered to be the bottom of the pyramid, implying a poverty line of R$2,000, equivalent to $2,000 at PPP per family per month.[26] However, later on the same page, he says that that the Casas Bahia customers individually have an "average monthly income twice the minimum wage (R$400)," which is equivalent to $800 per month. Either way, Casas Bahia customers (individually or as a family) fall well above the $2/day poverty line. Casas Bahia is a big, profitable retailer but has little to do with the BOP proposition if the poverty line is defined appropriately. The erroneous belief that Casas Bahia customers fall below the poverty line has helped to create the BOP fallacy that poor people buy top-quality products.

Hindustan Unilever Limited: Annapurna Salt

Many people in developing countries suffer from an iodine deficiency, which can lead to diseases such as goiter. Salt is an excellent carrier of iodine, which can be added to salt very inexpensively, although some is inevitably lost in the process of storage, transportation, and cooking. In an effort to solve this problem, Hindustan Unilever Limited (HUL), the Indian subsidiary of Unilever, has developed a proprietary microencapsulation technology to stabilize the iodine content in salt, and it markets this stabilized salt to the poor under the brand name Annapurna.[27]

Unfortunately, the penetration of Annapurna salt among the poor is miniscule at best. The branded-salt market in India accounts for only 20 to 30 percent of the total market; the rest of the market is served by the unorganized sector.[28] Within the branded sector, Annapurna is the second largest, with a market share of 35 percent, which translates to a 7 to 10 percent share of the total market for salt. Annapurna salt is priced at Rs. 7.5/kg, the same as the market leader Tata salt, whereas the small regional producers sell iodized salt at Rs. 2/kg.[29] The BOP proposition is adamant about selling high-quality products at a low price to the poor; yet, Annapurna sells its salt at a price premium of 275 percent! Annapurna may be a profitable business, with a good product employing a valuable technological innovation, but it is not a BOP success story. R. Gopalakrishnan, former vice president of HUL, states that the "illustration of Annapurna salt as co-creating a market around the needs of the poor [was] misplaced."[30]

Amul Ice Cream

Prahalad and Hart approve of Amul's efforts to market ice cream to the BOP in India. "Amul, a large Indian dairy cooperative, found an instant market in 2001 when it introduced ice cream, a luxury in tropical India, at affordable prices (2 cents per serving). Poor people want to buy their children ice cream every bit as much as middle-class families, but before Amul targeted the poor as consumers, they lacked that option."[31] According to Amul's website (http://www.amul.com), in 2006, their cheapest ice cream sold for Rs. 5 for a 50-milliliter (1.7 ounces) serving, which is equivalent to $0.34 at PPP. Not too many poor people living on less than $2/day can afford these prices.

Before Amul entered the arena, HUL was the largest firm in the Indian ice cream market. Prahalad and Hart commended HUL for a radical innovation that allowed ice cream to be transported cheaply across the country in nonrefrigerated trucks, and thus reach the BOP market.[32] What really happened is that HUL chose to market to the very top of the pyramid and did not expand into the BOP market. In 2002, HUL decided to compete on differentiation and premium price in the market rather than on low price. HUL also began to focus on six mainline cities, where 60 percent of the ice cream market exists, having realized that the returns from serving other less affluent markets were inadequate.[33] After this change in strategy toward the very top of the pyramid, HUL made a profit in the ice cream business for the first time ever.

Emerging Middle Class

The alleged large and lucrative market at the bottom of the pyramid is a mirage. Fueled by rapid economic growth, the shape of the economic pyramid is changing in many developing countries leading to a rapid emergence of the middle class. Companies seeking new profitable opportunities are much better off targeting this vast new pool of consumers—the fast-growing middle class—in the emerging economies, especially China and India.[34]

Single-Serve Revolution: A Dud

The most often cited example of BOP success is shampoo sold in single-use sachets to the poor, which is said to have begun a "single-serve revolution" that is sweeping through poor countries, as companies learn to sell small packets of various products such as shampoo, ketchup, tea, coffee, biscuits, and skin cream. "A rapidly evolving approach to encouraging consumption and choice at the BOP is to make unit packages that are small and, therefore, affordable."[35] It is interesting to note that the pioneer of this revolution was CavinKare, an Indian start-up firm that first introduced shampoo in sachets in 1983, and not MNCs with the technological and marketing prowess of, for example, Unilever or Procter & Gamble.

This claim of "affordability" is just marketing lingo. Companies may prefer to sell small packages at lower profit margins to encourage trial, brand sampling, and impulse purchasing. The poor may prefer these small packages because of convenience and managing cash flow. The poor find it difficult to save money due to lack of safe place to keep money and paucity of banking services. The poor may not have the money to buy a bottle of shampoo, but could buy shampoo sachets for occasional use. However, small packages increase consumption by facilitating impulse buying. It is common for *paanwallas* (small kiosks selling tobacco and other sundry products) in India to sell single cigarettes, resulting in increased consumption. In Malaysia, *samsu* (the generic name for cheap liquor) is sold in small bottles of 150 milliliters (5 ounces). It is also possible that a customer might be fooled into thinking the lower price of a smaller package makes it truly cheaper. (It is for this reason—to avoid consumer deception—that products sold in supermarkets in the United States are required to display the per unit price as well as the price per package.) While small packages probably create value by increasing convenience and helping the poor manage cash flow, even that might be debatable. An ACNielsen study on rural markets in India found that for several products the best-selling package size is the same across rural and urban markets.[36]

Whether or not they create any value for the poor, single-use packages do not increase affordability. The only way to increase real affordability is to reduce the price per use. HUL sells Annapurna salt in a small package size to target the BOP market, but at exactly the same price per kilogram as for larger packages. (Recall that Annapurna salt sells at a 275 percent price premium to unbranded salt.) As a result, small packages of Annapurna "have been slow to penetrate mass markets, although they have been successful in surprise niche markets, such as college students living in hostels."[37]

Companies need to reduce costs to make their products affordable to the poor. Larger packages usually lead to lower production and distribution costs per unit, which is why the per-unit price is usually lower for larger, economy-sized packages. In reality, single-use packages for most products are usually sold at a premium price. "In Mexico City, for instance, a full-size bottle of Head & Shoulders dandruff shampoo that lasts roughly 70 shampoos costs half as much, per ounce, as a single-use sachet."[38]

Prahalad states that "the entrepreneurial private sector has created a large market at the BOP; the penetration of shampoo in India is about 90 percent."[39] Although he recognizes the negative impact of the proliferation of single-serve packages on the environment, he then optimistically dismisses the problem by arguing that MNCs have both the incentives and resources to solve the environmental problem. Yet it has been almost thirty years since the first introduction of shampoo in sachets, and companies have not yet solved the environmental problem caused by plastic packaging. In fact, most single-serve packages are made from fused, multilayered, metalized polymer material that is impossible to recycle. This problem is exacerbated in poor villages and slums where trash collection facilities are grossly inadequate or nonexistent. A visit to any Indian village or town confirms the severity of the environmental problem.

During a recent visit to several villages in the Indian state of Rajasthan, it was obvious that single-serve packages are very common in the *kirana* shops (small kiosks selling general merchandise). Indeed, the single most common product category in single-use packages was chewing tobacco. This does not make chewing tobacco any more affordable, but it probably does increase the consumption to the detriment of the poor.

Financing Schemes

Prahalad has also praised Brazil's Casas Bahia: "More BOP consumers in Brazil are able to buy appliances through Casas Bahia because the firm provides credit even for consumers with low and unpredictable income streams....Casas Bahia is able to provide access to high-quality appliances to consumers who could not otherwise afford them."[40] Unfortunately, providing credit does not change the affordability of a product, even though it does provide some other value to the poor. The finance term for a Casas Bahia loan ranges from four months to one year, with an average of six months. The customer can choose between saving money for six months and buying the appliance later, or buying now and repaying the loan over the next six months. The financing terms do provide value: instant gratification; for the privilege of this instant gratification, the consumer pays an interest rate of over 4 percent per month.[41] While these customers often lack access to efficient credit markets, the interest rate charged by Casas Bahia is lower than that of informal moneylenders. However, this does not change whether the customer can really "afford" the appliance, which is a function of the price of the product. People with "low and unpredictable income" would be well advised to save and pay in cash, especially given the high interest rate. In a similar vein, consumer groups in the United States (e.g., Consumers League of New Jersey) advise low-income people not to buy appliances from "rent-to-own" stores. Unbundling the purchase price and the interest cost will enable the customers to do a better job of comparison shopping too. It is not surprising that Casas Bahia deliberately does not provide this information; many of its customers do not understand how to unbundle the purchase price and the interest cost, and instead focus on the monthly installment payment.[42]

Role of MNCs

An important element of the BOP proposition is that MNCs should take the lead role in selling to the poor.[43] In fact, to the extent that there are opportunities to sell to the poor, it is usually SMEs that are best suited to exploiting these opportunities. Because the BOP markets are small, they usually do not involve significant economies of scale. And the fact that they are often geographically and culturally fragmented, with weak infrastructure, also makes it hard to exploit economies of scale. Products sold to the poor are often less complex, reducing the economies of scale in technology and operations. As examples, bicycles are less scale-intensive than motorcycles; fans are less scale-intensive than air-conditioners; unprocessed food is less scale-intensive than processed food. Products sold to the poor are also usually less marketing and brand intensive, further reducing economies of scale.

Through their decades of on-the-ground experience in poor countries, MNCs have probably already realized that there is no great fortune at the bottom of the pyramid, and that they have no competitive advantage in that market. Thus, with just a few exceptions, they have avoided major investments in this illusory market. This may be a good thing, since MNCs might otherwise inhibit the emergence of local private entrepreneurs who provide economic, as well as noneconomic benefits to society (e.g., as community leaders).

One of the premises of the BOP proposition is the power of free markets, yet this supposition leads to a logical paradox. The business gurus exhorting companies to increase their profits by selling to the poor have fallen into an erroneous trajectory. These gurus have much faith in the power of markets and the invisible hand. Market efficiency implies that there are no easy ways to make profits because, in a competitive market, somebody would have already exploited these easy opportunities. Yet the BOP proponents argue that there are many profitable opportunities that the markets have not yet discovered—the markets can hardly be efficient in that case! In addition, the proponents proclaim that exploiting these opportunities is socially responsible and will reduce poverty. Yet, despite years of such exhortations, pervasive poverty persists; companies are not rushing in to exploit these alleged opportunities to make large profits and simultaneously reduce poverty. Maybe markets are efficient after all in that competent managers have concluded that these are not profitable opportunities!

There is an old, often-told joke about a market-oriented economist walking down the street who does not bend to pick up a $20 bill because he thinks that if the bill were real, somebody would already have picked it up. There are no easy unexploited opportunities to make money by selling to the BOP market.

Hindustan Unilever Limited

BOP proponents frequently praise HUL, the Indian subsidiary of Unilever, as a "pioneer among MNCs exploring markets at the bottom of the pyramid."[44] But in fact, most of HUL's "BOP initiatives were not proactive and intentional but a reactionary move as a result of competitive pressures."[45] As mentioned earlier, it was not HUL but the Indian firm CavinKare that came up with the innovation of shampoo sachets. CavinKare came up with another pricing innovation by launching a 4-milliliter (0.4-ounce) sachet of shampoo at Rs. 0.50 in 1999. This launch was a great success, and its market share jumped from 5.6 percent to 23 percent in four years. HUL responded by introducing its own shampoo sachets at the same price point. HUL's entry into low-priced detergents was also not proactive, but a response to the successful innovation of the Indian firm Nirma. Several years after Nirma's entry into this market, HUL launched its own brand, Wheel, as part of a project called STING—Strategy to Inhibit Nirma's Growth. Jaiswal concludes, "It is incorrect to give HUL pioneer-like status in tapping BOP markets, as reflected in Prahalad's work."[46]

It is certainly true that HUL has been a leader in penetrating the rural market in India. But, that is not the same as selling to the poor—a significant fraction of the rural population is not poor. A major BOP theme is that "quantum jumps in price performance are required to cater to BOP markets."[47] It is difficult to argue that HUL has achieved this jump often. Quite the opposite, in virtually all product categories, HUL sells products at a price premium—recall the examples of ice cream and iodized salt discussed earlier. This is probably good marketing strategy designed to maximize profits, but it is not a strategy for targeting the poor as a large market. Its market share in many product categories is dipping as new competitors have been offering rock-bottom prices in recent years. Even as sales slide, margins have grown. "We've been very careful to benefit shareholders," said then Chairman M.S. Banga.[48]

HUL is a well-managed company, motivated by profits. The problem arises when the BOP proposition paints HUL as a paragon of virtue that is eradicating poverty, which is largely hype.

Corporate Social Responsibility

While the BOP market is quite small and not very profitable for most big companies, there are some success stories. But these are isolated instances; for example, see the case of Nirma detergents, discussed in Chapter 5. Overall, however, although the BOP profit opportunities are not nearly as pervasive as the proponents argue, if a company is motivated by corporate social responsibility, not by economic profits, then of course, there are many opportunities for marketing to the poor.

It is interesting to note that, conceptually, the BOP proposition emphasizes the opportunity for significant corporate profits, and yet, in a search for empirical support, proponents often cite examples of not-for-profit organizations (see table 3.2). This is probably because there are very few successful BOP examples. After an extensive survey of 270 market-based solutions to reducing poverty in India, the consulting firm Monitor Group concluded that "only a small handful—mostly well-publicized ones like Grameen Bank and Aravind Eye Care—attained a scale sufficient to transform a 'business model' into a 'solution'."[49] It is true that both these examples, Grameen and Aravind, are "well publicized"—almost every BOP article or book cites them. But, it is ironic, and instructive, that both are not-for-profit organizations, and thus cannot be classified as commercial successes or as market-based solutions.

Raise Income

In fact, there is neither a fortune nor glory to be attained by selling to the bottom of the pyramid. It is erroneous to claim that there is much "untapped" purchasing power at the bottom of the pyramid. The poor obviously consume most of what they earn, and as a consequence have a low savings rate. Getting the poor to consume more will not eliminate their poverty. Their problem is that they cannot afford to consume more. The only way to help the poor and alleviate poverty is to raise their *real* income. There are only two ways to do this: (1) lower prices and (2) raise their incomes.

Lowering Prices

Reducing the prices of the goods and services the poor buy (or would buy) increases their effective income. Thus, to have a significant impact on the purchasing behavior of the poor, the BOP proposition calls for price reductions of over 90 percent.[50] This is a very ambitious and rarely achieved target. It would be useful to settle for lower, but still significant, price reductions of, say, 50 percent.

There are only three possible ways to reduce prices: (1) reduce profits; (2) reduce costs without reducing quality; and (3) reduce costs by reducing quality. If it is true that the average profit margin in a market is well over 50 percent, then working to make the market more efficient to reduce monopoly profits would result in significant price reductions. Even allowing that the poor are often subject to local monopolies, this is a rare situation. Therefore, the only realistic way to reduce prices to the poor consumer is to reduce the producers' costs. Unless all current producers are grossly inefficient, redesigning business processes will not reduce costs by over 50 percent without also reducing quality. A significant improvement in technology, however, could reduce costs dramatically. A good example is telecommunications, which is discussed in greater detail in

Chapter 5. Unfortunately, similar examples of technology leading to such dramatic cost reductions in other product categories
(besides electronics) are rare. The poor spend over 80 percent of
their income on food, shelter, clothing, and fuel—products that
have not benefited from such dramatic technological changes in
a long time. Back in the 1950s and 1960s, the "green revolution"
significantly reduced agricultural costs.[51] But it is often necessary to reduce quality in order to reduce costs; the challenge is
to do this in such a way that the cost–quality trade-off is acceptable to poor consumers.

Exaggerated Cost Reduction

At times, the BOP proposition exaggerates the price reduction
achieved, by making inappropriate comparisons. A frequently cited
example is the Aravind Eye Care System, a not-for-profit organization in India dedicated to eliminating unnecessary blindness,
especially among India's rural poor. It is claimed that Aravind has
reduced the cost of a cataract operation to $25 to $300, compared
to the $2,500 to $3,000 one costs in the United States.[52] Aravind
is an excellent organization that has reduced costs through economies of scale, specialization, and process design.[53] But these fig-
ures exaggerate its achievement. Comparing Aravind's costs to
costs in the United States does not by itself prove that Aravind
has been particularly innovative or effective. The cost of a haircut
is similarly dramatically lower in a small Indian town than in the
United States, yet this does not suggest any breakthrough achievement by Indian hair salons. The cost of many products and services, especially those that are labor intensive, is much lower in
poor countries simply due to the lower cost of inputs. Second, to
be consistent, Aravind's costs should be converted into dollars at
PPP rates, not at financial exchange rates BOP proponents use.[54]
Third, several factors lead to the high health care costs in the
United States, including high labor costs for medical personnel,
high administrative costs due to the third-party payment system,

and the high cost of malpractice insurance. Most estimates suggest medical treatment costs in India are about one-tenth of those in the United States[55] Finally, Aravind is subsidized by other nonprofit and charity organizations. It receives intraocular lenses and other medical supplies at a substantial discount from a nonprofit, Aurolab, for example. Aravind draws its patients to the hospitals from eye camps that are organized and paid for by various philanthropic organizations, such as the Lions Club and the Rotary Club.

The appropriate comparison is between Aravind and a hospital in India. Private hospitals in India charge about $350 for cataract surgery, which is about what Aravind charges its patients who are not indigent.[56] It is true that Aravind subsidizes poor patients—about 70 percent of the total patients—asking them to pay only $30 (and more if they can afford it). Aravind cross-subsidizes poor patients by charging higher prices to the more affluent patients. And, because they are highly dedicated to the cause, the surgeons and staff work grueling hours for pay comparable to government hospitals, which is much less than they would earn in most private hospitals. Still, retention is a problem, and a quarter of the staff defect annually to better-paying jobs in the private sector.[57] All this is not to detract from recognizing Aravind as an innovative organization —overall, Aravind is clearly more efficient than a typical hospital in India—but to show that the BOP proponents exaggerate the price reductions it achieves.

The Poor as Producers

The BOP proposition focuses on the poor primarily as consumers, as an attractive market. But the poor, like more affluent people, of course, are both consumers and producers. In discussing solutions to alleviating poverty, it is useful to conceptually separate the role of the poor as consumers and as producers. A concerted effort to view the poor primarily as producers, not as consumers, would go a long way toward alleviating poverty.

There are two ways for a person to be a member of the labor force: as an employee or as self-employed. As we saw in Chapter 2, microcredit, which aims to help poor people become self-employed, has not been effective. Creating opportunities for steady employment at reasonable wages is the best way to take people out of poverty.

Create Efficient Markets

The poor often sell their products and services into inefficient markets and do not capture the full value of their output. Any attempt to improve the efficiency of these markets will raise the income of the poor. Amul, a large dairy cooperative in India, is a great example of this approach.[58] Amul collects milk twice a day from over 2 million farmers in 100,000 villages. It started by selling milk, but has since forward integrated into more value-added products such as butter, milk powder, cheese, ice cream, and pizza. It has even entered direct retailing through franchising parlors. Amul is owned by the poor (it is a cooperative), and buys from the poor (the farmers, who are its members); however, its products are mostly purchased by the middle and upper income groups, or exported.

Another example, often discussed by BOP proponents, is e-Choupal, an initiative of India's large tobacco conglomerate ITC. Based on an innovative business model, e-Choupal has brought efficiency to the system for moving soybeans from the individual farmer to oil processing plants. It has reduced the role of, and the rents captured by, middlemen in this process. ITC views the poor farmers as producers. "Our e-Choupal is fostering inclusive growth and *enhancing the wealth creation capability of marginal farmers,*" [emphasis added] says Y.C. Deveshwar, Chairman of ITC.[59] However, only 10 percent of the users of e-Choupals are poor farmers, while 70 percent are middle income, and 20 percent are rich farmers.[60]

Table 3.3 summarizes the counterarguments to the "promises" of the BOP proposition. The poor cannot consume their way to

Table 3.3 Fortune or Mirage at the BOP?

Fortune at the BOP:	*Reality at the BOP:*
Large multinational companies can make a fortune by selling to the poor people at the bottom of the pyramid and simultaneously alleviate poverty.	*The alleged large and lucrative market at the bottom of the pyramid is a mirage; to alleviate poverty it is better to view the poor as producers.*
BOP market size is $13 to $15 trillion.	BOP market size is only $0.44 trillion.
There is much "untapped" purchasing power at the BOP.	The poor have a low savings rate, and little "untapped" purchasing power.
Profit margins in BOP markets are high.	BOP markets are not so profitable because the customers are price sensitive, and the cost of serving them is high given the small size of transactions and poor infrastructure.
The poor often buy "luxury" items.	The poor spend 80% of their meager income on food, clothing, shelter, and fuel alone, leaving little room for buying luxuries.
Companies should reduce prices dramatically without reducing quality.	A significant improvement in technology could reduce prices dramatically without reducing quality, such as in telecommunications. But, in most other product categories, the only way to reduce prices significantly is to reduce quality. The challenge is to do this in a way that the cost-quality trade-off is acceptable to the poor.
Single-serve packages increase affordability.	Single-use packages increase convenience and help the poor to manage cash flow. But, the only way to increase real affordability is to reduce the price per use.
Large MNCs should take the lead role in the BOP initiative to sell to the poor.	Markets for selling to the poor usually do not involve significant economies of scale, and small-to-medium-sized local firms are better suited to exploiting these opportunities.
Selling to the poor will alleviate poverty.	The best way to alleviate poverty is to view the poor as producers not as consumers, and to emphasize buying from the poor.

prosperity. One exception to this, however, is if private companies can profitably sell products that truly are beneficial to the poor and at prices the poor can afford. Unfortunately, there are only limited opportunities to do this, but it is feasible.

Harmless Illusion or Dangerous Delusion?

Private companies should try to market to the poor. However, the profit opportunities are modest at best and a cautious approach should be taken. The best opportunities exist when firms reduce prices significantly by innovatively changing the cost–quality trade-off in a manner acceptable to the poor. The private sector can help alleviate poverty by focusing on the poor as producers.

The BOP proposition is based on a creative illusion. There is no fortune to be made by selling to the poor. Neither will selling to the poor eradicate poverty. However, given the continuing problem of global poverty, perhaps it is a solution worth trying. Or, is it possible that the BOP proposition can hurt the very people it is trying to help? The BOP proposition is at best a harmless illusion, and probably a dangerous delusion.

CHAPTER 4

Romanticizing the Poor

E ven as the economic gap between the rich and the poor is growing steadily larger, the physical gap between the rich and the poor is narrowing.[1] Slums are often just a short walk from upscale beaches or border posh neighborhoods, and shantytowns can be found near luxury resorts. The media brings images of the poor into the living rooms of the advantaged everyday. It is not possible, nor politically correct, to just ignore poverty. The affluent can actually visit poor neighbourhoods and photograph or film the poor in their "natural habitat," either sanitizing or romanticizing their lives. Indeed, entertainment and poverty have come together: *poortainment.*

Poortainment

In 2008, the fashion magazine, *Vogue India*, featured a 16-page spread of poor Indians wearing ultra expensive accessories by top fashion designers such as Fendi, Burberry, and Marc Jacobs.[2] *Vogue India* editor Priya Tanna stated in the *Independent*: "For our

India issue, we wanted to showcase beautiful objects of fashion in an interesting and engaging context. This was a creative pursuit that we consider one of our most beautiful editorial executions."[3] Thus, in this "creative" outlet you can see the poor, but not really see them. Poortainment uses poverty as just another prop, a colorful backdrop for marketing to the rich.

The people in the *Vogue India* photographs are not that poor, at least not by Indian standards, and seem quite happy and dignified. The photographic spread, however, provoked much criticism from both Indian and foreign commentators, ranging from distasteful and vulgar to callous and exploitative. Surprisingly, the magazine was taken aback by the negative reaction to the photographs and even asked the critics to "lighten up." At a minimum, *Vogue India* needs to learn the first rule of global marketing: sensitivity to local culture and people.

Slumdog Millionaire

If you want to see real poverty in its gritty detail, filthy grime, and even its revolting brutality, then *Slumdog Millionaire* is the venue. The movie swept the Academy Awards in 2010 and became an international box office sensation. The film chronicles the rise of a young boy from the slums of Mumbai to riches and romance.

For the affluent with a weak stomach, poverty is made palatable by romanticizing it. Film critic Nikhat Kazmi of the *Times of India* calls the movie "a piece of riveting cinema, meant to be savored as a Cinderella-like fairy tale...It was never meant to be a documentary on the down and out in Dharavi [the slum]."[4] The critics and its own publicity materials branded it a feel-good movie. The desperate squalor of poverty is but an exciting backdrop for a traditional rags-to-riches fable.

Columnist Anand Giridharadas of the *New York Times* wrote that the movie portrays "a changing India, with great realism, as something India long resisted being: a land of self-makers, where a scruffy son of the slums can, solely of his own effort, hoist himself up, flout his origins, break with fate."[5] The movie does convey the message that the poor can bootstrap themselves out of poverty—this is the romanticization of poverty that makes for good poortainment. But it is not a realistic portrayal of the poor in India today.

This is the real poverty in India: 76 percent of Indians live below the commonly used $2/day poverty line;[6] 34 percent of adults are illiterate;[7] 15 percent of boys and 19 percent of girls do not attend even primary school; 48 percent of children are underweight for their age; 7 percent of children die in the first five years of their lives;[8] 79 percent of rural households and 46 percent of urban households do not have a toilet;[9] and 386,000 children die from diarrhea every year.[10]

There is no easy way to eradicate poverty, but expecting the poor to bootstrap themselves out of poverty is surely not the solution. "You cannot pull yourself up by your bootstraps if you have no boots."[11] But these illusionary bootstraps allow the middle and upper classes to cope with the poverty they see. Romanticizing poverty is appealing because it implies the poor can cope on their own.

Another way to romanticize poverty is to claim that the poor are still happy. The movie's screenwriter, Simon Beaufoy, said he wanted *Slumdog Millionaire* to convey "the sense of this huge amount of fun, laughter, chat, and sense of community that is in these slums."[12]

Poverty Tourism

A feature of all slums is the pervasive stench, and no movie can capture that. Dharavi (the slum portrayed in *Slumdog Millionaire*) has no discernible garbage removal and one toilet for every 1,440 people. In the opening scene, the protagonist drops into a pool of human excrement. The audience flinches, but it does not smell the stench. If you want that degree of reality, you have to visit the slums.

Poverty tourism is a fast-growing and trendy segment of the tourism industry offering "up close and personal" tours of a *favela* in Rio de Janeiro or Mumbai, or a visit to the township of Soweto near Johannesburg to see the "matchbox" houses.[13]

Not surprisingly, like other forms of poortainment, poverty tourism has come under attack as voyeurism. The tour organizers, of course, insist that their motive is to raise awareness of poverty rather than provide entertainment. Yet, they, too, often end up romanticizing poverty. For example, the founder of Reality Tours & Travel, which offers tours of the Dharavi slum in Mumbai, states that it is geared toward showcasing the human enterprise and industry within the area—those bootstraps again.

Salaam Balak Trust, an Indian charity for homeless children, organizes tours that feature the children living in and around Delhi's main railway station. Tourists are shown how the children scavenge for rubbish, sleep between gaps on the platform roof, get high on Eraz-ex [a white correction fluid] and struggle to survive among the gang leaders and policemen. The *Guardian* reporter tells of one tourist feeling a little disappointed that she wasn't able to see more children in action. "It's not like we want to peer at them in the zoo, like animals, but the point of the tour is to experience their lives."[14] Contrary to her protest, this is poverty in a zoo.

Real Poverty

This is not to suggest that the poor lack humanity, ambition, and enterprise. Quite the opposite is true, although this is not enough. Despite their ambition and enterprise, they are still poor and caught in a trap, victims of circumstances and institutional failures, especially of the governments. It is precisely why the poor need and deserve a helping hand to climb out of poverty, not a motivational speech. Poortainment leads one to believe the problem of poverty is not so bad after all and that it is improving without our intervention. But take off the rose-tinted designer glasses, and you see that real poverty is worse than we think it is, and it will not improve without our intervention. We should not romanticize the poor and celebrate the human spirit that survives in poverty. Rather, we should mourn the human spirit that is destroyed by poverty, and we should be enraged by the dehumanizing aspects of poverty.

Understanding Poverty

The romanticization of the poor, unfortunately, is not confined to popular culture. The libertarian approach to reducing poverty is just as guilty of romanticizing the poor. To successfully fight poverty it is necessary to understand poverty. One way to gain an understanding of poverty is to listen to the poor describe their experiences. In an unprecedented effort to understand poverty from the perspective of the poor themselves, the World Bank collected the voices of more than 60,000 poor women and men from 60 countries.[15] *Voices of the Poor* reveals that poverty is multidimensional and complex. Poverty is powerlessness, despair, insecurity, and humiliation, say the poor themselves. They talk about domestic violence, which is pervasive, and gender relations that are stressed. Table 4.1 shows some of the ways the poor have described their lives. They feel the new economic opportunities have bypassed them. They want more assistance from the governments and state institutions, and see corruption as a big problem. NGOs receive mixed ratings. The poor rely on informal networks to survive, but these too are fragile. There is nothing romantic about being poor.

As we saw in Chapters 2 and 3, the libertarian view that the poor are perfectly rational actors is used to justify company strategies that in some cases result in making the poor worse off, and the assumption that they are discerning consumers sometimes leads businesses to exploit them. In addition, the romanticized view that the poor cope well with poverty and will climb out of poverty on their own leads to governments treating the poor with

Table 4.1 How the poor describe poverty

Poverty is pain; it feels like a disease. It attacks a person not only materially but also morally. It eats away one's dignity and drives one into total despair.

Poverty is like living in jail, living under bondage, waiting to be free.

Lack of work worries me. My children were hungry and I told them the rice is cooking, until they fell asleep from hunger.

Everyday I am afraid of the next.

Problems have affected our relationship. The day my husband brings in money, we are all right together. The day he stays at home (out of work), we are fighting constantly.

Men rape within the marriage. Men believe that paying dowry means buying the wife, so they use her anyhow at all times. But no one talks about it.

People place their hopes in God, since the government is no longer involved in such matters.

Teachers do not go to school except when it is time to receive salaries.

The children keep playing in the sewage.

The NGOs give resources, they undertake research but there are also negative views because some are covers for businesses.

When food was in abundance, relatives used to share it. These days of hunger, however, not even relatives would help you by giving you some food.

No one helps, not anyone. I would gladly help someone, but how when I am in need of help myself?

This is misery. Our souls, our psyches are dead.

Whenever there is a funeral, we work together—women draw water, collect firewood, and collect maize flour from well-wishers—while men dig graves and bury the dead.

Source: Voices of the Poor. The World Bank, 2000.

malign neglect. Romanticizing the poor results in overemphasis on microcredit and underemphasis on fostering modern enterprises that would provide employment opportunities for the poor. It also results in too little emphasis on putting into place legal, regulatory, and social mechanisms to protect the poor, who are vulnerable consumers.

The Poor as Entrepreneurs

A key element of the libertarian approach to poverty reduction is to view the poor as effective entrepreneurs. It is a myth that most poor people are entrepreneurs, or even want to be entrepreneurs. The vast majority of the poor (as well as more affluent people) lack the skills, vision, creativity, and drive to be entrepreneurs. They would gladly take a job at steady wages if possible.

Another reason for preferring a job to a microenterprise has to do with issues related to self-control. All people have problems of self-control, with negative consequences. For example, affluent people might fail to get a medical check-up or not save enough for retirement. The negative consequences are more severe for the poor. A microentrepreneur does not know what she will earn next week or month and must have the willpower to save in good periods to survive the bad periods, while a salaried worker has a steady income. Behavioral economist Sendhil Mullainathan says, "Recognizing that salaried jobs remove one of the most basic self-control problems highlights an additional benefit of formal employment as a poverty alleviation tool."[16] He cites as an example the fact that very few farmers in south India plant sugarcane even though it is a profitable cash crop. The problem is that sugarcane is harvested once a year, requiring the farmer to exercise self-control to cover expenses over the entire year. Many farmers who own cows cite the daily income from milk as a primary benefit, even though cows are not as profitable as sugarcane.

The poor, of course, are neither stupid nor lazy, and they do not want to be poor. They are basically caught in a trap, victims of social and economic circumstances and institutional failures. Poverty makes life seem hopeless, and to a large extent it is hopeless.

It is a romanticized view that the poor have a long-term perspective and are focused on improving their future situation. The poor in fact are short-term oriented and not nearly that proactive. Amartya Sen states: "The deprived people tend to come to terms with their deprivation because of the sheer necessity of survival, and they may, as a result, lack the courage to demand any radical change, and may even adjust their desires and expectations to what they unambitiously see as feasible."[17] A study of farmers in Kenya found that few use fertilizers, even after the benefits—average return on investment of over 100 percent—have been demonstrated to them.[18] Not many Ghanaian farmers cultivate pineapples, which would achieve returns of 250 to 300 percent.[19] Banerjee and Duflo conclude that the poor have a "reluctance to psychologically commit themselves to the project of making as much money as they can."[20] This is perhaps understandable: the poor face such dismal circumstances that they come to believe the future is hopeless. George Orwell wrote over a hundred years ago that poverty "annihilates the future," and that bleak, trenchant observation is just as valid today. It is difficult, maybe nearly impossible, for the poor to be energized, motivated, and proactive. The few poor people who rise out of poverty on their own are to be congratulated. However, the rest of the poor should not be expected to similarly escape poverty.

The Poor as Value-Conscious Consumers

As previously discussed, the BOP proposition views the poor primarily as consumers, and as an untapped market suggesting that the consumption choices available to the poor can be increased by targeting various products and services, such as shampoo and televisions. Holding the poor consumer's nominal income constant, the only way a person can purchase the newly available product is to divert expenditure from some other product. Still, this increased choice will increase his welfare, assuming he is a rational and well-informed consumer. However, as a practical matter, this increase in choice is unlikely to result in a significant change in his poverty situation. A poor person is far more constrained by lack of income than by lack of variety of goods and services offered in the market.

Additionally, if for some reason, the poor consumer is deceived by marketing or is poorly informed, the BOP initiative might even reduce his welfare. Civil society organizations have often argued that targeting the poor as a market might cause them to wastefully spend part of their already meager income on low priority products and services.[21] It is almost an "item of faith" among development economists that the poor act rationally.[22] The libertarian view presumes that the poor hold coherent, well-informed beliefs and pursue their self-interest effectively. The BOP proposition argues that the poor have the right to determine how they spend their limited income and are in fact value-conscious consumers; the poor themselves are the best judges of how to maximize their utility.

This is free-market ideology taken too far, and it harms the poor. Even a stalwart proponent of neoliberal policies like *The Economist* concludes that the poor do make choices, and the empirical evidence suggests that "they are not always the best ones."[23] The assumption that the poor are value-conscious consumers is empirically false, and the implications of this assumption are morally problematic.

The poor in fact are vulnerable by virtue of a lack of education (often they are illiterate), lack of information, and economic, cultural, and social deprivations. People's utility preferences are malleable and shaped by their background and experience, especially so if they have been disadvantaged. It is not appropriate to assume that the expressed preferences are truly in the self-interest of the poor. We need to look beyond the expressed preferences and focus on people's capabilities to choose the lives they have reason to value. Amartya Sen eloquently argues that

> the mental metric of pleasure or desire is just too malleable to be a firm guide to deprivation and disadvantage.... Social and economic factors such as basic education, elementary health care, and secure employment are important not only in their own right, but also for the role they can play in giving people opportunity to approach the world with courage and freedom.[24]

The growing field of behavioral economics—the integration of psychological insights with economic analysis—empirically demonstrates that, contrary to the neoclassical assumption, people are not perfectly rational economic actors. Behavioral economists Bertrand, Mullainathan, and Shafir argue that the poor "exhibit the same basic weaknesses and biases as do people from other walks of life, except that in poverty, with its narrow margins for error, the same behaviors often manifest themselves in more pronounced ways and can lead to worse outcomes."[25] The poor are just as irrational as more affluent people, but their penalty for irrationality is more severe. For example, when a poor person spends too much on alcohol, it has a major detrimental impact on his and his family's lifestyle, which is an unlikely occurrence for an affluent family.

Empirical Evidence

Unfortunately, there are few micro-level studies on the purchasing behavior of the poor. In a survey of research on the consumption choices the poor make, Banerjee and Duflo show that the poor spend a "surprisingly large" fraction of their total income on alcohol, tobacco, and entertainment (be it televisions, weddings, or festivals).[26] The poor enjoy such products as much as affluent people do, and maybe even more so given their rather miserable lives. It is easy to rationalize any particular consumption choice of the poor. It is problematic that they do not spend enough on their own nutrition, health, and education.

One survey of the poor in Udaipur in India found that 55 percent of the adults were anemic, and that 65 percent of adult men and 40 percent of adult women were underweight.[27] The typical poor household in Udaipur could spend up to 30 percent more on food than it actually does, just based on what it spends on alcohol, tobacco, and festivals. Similarly, a study in rural India found that the poor are buying fewer and fewer calories over time.[28] Partly as a result of this general weakness, the poor are frequently sick.

A possible cause of this surprising under-spending on nutrition is the growing availability of consumption goods.

The evidence suggests that the poor lack self-control, yield to temptation, and spend to keep up with their neighbors.[29] One cause might be that they typically do not have bank accounts, and having cash at home makes it harder to exercise self-control. The poor seem to be aware of their vulnerability to temptation. In a survey in Hyderabad, India, the poor were asked to name whether they would like to cut particular expenses, and 28 percent of the respondents named at least one item. The top item that households would like to cut is alcohol and tobacco, mentioned by 44 percent of the households that want to cut on items, followed by sugar, tea, and snacks (9 percent), festivals (7 percent), and entertainment (7 percent). [30]

There is much evidence in the economics and psychology literature showing that people derive satisfaction not just from their own consumption but also from faring better than their peers.[31] Fafchamps and Shilpi show that this is equally true for the poor.[32] Keeping up with the neighbors seems to be a pervasive trait cutting across income brackets. Poor people in Nepal were asked to assess whether their level of income as well as their levels of consumption of housing, food, clothing, health care, and schooling were adequate. The answers to these questions were strongly negatively related to the average consumption of the other people living in the same village.

Spending on festivals is a surprisingly large part of the budget for many extremely poor households living on less than $1.25/day per person. In Udaipur, more than 99 percent of the extremely poor households spent money on a wedding, a funeral, or a religious festival.[33] The median household spent 10 percent of its annual budget on festivals. In South Africa, 90 percent of the extremely poor households spent money on festivals. In Pakistan, Indonesia, and Côte d'Ivoire, more than 50 percent did likewise.[34] Spending on festivals is a form of entertainment, especially in the absence of movies and television. There appears to be a strong need to spend more on entertainment. One possible reason is that the poor (like everyone) want to keep up with their neighbors.

Mounting evidence suggests that just being poor hinders people's ability to make good decisions. Dozens of psychological studies find that, compared to wealthier people, poorer people feel more powerless, depressed, and anxious, and believe that they have less control, mastery, and choice.[35] "Perhaps at some level, this avoidance is emotionally wise," write Banerjee and Duflo: "Thinking about the economic problems of life must make it harder to avoid confronting the sheer inadequacy of the standard of living."[36]

The empirical evidence does not support the romanticized view of the poor as "value conscious consumers." The problem is that the poor often make choices that are not in their own self-interest. Selling to the poor in some cases can result in reducing their welfare. Therefore, there is a need to impose some limits on free markets to prevent exploitation of the poor. Markets work best when appropriately restricted to protect the vulnerable.

Poverty and Alcohol

Alcohol consumption is a financial drain for the poor. The reported share of household income spent on alcohol and tobacco by the poor is high in many countries, ranging from 6 percent in Indonesia to 1 percent in Nicaragua.[37] The poor in India spend about 3 percent of their household income on alcohol and tobacco.[38] These numbers understate the true consumption level since it is usually only the man in the household who engages in this consumption. An in-depth field study in Sri Lanka found that "money spent on alcohol by poor families and communities is underestimated to a remarkable degree.... A large part of alcohol expenditure is unseen.... Over 10 percent of male respondents report spending as much as (or more than!) their regular income on alcohol."[39] Sadly, the poorer people spend a greater fraction of their income on alcohol than the less poor.

Given their bleak lives, it is understandable why the poor spend so much on alcohol and tobacco. These addictive substances often enter their lives as analgesics from extreme labor. In addition, poor people often encounter stressors including hunger, pollution, overcrowding, and violence that lead them to act in ways that may alleviate suffering in the short term, but hinder economic prosperity in the long term. While such behavior is understandable, that does not reduce its negative consequences. Public health experts Efroymson and Ahmed tell a moving, but not uncommon, story of Hasan, a rickshaw puller, who spends $0.20/day on tobacco.[40] When asked if his three children ever eat eggs, he exclaimed, "Eggs? Where will the money come from to buy them?" If Hasan did not buy tobacco, each of his children could eat an egg a day, or other nutritious foods, and be healthier as a result. For more affluent people, the consequences of cigarette smoking are not as dire as children's malnutrition.

Aside from the direct financial cost, alcohol abuse imposes other economic and social costs such as work performance, health, and accidents. "Domestic violence and gender-based violence was almost taken for granted in nearly all settings as an automatic consequence of alcohol use. Deprivation of the needs of children due to the father's heavy alcohol use was regarded simply as a misfortune of the children concerned." There is much evidence showing alcohol abuse exacerbates poverty.[41]

The Economist approvingly cites SABMiller, which has succeeded in several African countries with Eagle, a cheap beer made from locally grown sorghum (rather than imported malt).[42] SABMiller is able to price the beer at a level below that of mainstream clear beers in Uganda, Zambia, and Zimbabwe partly because it has obtained a reduction in excise duties from the governments involved. Andre Parker, managing director for the company's Africa and Asia divisions, says, "The brand is reliant on the excise break, so we are working with the governments to lower the excise rate so that the retail price is below that of clear beer. The margin, though, is at least as good as our other brands."[43] Eagle beer is profitable for SABMiller and a practical example consistent with the BOP proposition, but it is probably detrimental to the overall welfare of the poor consumers. Activist consumer organizations advocate higher (not lower) taxes on alcohol to support public education and rehabilitation programs.[44]

The poor, of course, have the right to consume, and even to abuse, alcohol. But, it is not in their self-interest to do so, at least not at the levels typically drunk. Companies have the right to profit from the sale of alcohol to the poor. But even in rich, capitalist economies the governments put some constraints on this right, such as "sin taxes," and by restricting advertising and sales to minors. The industry prefers voluntary constraints rather than regulation. The U.K. House of Commons health select committee recently examined the practices of some British alcohol producers and communications agencies to determine whether the industry's system of self-regulation and codes of conduct are effective.[45] The committee looked at four themes that are banned by the industry's self-regulated advertising codes of conduct: (1) targeting and appealing to young people; (2) attitudes to drunkenness and potency; (3) association with social success; and (4) sexual attractiveness. The committee found that the codes of conduct are systematically violated in all of these areas. The committee recommended that regulation of advertising practices for alcohol should be independent of the alcohol and advertising industries. The need for regulation of the alcohol industry is even greater in developing countries than in the United Kingdom

In many developing countries, regulatory constraints on the alcohol industry are sometimes missing; even when they do exist, they are poorly enforced, especially in the context of marketing alcohol to the poor. For example, in Malaysia, bottles of *samsu* (the generic name for cheap spirits) advertise outrageous claims that it is "good for health, it can cure rheumatism, body aches, low blood pressure, and indigestion. Labels also claim it is good for the elderly, and for mothers who are lactating."[46] Even MNCs have gotten into the act. DOM Benedictine, which contains 40 percent alcohol, claims health-giving and medicinal properties. Guinness Stout suggests it is good for male fertility and virility. Alcoholic drinks are easily available in Malaysian coffee shops and sundry shops without a liquor license. Forty-five percent of Malaysian youth under age 18 consume alcohol regularly. In an ironic twist on the single-use packaging discussed in Chapter 3, *samsu* is available in small bottles of about 150 milliliters (5.1 ounces) and "sold for as little as $0.40–0.80.... It is obvious that these potent drinks are packaged to especially appeal to the poor."[47]

Aside from the government, activist movements also play a role in protecting the consumer. Alcoholics Anonymous is a fellowship of men and women who share their experiences, and help each other that they may solve their common problem with alcoholism. The poor in emerging economies usually do not have access to such rehabilitation programs. In 1991, Heileman Brewery in the United States introduced PowerMaster, a malt liquor with a high alcohol content, targeted to African Americans community. Community leaders began a campaign that resulted in the product being withdrawn from the market within a few months. Such social mechanisms for consumer protection are often very weak in developing countries, and even more so with regard to poor people.

Carlsberg in Malawi

In May 2009, the national Swedish broadcasting corporation Radio Sweden aired a very interesting in-depth documentary on the alcohol industry in Malawi.[48] Malawi is one of the poorest countries in the world; more than half the population lives on less than $2/day. Nelson Zakeyu, the founder and head of Drug Fight Malawi, which is dedicated to fighting alcohol problems, says that alcohol has an important impact on the three main social problems in Malawi: poverty, HIV epidemic, and the maltreatment of women. In the documentary, reporters interviewed several women who told stories in which women and children pay the price—domestic violence, child neglect, and malnourishment—for the men's alcohol addiction. Carlsberg, the large Danish beer MNC, started in Malawi about 40 years ago as an aid project, now controls 97 percent of the bottled beer market. What was the logic for a brewery being an aid project? Carlsberg is certainly not aiding Malawi today.

The alcohol policy in Malawi is very liberal; the prices of beer and liquor are low; alcohol is available almost everywhere, and to anyone, at any time of the day. The reporters for Radio Sweden were struck by the extent of poverty and alcohol addiction in the capital city of Lilongwe. Yet, the marketing director of Carlsberg in Malawi claims that there are no addiction problems in Malawi. Dag Endahl, an official with the Norwegian aid organization FORUT that specializes in alcohol problems in developing countries, says "Carlsberg ought to take a walk outside the office and talk to people."

The marketing director also claims that Carlsberg applies the same restrictions on advertising in Malawi as it does in Europe. The documentary reports facts to the contrary; the company's marketing tactics in Malawi are inconsistent with Carlsberg's corporate code. For example, the code prohibits advertisements from implying that drinking the brand is linked to wealth or professional success. However, Carlsberg Malawi published a full-page advertisement showing students celebrating their graduation, which is an obvious sign of success in a country where over the half population is illiterate. The code also prohibits placing emphasis on the alcoholic strength of the beer, as well as to avoid implying it is to be preferred because of its high alcohol content. In 2008, Carlsberg Malawi launched a new, even stronger beer with the advertisement "Drink Elephant beer when you want a beer with more alcohol than in other beers! A real Elephant person is someone who is strong and full of character." The code says that advertisements should not show or encourage excessive or irresponsible drinking. Carlsberg Malawi sells a slightly cheaper beer for the local market called Kuche Kuche, which means "drink until dawn" in the local language, Chichewa.

The major global alcohol companies finance the Washington-based lobbying organization International Center for Alcohol Policies (ICAP). ICAP is active in many African countries, lobbying to limit state regulation of the alcohol industry and promoting policies that encourage "responsible drinking." However, research shows that educational approaches are not that effective. Experts on alcohol policies and social activists argue that higher taxes and restrictions on the availability of alcohol are the most effective ways to reduce the negative impacts of alcohol. Endahl claims that ICAP advocates policies that do not take into account the effects of alcohol on public health, violence against women, HIV, and poverty. "They [ICAP] are extremely keen to avoid regulations of the market through increased taxes, a change of opening hours and age limits, etc."

It is not only tobacco and alcohol companies that exploit the weaknesses of the poor. Even Unilever, a consumer products company, preys on the anxieties of disadvantaged people by marketing a highly profitable skin-whitening cream, Fair & Lovely.

Fair & Lovely

Created by Unilever's research laboratories in India, Fair & Lovely claims to offer dramatic skin-whitening results in just six weeks. On its website, the company calls its product "the miracle worker," which is "proven to deliver one to three shades of change."[49] Fair & Lovely, the best selling skin whitening cream in the world, is clearly doing well. First launched in India in 1975, it held a commanding 50 to 70 percent share of the skin whitening market in India in 2006, a market valued at over $200 million and growing at 10 to 15 percent per annum.[50] Fair & Lovely is marketed by Unilever in 30 countries across Asia, Africa, and the Middle East, with India being the largest single market.

Claims of Doing Good

Hindustan Unilever Limited, Unilever's Indian subsidiary, claims Fair & Lovely is doing good by fulfilling a social need. HUL research says that "90 percent of Indian women want to use whiteners because it is aspirational, like losing weight. A fair skin is like education, regarded as a social and economic step up."[51]

This is a deeply racist view and hopefully not shared by HUL management.

More importantly, BOP proponents Hammond and Prahalad have applauded Fair & Lovely for doing good. They claim a poor woman now "has a choice and feels empowered because of an affordable consumer product formulated for her needs," and that HUL is making the poor better off by providing "real value in dignity and choice."[52]

Unilever was the lead company mentioned in a 2007 *Business Week* cover story on corporate social responsibility.[53] "You can't ignore the impact your company has on the community and the environment," said the then CEO Patrick Cescau. However, contrary to all these claims, Fair & Lovely is not doing good, and has a negative impact on public welfare.

Target Market

The target market for Fair & Lovely is predominantly women aged 18 to 35 years. Disturbingly, "there is repeated evidence that school-girls in the 12 to 14 age range widely use fairness creams."[54] The poor are also a significant target market for Fair & Lovely. HUL marketed the product in "affordable" small-size pouches to facilitate purchase by the poor. Sam Balsara, president of the Advertising Agencies Association of India said, "Fair & Lovely did not become a problem today. It's been making inroads into poor people's budgets for a long time. I remember being told back in 1994 by mothers in a Hyderabad slum that all their daughters regularly used Fair & Lovely." It is a romanticized view that these poor girls and women are rational discerning consumers acting in their true self-interest.

Product Efficacy

Many dermatologists, including Professor A.B.M. Faroque, chair of the Department of Pharmaceutical Technology, the University of Dhaka, Bangladesh, have questioned the efficacy of Fair & Lovely and other skin whitening creams.[55] Since Fair & Lovely is categorized as a cosmetic product, not as a pharmaceutical, Unilever has not been required to prove efficacy. Professor Faroque adds that, ironically, despite the obsession with fair skin, dark skin is actually healthier and less vulnerable to skin diseases than lighter skin because it contains more melanin that provides protection from the sun. Unilever claims that the technology used in its Fair & Lovely products has been sold in over 30 countries for the past 30 years to millions of satisfied customers, who bear testimony to the safety and efficacy of its product. This is a yet another romanticized view of the poor as consumers: Just because they buy the product, it does not mean that it is efficacious or good for them.

Controversial Advertisements

Fair & Lovely's heavily aired television commercials typically feature a depressed-seeming woman with few prospects, who achieves a brighter future by either attaining a boyfriend/husband or a job after becoming markedly fairer, which is shown in the advertisements with a silhouette of her face lined up dark to light. A BBC television report on the subject of racist advertising in India, highlighted one notorious TV commercial in India (often referred to as the Air Hostess advertisement), which "showed a young, dark-skinned girl's father lamenting he had no son to provide for him, as his daughter's salary was not high enough—the suggestion being that she could not get a better job or get married because of her dark skin. The girl then uses the cream [Fair & Lovely], becomes fairer, and gets a better-paid job as an air hostess—and makes her father happy."[56] Such advertisements have attracted much public criticism, especially from women's groups, in many countries including India, Bangladesh, Malaysia, and Egypt.

Brinda Karat, general secretary of the All India Democratic Women's Congress (AIDWC), called the Fair & Lovely advertising campaign "highly racist,...discriminatory on the basis of the color of skin,...[and] an affront to a woman's dignity."[57] The AIDWC campaign against Fair & Lovely advertising culminated in the Indian government banning two Fair & Lovely commercials, including the notorious Air Hostess advertisement, in 2003. Ravi Shankar Prasad, India's information and broadcasting minister, said at the time, "I will not allow repellent advertisements such as this to be aired."[58] "Fair & Lovely cannot be supported because the advertising is demeaning to women and the women's movement," the minister said.[59]

In October 2008, the Advertising Standards Authority in the UK said that a Fair & Lovely commercial made claims that were "misleading," and ruled that it should not be broadcast again.[60] The advertisement had been broadcast in the UK on Nepali TV in the Bengali language. Unilever responded that the ad was created for use in India and Bangladesh and was not supposed to be shown in the UK. It seems Unilever has a double standard; misleading advertisements that cannot be shown in the UK are designed for poor countries where there are more disadvantaged consumers, and the regulatory standards are either lax or not enforced.

Empowerment for Women

Unilever's response to the criticism it has received for its Fair & Lovely advertisements assumes a view that the poor are rational, well-educated consumers. Arun Adhikari, executive director for personal products at HUL, said, "We are not glorifying the negative but we show how the product can lead to a transformation, with romance and a husband the pay-off."[61] The creator of the Air Hostess advertisement, R. Balakrishnan, argued that "the consumer automatically regulates advertising...[and] is extremely mature, as she is shelling out money for our product."[62] It is a romanticized view that sees the poor consumers as powerful enough to regulate advertising. After the Indian government banned two Fair & Lovely commercials, HUL was unrepentant and argued that its commercials were about "choice and economic empowerment for women," and the company has continued to produce similar advertisements.

The women's movements obviously do not buy this argument. This is not empowerment; at best, it is a mirage; at worst, it serves to entrench women's disempowerment. The way to truly empower a woman is to make her less poor, financially independent, and better educated; social and cultural changes also need to occur that eliminate the prejudices that are the cause of her deprivations. If she were truly empowered, she would probably refuse to buy a skin whitener in the first place.

Constraints on Free Markets

Fair & Lovely is clearly doing well; it is a very profitable and high-growth brand for Unilever in many countries. The company is not breaking any laws; millions of women voluntarily buy the product and seem to be loyal customers.

In a classic free market argument, HUL says, "The protests of women's activist groups bear no relationship to the popularity of Fair & Lovely."[63] Unilever is behaving legally, as a capitalistic firm in a free market. But there is an evident contradiction between this argument and HUL's explicit and vociferous espousal of corporate social responsibility. The free-market approach does not work well in this case because of the vulnerability of the consumers—poor girls and women—who are also victims of racist and sexist prejudices within the society. This concern is greater when children use the product. Unilever did not create the sexist and racist prejudices that, at least, partially feed the demand for this product. However, it is likely that the company has helped to sustain these prejudices even if unwittingly.

When there is a divergence between private profits and public welfare, markets should not be left totally free, and some intervention is warranted. When the profit-maximizing behavior of firms results in negative consequences to public welfare, as in the case of Fair & Lovely, constraints need to be imposed on the behaviors of firms. Constraints can be achieved through four mechanisms: corporate social responsibility, self-regulation by industry, activism by civil society, and government regulation. First, a firm could voluntarily constrain its own behavior and act in the public interest. The firm might choose to do so because it exercises corporate social responsibility even though it involves some financial penalty. A second possibility is for firms in an industry (or industries) to self-regulate their conduct perhaps to reduce free-rider problems and to pre-empt government regulation. The third possibility is for civil society to pressure companies to act in the public interest. Finally, the government could regulate firm conduct to achieve public welfare. Unfortunately, none of these constraints is working well in this case so far.

More Government, Please

There is a strong need for checks and balances on powerful companies, especially MNCs, marketing to the poor. The romanticization of the poor as "value-conscious consumers" has resulted in too little emphasis on legal, regulatory, and social mechanisms to protect these vulnerable consumers. In the absence of such protective mechanisms, even companies that proclaim to be socially responsible market products to the poor that are of dubious value and possibly even harmful.

In recent years, the political ideology of the world has shifted decisively toward an increased role for markets.[64] There is a growing libertarian movement that seeks to decrease the role of the state and to "marketize" all public sector functions. In particular, the BOP proposition argues that the private sector should play the leading role in poverty reduction; "governments and donors become mere catalysts of business activity."[65] This libertarian perspective is intrinsically flawed and problematic because it grossly underemphasizes both the role and the responsibility of the state for poverty reduction.

There is much ideological debate about the roles of free markets and the state in achieving overall economic growth and development. Regardless of one's position on this ideological debate, there is no denying a much-needed role for the state. Financial economists Rajan and Zingales, from the University of Chicago, persuasively argue, "markets cannot flourish without the very visible hand of the governments."[66] It is the role of the state to mediate the relationship between markets and society. There is also a need to impose some restrictions on free markets to prevent exploitation of the vulnerable. Another vital role of the state is to provide basic services such as infrastructure, public health, and education. Both these responsibilities of the state are even more critical in the context of poverty reduction.

Broad View of Poverty

Poverty cannot be defined only in economic terms; it is about a much broader set of needs that permit well-being. The words of Amartya Sen, quoted in Chapter 1, bear repeating: "The point is not the irrelevance of economic variables such as personal incomes, but their severe inadequacy in measuring many of the causal influences on the quality of life and survival chances of people."[67] The BOP proposition focuses on companies, marketing, and financial outcomes; it sees the social, cultural, and political benefits, at best, as by-products of economic gains. In contrast, social, cultural, and political freedoms are desirable in and of themselves, and they also enable individual income growth. Government and public policy should take a more active role in cultivating and safeguarding these other noneconomic freedoms.

The improvement in social indicators in many developing countries has not kept pace with economic growth and the decline in income poverty. This is the result of government failure, for example in India, to "fulfill the traditional, accepted functions...like public safety and security, universal literacy and primary education, public health education, provision of drinkable water, sanitation drains and sewage facilities, public health (infectious and epidemic diseases), building roads, and creating and disseminating agricultural technology."[68] These functions have a direct and significant impact on productivity. While there has been a distinct worldwide shift in political ideology toward an increasing role of the market (as opposed to the government), providing the above functions still needs to be in the public domain, especially in the context of helping the poor and alleviating poverty. There is much controversy surrounding the issue of privatizing these functions, especially in countries with "failed" governments.[69] Even with privatization, it is difficult to eliminate the role of the government. For example, if the water supply is privatized, the government still needs to regulate rates or ensure that the poor have enough purchasing power to buy water.

The empirical evidence supports a larger role for the state in providing social services in developing countries. Public expenditure on education as a percentage of GNP for developed countries was 5.46 percent in 1980 and 5.54 percent in 1997; the comparable numbers for developing countries were 3.99 percent and 3.92 percent.[70] World Bank data indicate public education expenditure to be 5.6 percent of GDP for developed countries and 4.1 percent for developing countries, in 2004. Similarly, public health expenditure accounted for 6.7 percent of GDP in 2004 in high-income countries compared to 1.3 percent in low-income countries.[71] Governments in developing countries need to play a larger role in both education and public health.

BOP proponents argue that the poor accept that having access to running water is not a "realistic option" and therefore spend their income on things that they can get now that improve the quality of their lives.[72] In 2005, Prahalad said: "If people have no sewage and drinking water, should we also deny them televisions and cell phones?"[73] This is at best a disingenuous argument; and at worst, cynical exploitation.

The real question is: Why do the poor accept that access to running water is not a "realistic option"? We should not accept this bleak view, even if they do. Instead, we should acknowledge the failure of government and attempt to correct it. We need to give a voice to the poor—this is a central aspect of the development process. By emphatically focusing on the private sector, the libertarian approach ignores the imperative to correct the failure of government to fulfill its traditional and accepted functions, such as public safety, basic education, public health, and infrastructure. There is no viable alternative mechanism for achieving these results.

According to a popular myth, upon being told that the peasantry had no bread to eat, Marie Antoinette callously said, "Let them eat cake." Upon being told today that the poor have no drinking water, presumably she would say, "Let them drink Evian." The BOP proposition goes a step further and suggests "Let them watch television." Adding to the ideological quagmire, it argues that the television manufacturers are being virtuous because selling to the poor helps alleviate poverty. Even if we concede that televisions help the poor to escape the burden of their bleak lives, and thus provide some value to them, how do they help eradicate poverty?

The libertarian approach grossly underemphasizes the critical role and responsibility of the state to reduce poverty. The support for the libertarian approach is *intellectually* problematic; its implications are *morally* problematic. Instead of relying exclusively on the invisible hand of free markets to alleviate poverty, it would be much more appropriate to require the state to extend a very visible hand to the poor to help them climb out of poverty.

The downside of the libertarian approach can be illustrated by the following parable.

A seriously wounded person is being tended by an ineffective doctor (either incompetent or corrupt or both). A Good Samaritan is appalled by the situation and takes charge—and puts a Band-aid on the patient. The doctor walks away thinking somebody else is now responsible for the patient. The Samaritan feels good about his actions. A management consultant advises the Samaritan to start a business of selling Band-aids. The patient continues to deteriorate.

PART II

Effective Strategies

Part I of this book presented the reasons the libertarian approach to reducing poverty is not effective. The second part of the book explores strategies for poverty reduction that are effective and outlines the appropriate roles for business, government, and civil society.

To reduce poverty it is necessary to focus on increasing the income of the poor by viewing them as producers. The primary emphasis in poverty reduction must be on creating employment opportunities for the poor. The private sector is clearly the best engine for job creation. Business needs to create jobs suited to the poor in labour intensive, low-skill sectors of the economy. The government should facilitate job creation by fostering an environment conducive for business to grow and thrive. The government also needs to increase the employability of the poor by improving their skills and capabilities, and by reducing friction in labour markets.

As noted in Chapter 1, another role of the government is to provide basic public services, such as education, public health, sanitation, and infrastructure, and it is the poor who bear a disproportionate share of the burden when the government fails in this responsibility. While having access to these services probably leads to increasing the productivity of the poor, it is important in and of itself. Although there is no fortune to be made by marketing to the poor, it is possible, on a limited scale, for companies to make profits by selling to the poor, and we need to ensure that the products and services targeted to the poor really benefit them. Markets often fail, and it is another role of the government to enact appropriate regulations that will protect the vulnerable consumers, especially the poor.

Civil society plays a critical supporting role, which is to be a catalyst for action, advocate, and watchdog, ensuring that both business and government fulfill their responsibilities. Figure II.1 summarizes the roles of the three actors.

	Poor as Producers	Poor as Consumers
Business	• Provide employment opportunities. (Chapter 6)	• Sell products and services that the poor can afford and that are beneficial to the poor. (Chapter 5)
Government	• Facilitate business growth and job creation. (Chapter 6) • Increase employability of the poor, and reduce friction in labour markets. (Chapter 6)	• Provide basic public services. (Chapter 7) • Regulate markets to protect vulnerable consumers. (Chapter 7)
Civil Society	• Catalyst, advocate, and watchdog to ensure that both business and government fulfil their responsibilities. (Chapter 8)	

Figure II.1 Framework for fighting poverty

CHAPTER 5

Selling Beneficial Goods to the Poor

The poor, of course, have many unmet needs.[1] It would be a painless solution to the problem of poverty if business could satisfy all (or most of) these needs and make a profit in the bargain. That, as we saw in Chapters 3 and 4, is the seductive appeal of the BOP proposition. However, while the BOP proposition is not the solution, and while there are too many examples of businesses that profit by exploiting the poor, some opportunities do exist for firms to make profits and simultaneously help alleviate poverty. We need profitable businesses that sell products and services that benefit the poor and genuinely improve the quality of their lives, at prices they can afford. After an extensive survey, Monitor Group, a consulting firm, concluded that there are very few examples of profitable large-scale businesses that market truly beneficial goods in low-income markets.[2] The challenge is to design creative market-based solutions for alleviating poverty.

This chapter examines three business ventures that market beneficial products to the poor, which have not been commercial successes. The multinational companies Procter & Gamble,

Essilor, and Danone each launched initiatives, which so far, have failed to generate adequate profits. As a result, the companies have significantly scaled back their initial plans and converted their efforts into small experimental operations. There is nonetheless much to learn from these failures about how to design profitable businesses targeting the poor. Conclusions from these three examples are then reinforced by analyzing more successful ventures: mobile phones and Nirma (a low-cost detergent marketed by an Indian firm).

Far from triggering a revolution in business thinking, developing successful strategies requires firms to "get back to basics." Low-income markets are different than affluent ones; however, although the context changes, the logic of business does not change: Durable business principles are still effective guides to strategy development. The generous and well-intentioned social objective of addressing the needs of the poor must not hide the fact that these opportunities present tough economic and strategic challenges. The desire to do good should not blind managers to the realities of the underlying economic forces that determine business success and failure.

The first lesson in designing market-based solutions for alleviating poverty is that the unmet needs of the poor (such as clean drinking water) do not necessarily constitute a market. A market can exist only if there are buyers willing and able to pay a price that covers the total cost of production, including the opportunity cost of capital used. Unfortunately, because of the very meager income of the poor, markets for many socially useful goods simply do not exist. The second and most important lesson is that firms have to dramatically reduce costs, even if this means reducing quality, in order develop the poor as a market. This does not mean selling shoddy or dangerous products. As noted earlier, it means that firms need to make the appropriate cost–quality trade-offs. The third lesson is that creating efficient distribution networks is critical to the success of such initiatives. Vertical integration into proprietary distribution channels is probably not a good solution. The final lesson is that trying to achieve multiple social objectives, such as environmental sustainability, makes it even harder for the initiatives to succeed. It is difficult enough to combine profitability with selling beneficial goods to the poor without adding more constraints.

The 4 Cs of Marketing

It is quite easy to make profits by exploiting the poor by selling them harmful products (I am using the term "product" here generically, to include services). To understand the poor as a market, we need to start by making some judgments about whether the products are beneficial or harmful to them. The libertarian approach argues that if the poor buy the products, then they must be beneficial. Development economist Esther Duflo calls this the "moronic revealed-preferences" argument.[3] The poor, like everyone else, sometimes make bad choices. What is really needed is to look beyond the expressed preferences and focus on what is truly in the self-interest of the poor.

The second dimension in understanding the poor as a market is whether selling them a particular product is profitable or not for companies. Figure 5.1 categorizes the markets of the poor along these two dimensions. The iconic products in the four quadrants are cigarettes, colas, cell phones, and condoms, and constitute the 4 Cs of marketing to the poor.

The *cigarettes quadrant* includes products that are profitable for firms but harmful to the poor. Given that the poor are vulnerable consumers, it is quite easy to make profits by selling tobacco and alcohol to the poor, which are obviously bad for them. Another way a product can harm the poor is by diverting their scarce money from more useful expenditures. The poor might be better off spending less on cosmetics and more on nutrition.

The *colas quadrant* includes products that are neither profitable for companies nor beneficial for the poor. The most common examples in this quadrant are various consumer-packaged goods, such as ice cream. The poor have higher-priority needs, nutrition,

	Beneficial for the Poor	Harmful for the Poor
Profitable	**Cell Phones** Nirma detergent Markets at their best No need for intervention	**Cigarettes** Alcohol Fair & Lovely High interest consumption loans Need for constraints on markets: corporate social responsibility, self-regulation, social activism, government regulation
Not Profitable	**Condoms** Clean water Eyeglasses Need for government or civil society to subsidize Challenge: Creative business models that are profitable	**Colas** Ice cream Candy Markets penalize business No need for intervention

Figure 5.1   The 4 Cs of marketing to the poor

for instance, and would be better off not buying these products. The reality is that many of these products are too expensive, and so the poor do not buy them; hence companies that manufacture and sell them are not profitable. In this case, there is no need for outside intervention; free markets self-regulate, penalizing the firms with losses and keeping the market size small. A representative example of this is Coca-Cola's experience in India.

Balakrishna and Sidharth applaud Coca-Cola in India for launching in 2003 its low-price, affordability strategy, which hinged on increasing the overall consumer base by offering carbonated soft drinks in smaller cans and bottles that presumably the poor could afford: 200-milliliter (6.75 ounces) at Rs. 5, which is equivalent to $0.34 at PPP.[4] Compare this to the United States, where a 355-milliliter (11.8 ounces) can of Coca-Cola typically sells for $0.25. This is "affordability" for the Indian poor? Coca-Cola's initiative certainly did not help the poor. Nor did it help Coca-Cola. Facing complaints from its bottlers and retailers, the company reversed this low-price strategy and began to raise prices in India by August 2004.[5]

The *cell phones quadrant* includes products that are both profitable for firms and beneficial for the poor; Nirma detergent is an example. Cell phones have achieved significant penetration among the poor, and at the same time have improved their quality of life. This is a win-win solution, an example of free markets at their best. There is no need for outside intervention here. The problem, however, is that there are very few examples in this quadrant. The challenge is to create more opportunities in this quadrant.

The *condoms quadrant* includes products that are unprofitable for companies but beneficial for the poor, and they are products that meet the unmet needs of the poor. Unfortunately, this quadrant is filled with products that cost more to produce than the poor consumer is able to pay. It is not that the poor do not value the products; they just do not have the money to be able to afford them. Condoms are clearly beneficial for the poor for two reasons: pregnancy avoidance and prevention of sexually transmitted diseases. The prices of condoms, however, are very high and many poor people cannot afford them.

In India, the market for condoms is divided into three segments. The first segment began in the 1960s with a government program to distribute free Nirodh condoms through government hospitals and health centers. Making this supply available for free was intended to address the unmet needs of 40 percent of the population living below the official poverty line. In 2003, the Indian government distributed 891 million free condoms. The second segment is social marketing programs launched by the Indian government in 1968 to cater to people who can afford to pay for condoms, but cannot afford the market price. The government supplied condoms to marketing companies and NGOs at subsidized rates for sale in the open market. The intention was to target people living above the poverty line, covering 47 percent of the population. In 2003, 513 million condoms were sold at subsidized prices. The third segment consists of condoms sold by private companies in India at free market prices.

In this quadrant, free markets do not work to satisfy the unmet needs of the poor. There is a strong need for governments or civil society to subsidize these products. Civil society, however, usually does not have the resources to do this on a large scale, which leaves government to play the critical role. It is only a second-order question whether the government directly provides the products or subsidizes a private firm (or civil society) that provides them.

The only other alternative is to creatively design a profitable business model that moves a product from the *condom* quadrant into the *cell phone* quadrant. My objective in this chapter is to analyze several case studies and derive some insights for potential business models that address this challenge.

Case Studies

The three case studies described below are based on data from published sources and private conversations with senior executives from the companies.

Essilor and Vision Correction

About 2.3 billion people in the world suffer from poor vision due to refractive error, a common disorder of the eye that causes blurred vision. The treatment for refractive error is simple and cost-effective: eyeglasses. Nevertheless, in 2009, it was estimated that 564 million people who need eyeglasses do not have access to them.[6] In the mid-2000s, only 7 percent of the Indian population actually wore glasses, whereas about 65 percent of the population needed them.[7]

Essilor International is a large French company that designs, manufactures, and sells plastic corrective opthalmic lenses and instruments in over 100 countries worldwide. With revenues of about $4.2 billion in 2009 and a global market share of about 30 percent, Essilor dominates the ophthalmic lens industry.

In 2005, Essilor partnered with the Indian not-for-profit eye hospitals Aravind (discussed in Chapter 3) and Sankara Nethralaya to launch an initiative to bring corrective lenses to India's rural poor. The project started with four "refraction vans," that is, mobile optician shops, which visited villages to prescribe and sell corrective eyeglasses to poor people suffering from visual disorders. Initially, a pair of eyeglasses was priced at less than 200 rupees ($4). Essilor considered scaling up the operation; the company estimated with 1,000 vans it could reach all 600,000 villages of India. However, even with donations/sponsorships and despite significant price increases, the project hardly earns its cost of capital. After trying to franchise the vans to local opticians, Essilor decided to operate them on its own and to limit future investments to the amount of cash generated by the existing vans. In 2010, Essilor was operating only eight refraction vans.

Procter & Gamble and Clean Drinking Water

In 2002, 18 percent of the world's population (1.1 billion people) did not have access to a safe, affordable, sustainable source of drinking water.[8] Lack of clean drinking water is not just an inconvenience; it has major health implications and consequences. Approximately 1.6 million people, over 90 percent of whom are children, die every year from cholera and other diarrheal diseases, which are waterborne diseases. Other diseases that can be picked up from unsafe drinking water include the parasitic diseases intestinal helmints and schistosomiasis (snail fever), trachoma (a bacterial infection of the eye and a leading cause of blindness), hepatitis A (an acute infectious disease of the liver), and arsenic poisoning.

In 1995, P&G, which had been researching new water-purifying technologies since 1991, formed a partnership with the Centers for Disease Control and Prevention (CDC) in the United States to develop a low-cost water purification technology to deliver commercial and public health benefits.[9] In 2000, after some failed attempts, these efforts culminated in the launch of a product it called PUR: Purifier of Water, a powder that, when mixed with water, leaves it visibly clean and produces no unpleasant aftertaste. PUR was easy to use, requiring only basic household equipment: a bucket and tightly woven cloth. P&G originally sold PUR in a small sachet, enough to purify 10 liters of water, which was priced at US$ 0.10 per sachet. Following positive test marketing in Guatemala, P&G rolled out PUR on a larger scale in 2001. These larger tests, however, only yielded market penetration rates of about 15 percent in the Philippines and 5 percent in Guatemala. In 2002, P&G decided to stop the large-scale tests and to conduct further tests in Morocco and Pakistan. In 2004, P&G launched PUR on a mass scale in Pakistan. However, repeat purchase rates hovered around 5 percent; the scale-up in Pakistan failed.

In 2005, P&G officially abandoned attempts to commercialize PUR, and transformed the project into a corporate social responsibility program.[10] P&G announced its new noncommercial approach and its decision to sell PUR at $0.04 per sachet, the cost of production, to nonprofit humanitarian organizations.

Grameen Danone Foods and Child Nutrition

Good nutrition, especially for children, is the cornerstone of survival, health, and development. Undernourished children have lowered resistance to infection and disease and are more likely than well-nourished children to die from common childhood ailments. Recurrent illness saps nutritional status, locking those who survive into a vicious cycle of sickness and faltering growth. In 2007, 23 percent of children in the world under the age of five years suffered from malnutrition, as measured by WHO standards; in Bangladesh, the comparable number was 41 percent.[11]

In 2006, Danone, a large food and beverage MNC, teamed with Grameen Bank to create Grameen Danone Foods Ltd. (GDFL), with the mission of alleviating "poverty by implementing an innovative business model which will bring healthy and wholesome food to the poorest everyday."[12] GDFL developed a yogurt product called Shoktidoi (which means "strengthening yogurt"), which was specifically designed to address the problem of malnutrition in children. Shoktidoi is rich in protein and calcium, and contains active bacteria that help curtail the severity and duration of bouts of diarrhea.

As a "social business," GDFL was set up to generate enough revenue to sustain itself but not to earn economic profits nor to pay dividends. Danone and Grameen Bank agreed to reinvest all the cash the project generated back into the business. The expected profits were 3 percent of sales over the long term. The business plan called for the venture's first plant to begin operating in early 2007, to break even in 2008, and to run at full capacity in 2010. The long-term plan was to expand to 50 factories located throughout Bangladesh.

The first GDFL factory in Bangladesh is smaller, simpler, and less automated than Danone's usual plants, with a capacity of 3,000 tons per year compared to 400,000 tons at Danone's biggest dairy plant in Europe. The Shoktidoi brand yogurt was introduced at a price of 5 takas ($0.07) per 80-gram serving (2.8 ounces). In 2008, the price was changed to 6 takas per 60-gram serving (2.1 ounces). GDFL's initial plan was to distribute the yogurt only through female sales representatives, dubbed "Shokti Ladies," who would sell the product door-to-door.

Sales have been disappointing, and the Shokti Ladies distribution strategy has not worked as expected. GDFL sold only 150 tons of yogurt in 2008 and expected to sell 500 tons in 2009, compared to the plant capacity of 3,000 tons. Sales through urban grocery stores targeted at the middle class account for 80 percent of sales, and only 20 percent of its sales are through Shokti Ladies to the rural market. Danone executives now believe that urban sales are needed to subsidize the rural sales. GDFL had an operating loss of 21 million takas ($0.3 million) in 2008, and losses are expected to remain at roughly the same level in 2009, even though volumes are supposed to grow. GDFL nevertheless decided to build a second factory in Bangladesh.

The Cost of Capital Trap

The notion of a "social business," as put forth by Muhammad Yunus,[13] is based on the theory that the poverty problem can be solved by creating what he calls "not-for-loss" businesses. While traditional not-for-profit initiatives might not be sustainable in the long run because they depend on donations, he says, not-for-loss businesses are viable because they cover their operating costs.

However, Yunus deliberately ignores the cost of capital. The objective of private firms is not just accounting profits, but rather "economic profits," defined as accounting profits minus the opportunity cost of capital. The logic for determining the cost of capital is the opportunity cost of foregoing other alternative investments, adjusted for risk. The ability to generate accounting profits is not enough; economic profitability is necessary to make a project truly viable in the long run, along with being scalable by attracting additional capital. Regardless of the social (or environmental) benefits of a project, if it generates return on investment lower than the cost of capital, it is doomed to remain underfunded and to operate on a small scale, because it will have access mostly to donations, not free-market equity funding. Investors in social businesses are really acting as philanthropists.

Vikram Akula, the CEO and founder of SKS Microfinance, a $250 million microfinance firm in India, challenges Yunus's view: "When I started SKS ten years ago, [...] I established it as a nonprofit with lots of small donations from friends and relatives. I had certainly admired Grameen Bank's group-lending model, but wasn't a big fan of Yunus's theory that microfinance firms should be merely self-sustaining companies—what he calls "social businesses." I felt that if the industry were going to provide the estimated $300 billion of credit needed by the poor, it would have to tap larger, commercial capital markets—and that meant structuring our business so that investors could expect significant returns."[14]

An organization that earns accounting profits but not economic profits still needs philanthropic donors to survive. There is no conceptual difference between a not-for-profit that incurs an accounting loss of, say, $1 per year and needs philanthropic donors to cover this operating loss versus a not-for-loss organization that covers its operating costs every year but needs $10 of philanthropic capital at the beginning, assuming the cost of capital to be 10 percent. Or, put differently, there is little difference to a philanthropist between donating $1 per year forever and donating $10 of capital up front, assuming the cost of capital to be 10 percent.

One way to support initiatives for which the return on capital is not expected to be sufficient is to fund them as social businesses through separate foundations. For example, Danone has created the Danone Communities fund in order to decouple such social business initiatives like the Grameen–Danone joint venture from its mainstream business operations. The Danone Communities fund invests in social business initiatives, as well as in financial securities. Its overall return is supposed to just beat the risk-free rate of return. Shareholders thus do not donate the money; they entrust the money to the fund. However, they are, in effect, making a charitable donation: the difference between the cost of capital and their return. It is worth noting that, in 2009, only 10 percent of Danone Communities' resources are allocated to social businesses, the rest being invested in risk-free placements.

Social businesses are not good examples of market-based solutions to poverty. Surely, the market-based or libertarian approach implies that companies achieve economic profits, not just that they do not have an operating loss.

The Unmet Needs Trap

Paramount among the unmet needs of the poor is vision care. Half of the world population on average needs to wear spectacles, but in India, for example, the market penetration of eyeglasses is dramatically lower, at only 7 percent, because the poor do not have access to eyeglasses and/or cannot afford them. This is often seen as a huge business opportunity for a firm to market eye-glasses to the needy.

But a market exists only to the extent that there are buyers willing and able to pay a price for a product that exceeds what it costs the seller to produce it, including the opportunity cost of capital. The perceived consumer value must exceed the price; and the buyers have to be willing and able to pay this price. A firm is willing and able to sell at this price only if its revenues exceed its total costs. The size of a market and the price of the product are determined by the intersection of the demand and supply curves. If these curves do not intersect, there will be no market for a product, even if it fulfills an unmet need. For example, there is a need for homes that utilize only solar energy. But the price consumers are willing to pay for solar energy is low compared to the cost of manufacturing solar panels and energy-storage devices—there is an unmet need but no appreciable market. The basic rules of economics have not been repealed for the poor. The poor clearly have unmet needs for eyeglasses, clean water, and nutritious food; however, the three case studies demonstrate that Essilor, P&G, and Danone are struggling to find business opportunities here.

Assessing the size of the unmet need should not be confused with an estimate of the potential market opportunity. For example, when assessing the size of the unmet need for eyeglasses in India, a plausible starting assumption is that the percentage of the population having refractive problems is the same in India as in other countries for which detailed data are available. Information about the number of eyeglasses sold in India is also readily available. Hence, it is fairly easy to assess the size of the unmet need for eyeglasses. Estimating the size of the potential market, however, is far more difficult. Assuming a price of $4 per pair of eyeglasses, it is not easy to figure out how many poor people will be able and willing to buy them. Conducting market research is significantly more difficult among the poor than in more affluent and devel-oped markets. The logistics of reaching the poor is more demand-ing and expensive. Because the poor are often not well informed about a product, they cannot easily answer a questionnaire about their future willingness to buy it. There are few comparable products from which one can extrapolate by analogy.

A more extreme reason these markets are so small is that many poor people are not well informed or well educated enough to fully appreciate the value of the product or service being offered. For example, a survey conducted by the Monitor Group in 2009 in India found that 60 percent of the respondents would not switch to purified water "even if it was free."[15] It is difficult to understand such responses given the evidence that waterborne diseases are a major cause of bad health among the poor. In a similar vein, a survey in Timor-Leste found that 55 percent of rural women were unwilling to pay even $1 for eyeglasses, despite the significant impact of eyeglasses on worker productivity and quality of life.[16] A major cost for firms serving these markets is the cost of educating the potential consumers.

Confusing unmet need and market size leads to disappointing performance. For example, while child nutrition is obviously a salient need in Bangladesh, the market for GDFL's Shoktidoi yogurt was grossly overestimated. Since its launch in February 2007, the factory has never operated at more than 25 percent of its production capacity, even though the plant is dramatically smaller than Danone's traditional units in developed countries. This is even more disappointing since 80 percent of the current sales are to the urban middle class rather than to the rural poor, the primary target of the original project.

The size of the unmet needs market, like any other market, can grow bigger if the supply or demand curves shift outward. The demand curve can shift out if the income of the poor increases, or if the poor assign a higher perceived value to the product because they have become better educated about its benefits. Educating the poor about product benefits is expensive, and increases the costs of the firm taking on this task. The supply curve can shift out if technological innovation significantly reduces costs, such as is the case in mobile telecommunications. Unfortunately, such shifts in the supply curve have not occurred for the great majority of the unmet needs of the poor, and certainly not for the three case studies involving eyeglasses, clean water, and child nutrition.

Moral indignation and a righteous sense of social injustice are appropriate responses to the extent of unfulfilled basic human needs of the poor, such as safe drinking water, sanitation, nutrition, shelter, energy, basic health care, and education. If the market size is too small compared to the unmet need, market-based solutions are not a feasible way to alleviate poverty. Philanthropic responses—traditional charity organizations or social businesses—will work better. The problem with that is "scalability." Unfortunately, the scale of philanthropy—even taking into account large donors like Bill Gates and Warren Buffet—is too small compared to the immense size of the unmet needs. Governments must play a critical role in this context.

Private companies trying to implement market-based solutions to alleviate poverty by marketing socially useful goods to the BOP have to create the appropriate market. The key issue is designing a much-needed product in such a way as to make the price truly affordable by the poor.

The Affordability Trap

Firms targeting the BOP often fail because the products are much too expensive and not affordable by the poor. There are two lessons here. First, firms should not overestimate the purchasing power of the poor. Second, firms should adjust the cost-quality trade-off much more significantly to conform to the lower purchasing power of the poor.

Overestimating Purchasing Power

A surprisingly common mistake is that firms and researchers convert the income of the poor using purchasing power parity (PPP) exchange rates, but convert product prices using financial exchange rates. This mistakenly makes products seem more affordable by the poor. Since financial exchange rates are about two to five times higher than PPP exchange rates for most developing countries, this has a big impact on the apparent affordability of products.

The World Bank's commonly used $2 PPP per day standard translates to about Rs. 30 per day in India, using the approximate PPP rate of Rs. 15 per dollar in 2005. Pricing a sachet of PUR at $0.10 makes it seem that the sachet costs 5 percent ($0.10 divided by $2.00) of the poor person's daily income. But since the price was converted at the financial exchange rate of Rs. 45 per dollar, the sachet actually costs Rs. 4.5, which is 15 percent of the poor person's daily income. This is one reason the repeat purchase rates for PUR were very low.

Another cause of overestimating the purchasing power is that firms do not fully appreciate the consumption patterns of the poor. Because basic necessities account for a large fraction of their meager income, there is not much room left for other expenditures.

Essilor justifies setting the price of eyeglasses at Rs. 200 on the grounds that they are priced at around one week of base salary in developed countries. This Rs. 200 per week is roughly consistent with the poverty line of Rs. 30 per day mentioned above. A European can afford to spend 200 euros, about 2 percent of his annual income on eyeglasses. Essilor uses appropriate exchange rates and takes into account the low income of the poor by considering prices as a fraction of income; it thus avoids the PPP exchange rate mistake discussed above, although even then it ends up overestimating the market potential. A poor person in India cannot afford to spend the same percentage of his annual income on eyeglasses since a much larger fraction of his income is needed for more "necessary" needs. The poor in India spend about 80 percent of their income on food, clothing, and fuel, making it difficult to buy a product even as useful as eyeglasses.[17] This partly explains why the proportion of prescriptions that convert into actual purchases in Essilor's initiative is below 40 percent.

Adaptation Trap

All three companies in the case studies fail to achieve the appropriate cost-quality trade-off and end up trying to market products that are too expensive and not affordable by the poor.

Shoktidoi is a dairy product and its storage and transportation require refrigeration, which is obviously a problem given the climate and infrastructure in Bangladesh. Marketing a dry or stable grocery product for child nutrition that does not require refrigeration would have been much less costly. GDFL's choice of yogurt was probably driven by the fact that Danone had divested its biscuit and grocery businesses several years before, and dairy products are currently one of its main business lines. Rather than starting with the problem—child nutrition—and finding the most cost-effective solution, Danone started with the product it markets in affluent countries and tried to adapt it to the low-income markets. The other two companies, P&G and Essilor, fall into the same "adaptation trap."

Essilor's initiative sells polycarbonate-based lenses, which are more expensive (and better quality) than simple glass lenses, probably because Essilor no longer manufactures glass lenses. The Essilor refraction vans are staffed by an optometrist and a technician who perform an eye test for each patient and then prescribe and deliver customized eyeglasses. This is an expensive business model. An alternative and cheaper approach would be to sell pre-manufactured reading glasses that do not require individual customization. The appropriate strength of eyeglasses can be chosen based on a simple test such as looking at a newspaper or threading a needle, and does not require a trained optometrist. Even in developed countries, many people buy reading glasses off the shelf without needing a prescription. The limitation, of course, is that reading glasses are useful only for presbyopic (or farsighted) people. Of patients requiring eyeglasses, about 75 percent suffer from presbyopia, which is an almost inescapable consequence of aging. Thus, a very simple low-cost solution would be effective for 75 percent of the patients. There might even be the potential to sell premanufactured eyeglasses for myopic (or nearsighted) patients; this obviously implies less precision in vision improvement, but at a much lower cost. Realizing that it was falling into the adaptation trap by offering to the poorer market the same degree of customization it offers to more affluent markets, and thereby making the product too expensive for the poor, Essilor recently decided to allow the refraction vans to also distribute ready-made glasses without prescription. These low-range products are outsourced from external low-cost providers. Essilor also has broadened its range of prescription eyeglasses while increasing the average price to $10, which resulted in a 40 percent decrease in volume. Thanks to these changes in pricing and product mix, in addition to its cost reduction initiatives, Essilor's operation has finally turned profitable in an accounting sense. However, Essilor is unwilling to commit new capital to the project since it does not earn more than its cost of capital.

A major cause of the commercial failure of PUR was that the product was too expensive at $0.01 per liter of purified water. P&G used flocculation technology that is superior to simple chlorination of water.[18] A bottle of locally produced hypochlorite solution that chlorinates 1,000 liters of water costs only $0.10 and is effective at killing most bacteria and viruses that cause diarrhea.[19] Some users object to the taste and odor of chlorine. There are also concerns about the potential long-term carcinogenic effects of chlorination. The poor, unfortunately, face a choice between a superior product that they cannot afford and a less effective product, with negative side effects, that they can afford. The CDC considers chlorination a viable option depending upon local conditions because of the immediate and larger benefits of reducing diarrhea. A different low-cost approach is community filtration plants that sell purified water at $0.0025 per liter, which is one-fourth the price of PUR.[20] P&G, too, falls into the adaptation trap. Rather than starting with the problem—the need for safe drinking water—and finding the most cost-effective solution that the poor can afford, P&G starts with the business model it uses in affluent markets. As part of its expansion efforts in the late 1990s,

P&G purchased Recovery Engineering Inc. and its PUR brand water treatment appliances. These products were designed primarily for consumers in the United States who wanted to improve the taste and health safety of tap water.

Firms targeting the markets of the poor need to emphasize the appropriate cost–quality trade-off from the perspective of the poor. A simple or minor adaptation of the business model from affluent markets usually results in products that are too expensive and not affordable by the poor. A significant reduction in quality might be necessary. Selling low-quality products to the poor might seem unethical. However, selling products at the appropriate cost–quality trade-off is not only ethical, it is socially virtuous. If the poor cannot afford customized eyeglasses, they are better off with approximately correct premanufactured eyeglasses than none at all. The appropriate reference point for quality is not the standard prevailing in affluent markets, but rather the status quo in markets of the poor, which is usually unfulfilled basic needs. A low-quality product is better than no product at all.

The dilemma for MNCs is that at the appropriate cost–quality trade-off, the price and the margin may be too low to earn significant profits. PUR does not generate enough sales volume at the price of $0.01 per liter to be commercially viable. The market for hypochlorite solution has very low entry barriers, many local small producers, and is not profitable enough to attract P&G. This is the central dilemma of marketing socially useful goods to the poor. The core challenge of market-based solutions to poverty is finding business models that sell socially virtuous products to the poor and are *simultaneously* profitable for private companies.

Moreover, the new business model required to target the poor consumers may conflict with the established strategy and brand image of the firm. It is unlikely that P&G would risk its global brand image by marketing a water-chlorination product with potential long-term carcinogenic effects, even if the immediate gains from reducing diarrhea were, on balance, greater. Essilor's core business all over the world uses the distribution channel of opticians and optometrists to sell value-added, customized eye-glasses. Essilor has been understandably reluctant to market pre-manufactured, standardized eyeglasses through direct distribution to the poor; this conflict might be confusing and upsetting to the end consumers and the distribution channels, and may endanger its core business.

The Distribution Trap

Creating efficient and viable marketing and distribution support networks is an even bigger challenge than reducing manufacturing costs. Distribution networks to serve the poor, especially in rural areas, do not exist or are very inefficient, and MNCs are forced to create them. Creating socially responsible distribution is essential for the success of market-based solutions to poverty.[21] At the same time, creating a distribution network to reach the poor might be too expensive and contribute to the commercial failure of the project.

The strategic trend among large companies in developed countries has been to deintegrate their activities: Unbundle the value chain, outsource what they can, and focus on their core business. Multinational firms are often ill equipped to forward integrate into distribution, especially in the unfamiliar environment of the poor in emerging economies.

Essilor's core strategy is to sell all its lenses through its own prescription laboratories, but not to integrate forward into retail, which remains the job of independent opticians or chains of optical shops. Essilor's traditional clients are opticians, not patients. When considering the BOP opportunity in India, Essilor first went to Indian opticians and tried to get them engaged in the project. However, most of them rejected the idea, arguing that serving the rural poor was too costly, too demanding, and would be unprofitable. It was then that Essilor decided to forward integrate into retail distribution by operating the refraction vans. With this move, Essilor entered a business that the local specialists deemed unprofitable, and was beyond the company's core competencies; it also became a low price competitor to its traditional customers.

GDFL did not initially consider supermarkets and grocery stores to market Shoktidoi because they operate only in urban areas and serve the middle class, rather than the poor population. Like Essilor, the company tried to meet this challenge with an innovative distribution plan. Building on Grameen's microfinance experience (micro-loans distributed by the Grameen Ladies), GDFL decided to create its team of independent female sales representatives, Shokti Ladies, to sell Shoktidoi door-to-door, directly to the consumers. Danone executives now acknowledge that the Shokti Ladies strategy has been a failure. GDFL started with 60 Shokti Ladies in February 2007, who all left in April 2007 when production at the factory stopped. A new hiring campaign was then launched, and the number of Ladies peaked to 273 in February 2008, but dropped to 17 in September 2008 when demand decreased dramatically, following a price increase that was triggered by a sudden rise in the price of milk. By December 2008, GDFL had only 37 Ladies.

The best-performing Shokti Ladies sold 100 yogurt packages a day, which was half the expected sales level. And because selling Shoktidoi is not a full-time job; Shokti Ladies cannot make a living working for GDFL alone. In 2008, when GDFL realized that the Shokti Lady scheme was not sustainable, it decided to market Shoktidoi through small general stores concomitantly. In June 2009, shops accounted for 80 percent of sales of Shoktidoi, but by using this distribution network, GDFL is marketing to the urban middle class much more than to the rural poor. GDFL has, in fact, created a traditional consumer goods business that subsidizes the money-losing operation targeting the poor. Shoktidoi prices are significantly higher in urban areas: 12 takas per 80-gram serving (2.8 ounces) in the capital Dhaka, compared to 6 takas per 60-gram serving (2.11 ounces) in rural areas. Moreover, urban sales are supported by traditional marketing techniques targeting middle class consumers, such as TV advertising campaigns and product range extensions (e.g., flavored yogurts and drinks).

Thanks to this new revenue stream, GDFL forecasts to sell 1,500 tons of yogurt in 2010 (i.e., 50 percent of the factory's capacity) and to break even in 2011.[22] Meanwhile, it has relaunched its rural marketing initiative: By October 2009, 560 Shokti Ladies were in business, with a new management and a revised training program and compensation scheme.

Proprietary, exclusive, one-product distribution channels do not enjoy economies of scope, are very expensive, and are unlikely to be the solution to the distribution challenge. This is part of the cause of the lack of profitability of the GDFL and Essilor ventures. The exclusive one-product distribution channel of Shokti Ladies is unfeasible because of very high costs: no economies of scope, and inadequate economies of scale due to low volumes. Essilor understood this problem and tried to deintegrate from distribution by franchising its refraction vans to opticians. Potential franchisees immediately asked for permission to use the vans to distribute other products than spectacles equipped with Essilor lenses—they immediately realized the need for economies of scope. In addition to reading glasses, some opticians also suggested selling noncompeting items such as cell phones. Essilor management has been reluctant to accept these proposals.

Some corporations try to solve the problem by partnering with local nonprofit institutions that benefit from strong legitimacy and are already in contact with clients. Danone partnered with the Grameen Bank, which is highly respected in Bangladesh thanks to Muhammad Yunus' reputation. Essilor piggy-backed on the existing "tele-ophthalmology" operations of two hospital chains, Aravind and Sankara Nethralaya, which are also highly respected for their ability to provide the poor with affordable cataract surgery. In both cases, these alliances were instrumental in making "pilot" operations happen by taking advantage of existing nonprofit distribution channels.

While alliances with nonprofit organizations may be instrumental to igniting operations, they cannot be relied on to scale up the business. As discussed earlier, social businesses have problems attracting enough capital to grow a business to a large scale.

Aravind and Sankara Nethralaya were able to partner with Essilor to initiate the project with four refraction vans. It is unlikely they would have been able to participate equally if the project were to expand to 1,000 vans to cover all of India. If a project is to grow as a purely commercial venture, then it has to overcome the "distribution trap."

The Multiple Objectives Trap

While trying to combine socially useful products with firm profitability is a major challenge, initiatives for selling to the poor often make this even harder by adding other social and environmental objectives.

GDFL started out with ambitious environmental sustainability objectives. The initial plan was to package Shoktidoi in cups made of polylacticacid (PLA), which is manufactured from corn and is biodegradable. The plant would recycle PLA waste to produce biogas that would be used for lighting and heating purposes. Delivery would be done by cycle rickshaws to avoid fuel consumption. GDFL also planned to encourage customers to use their own containers to fill with yogurt rather than buy it prepackaged. Most of these environmentally friendly plans have been abandoned because they increased the complexity and cost of the project. GDFL now uses polystyrene (an oil derivative) packaging.

GDFL also wanted to create jobs for poor women as a social objective of the venture. This was consistent with the Grameen philosophy of developing and empowering women through microentrepreneurship as way to fight poverty. As discussed above, the Shokti Ladies scheme too has proven to be problematic.

Because of the alliance with eye care hospitals, Aravind and Sankara Nethralaya, the Essilor venture also had the social objective of diagnosing eye diseases. All "eye camps" therefore involved two vans, operated by six people: Essilor's "refraction van" focused on mounting and selling spectacles while the hospital's "tele-ophthalmology van" performed eye-disease diagnosis. However, the staff included only an optometrist, whose training focused on refractive error, not on eye diseases. When the optometrist suspected an eye disease (in particular cataracts, which is a major cause for blindness in India), the optometrist could route the patient to the "tele-ophthalmology van" to perform an examination of the eye fundus (the interior of the eye). The technician conducting the eye examination was in contact with an ophthalmologist in the base hospital using a satellite communication link, hence the "tele-ophthalmology" concept. This, of course, increases the cost and complexity of the initiative. It might have been more profitable to focus on correcting refractive problems, without adding other public health objectives.

Multiple objectives, such as profitability, generating employment, environmental sustainability, and public health, are often in conflict, at least in the sense of drawing on a pool of limited resources, and impose trade-offs. The danger is that attempting to achieve too many objectives simultaneously leads to the project's commercial failure and demise, and none of the objectives being achieved. Perfection is the enemy of the good. Much of the strategy literature emphasizes the value of "focus." Initiatives for selling to the poor are well advised to focus on ensuring the product being marketed is in fact useful to the poor, affordable by the poor, and that the project is economically profitable to enable scaling up.

Sidebar 5.1   Designing a Business Model to Profitably Sell to the Poor

The Cost of Capital Trap

To be sustainable in the long term, a business has to earn more profits than the opportunity cost of capital employed in the business. It is not enough to just cover operating costs.

The Unmet Needs Trap

The size of a market is determined by the number of people willing to pay a price for the product that is higher than the cost of producing the product, not by the number of people who need the product.

The Affordability Trap

The poor can afford only low-priced products because they have very little purchasing power and many competing demands on their meager income.

The Adaptability trap

It is usually necessary to reduce quality in order to significantly reduce costs; the challenge is to make the cost–quality trade-off acceptable to the poor. Starting with the product sold to affluent markets and adapting it to the poor often does not work.

The Distribution Trap

Successful business models often piggyback on existing distribution networks and try to achieve economies of scope. Distribution networks to serve the poor often do not exist or are very inefficient.

Multiple Objectives Trap

Successful ventures have a narrow focus on profitably selling beneficial products to the poor. Trying to serve multiple social objectives usually leads to failure.

Positive Examples

While not common, there are some positive examples of profitable business ventures that provide beneficial products and services to the poor. Two good examples are mobile phones and Nirma (an Indian producer of detergents).

Mobile Phones

Mobile telecommunications is probably one of the best, and well-publicized, examples of successful BOP ventures. In 1995, there were more phone lines in Manhattan than in all of sub-Saharan Africa. Today, the penetration of mobile phones in Africa is 28 percent. More people in China and India own mobile phones than in North America and Europe combined.[23] In India, about 45 percent of poor households own a mobile phone, a penetration rate greater than that for radios, and second only to televisions.[24]

The main perceived benefit of mobile phone usage among the poor is improved communication with family and friends. In addition, several studies have focused on the positive impact of mobile phones on the livelihoods of farmers, fishermen, and small entrepreneurs. There is also much enthusiasm about the potential for mobile phones to deliver other services to the poor, such as public health, financial services, education, government services, and disaster warnings.[25]

It is easy to argue that the poor need mobile phones. The industry has successfully avoided both the unmet needs trap as well as the affordability trap by reducing the total cost of ownership (TCO). According to Nokia research, the TCO across 77 developing countries was $10.88 per month in 2008, down by 20 percent from 2005.[26] Nokia believed that a TCO of $5 or less per month would enable the poor to purchase a mobile phone. In 2008, 12 countries had achieved this $5 target, including in addition to India and China, Pakistan, Bangladesh, and Indonesia.

The TCO comprises three elements: handset (7 percent), service (79 percent), and taxes (14 percent). Technological advances, the learning curve, and economies of scale are largely responsible for the tremendous decrease in the cost of the handsets and mobile services over the last few decades. The worldwide mobile communications industry association's Emerging Market Handset program achieved its goal of reducing the price of entry-level handsets to less than $30 in 2006.[27] The cost structure of mobile phone service has two important characteristics: (1) high fixed costs and low marginal costs, and (2) services sold to affluent people and to poor people use the same capital-intensive infrastructure. This implies that it is economically profitable to cross-subsidize and sell services to the poor even at very low prices, so long as the price is above marginal cost. According to a study conducted by the consulting firm BDA with chamber of commerce Ficci in India, the top 9 percent of mobile phone users contribute 29 percent to the industry revenues and 45 percent of the profits; the lower end of the pyramid—71 percent of subscribers—contributes a mere 27 percent to revenues and only 15 percent to profits.[28]

The industry has further reduced the cost of serving the poor, especially the marginal cost, by selling prepaid phone services. This reduces the phone operator's costs involved in credit checks, billing, and bad debts; instead of paying interest on working capital, the firm earns interest on the prepaid balances. Virtually all poor customers are prepaid subscribers.

In addition, in many developing countries there is a flourishing market for used mobile phones that further reduces the entry price for poor consumers. An innovative approach to reducing costs has been the shared-access model, whereby one person or organization owns the mobile phone subscription and rents airtime to others. Grameenphone has formalized this on a large scale through its Village Phone initiative, which makes microloans to poor entrepreneurs to buy a mobile phone, an external antenna (for better reception), and a discounted subscription. The Village Phone program has more than 362,000 operators in Bangladesh, and has been replicated in several other countries.

The poor have low costs because their usage of value-added and more expensive services such as financial payments, government services, downloading music, email, and Internet browsing is "extremely low."[29] In Bangladesh, 94 percent of the phone users who are poor further lower their cost by sending and receiving "missed calls," that is, calling a number, letting it ring an agreed-upon number times, and then hanging up before the other person answers. Missed calls can be used to send a prenegotiated message (such as "pick me up now"); a relational sign (such as "I am thinking of you"); or to request a call back. This practice is growing rapidly throughout developing countries and is known by several names: beeping, flashing, pranking, and fishing. This is of growing concern to network operators since missed calls burden the infrastructure and do not generate revenues.[30]

The industry has clearly avoided the affordability trap and created a real market for mobile phone services to the poor. It has also avoided the distribution trap by selling prepaid phone cards through a large variety of retail shops, including general merchandise kiosks. It is even possible to electronically buy prepaid credits and to transfer credits from one phone to another, further facilitating distribution. Even though mobile phones can be used to deliver other services (such as public health) that would be socially valuable, the industry did not weigh down the BOP venture with multiple objectives.

Nirma

Unfortunately, the tactics used by the mobile telecommunications industry to reduce costs are not transferable to most other industries, especially the significant improvements in technology. So Karsanbhai Patel took another approach. In 1969, he started a small business selling a cheap powdered detergent, Nirma, which he had formulated in his kitchen. The quality of Nirma was clearly inferior to that of Surf, the product marketed by Hindustan Unilever Limited (HUL). "Nirma contained no 'active detergent,' whitener, perfume, or softener. Indeed tests performed on Nirma confirmed that it was hard on the skin and could cause blisters."[31] Nirma also spent less on advertising and promotion than HUL. Largely because of this, Nirma sold for about one-third the price of Surf. Nirma rapidly became a success. In 1977, Surf had a market share of 31 percent compared to 12 percent for Nirma. Ten years later, in 1987, the market share of Surf had decreased to 7 percent, while Nirma's had risen to 62 percent. By reducing the price, Nirma had succeeded at creating a new market: a lower-cost detergent targeted at the BOP. Reacting to Nirma, HUL entered this market in 1987 with a new brand: Wheel.

The primary common element between these two successful examples is the tremendous emphasis on cutting costs and hence reducing prices. It seems the poor like inexpensive, low-quality products, not because they cannot appreciate or do not want good quality; rather, they simply cannot afford the same quality products as the affluent; so they have a different price–quality trade-off. They are even willing to put up with a detergent that sometimes causes blisters! The acceptability of a product has to be seen from the perspective of the poor consumer who had not been able to afford any detergent before Nirma came on the market, and not from the perspective of an affluent person who routinely buys a high-quality detergent.

Nirma's "extremely simple distribution system stood in sharp contrast with HUL's multilayered system."[32] When Patel started the company, to reduce costs, he did not employ a field sales force or own a distribution network. And he negotiated prices with trucking suppliers on a daily basis. This reinforces the earlier discussion about carefully managing distribution channels to reach the poor.

Appropriate Low-Quality Products

The dominant conclusion from the above case studies and analysis is that the central element of the new business model is a dramatic reduction in costs such that firms can earn a reasonable profit margin and still price the product at a level that the poor can afford. Since technological leaps that result in dramatic cost reduction (such as in mobile telecommunications) are rare, it is necessary to reduce quality in order to reduce costs significantly in most cases. The challenge is to do this in such a way that the cost–quality trade-off is acceptable to poor consumers.

Selling cheap, lower-quality products does not hurt the poor. Insisting on not lowering the quality actually hurts the poor by depriving them of a product they could afford and would like to buy. The BOP proposition argues that selling low-quality products to the poor is disrespectful. Quite the contrary, imposing our price–quality trade-off on the poor is disrespectful of their preferences and needs. The poor are better off now that they can buy an affordable detergent. In a real sense, they are economically better off. We need more products like Nirma. Unfortunately, examples like Nirma are not common. The myth is that low quality implies terrible, shoddy, or dangerous products. It is better to think of quality as a relative concept.

Quality Broadly Defined

Business professor David Garvin develops a framework for analyzing quality by considering eight dimensions of quality: performance, features, reliability, conformance, durability, serviceability, aesthetics, and perceived quality.[33] To further expand this concept, we might add other dimensions such as availability, timeliness, convenience, and customization. The customer takes into account all these dimensions and arrives at a subjective judgment of the overall quality of the product (or service), and is, by definition, willing to pay a higher price for a product with higher quality—this is the price–quality trade-off. Holding technology and firm capabilities constant, it costs more to produce higher quality products—this is the cost-quality trade-off. To profitably serve the poor, a firm needs to make the cost–quality trade-off in a manner consistent with the price–quality trade-off made by the target customer.

The BOP proposition correctly celebrates the "shared access" model as a way to make products more affordable to the poor. The poor, like the rich, would prefer to exclusively own a cell phone; the poor make a price–quality trade-off, however, and opt to share a phone. The shared access model is not confined to the poor. Very rich people can choose to own private jets, while the merely rich often settle for a fractional ownership. Rich people often own vacation homes, while less rich people settle for time-share ownership.

Even the Aravind Eye Care System achieves its low cost structure partially by trading-off quality. Prahalad in his book argues that the quality of treatment at Aravind is as good as or better than at the best eye care centers in the world by considering the rate of medical complications.[34] This is too narrow (and technical) a view of quality. Aravind achieves economies of scale through specialization and attracting patients from a wider geographic radius. The patients therefore give up something in terms of convenience—an aspect of quality broadly defined. It is, of course, a trade-off that the patients of Aravind like, but a trade-off nonetheless.

In Conclusion

Companies, academia, civil society, and governments have devoted increasing efforts and attention to generating market-based solutions to alleviate poverty. Unfortunately, there are very few examples of profitable businesses that actually market beneficial goods in low-income markets and operate at a large scale. Combining social virtue with profitability while achieving scale is a major challenge. The desire for a positive outcome should not blind managers and policymakers to the difficulty of the challenge.

Developing sound market-based strategies requires firms to get back to the basic principles and logic of economics and business: focused objectives, understand the customers, and appreciate the role of economies of scope and scale. The biggest difference between the markets of the poor and of affluent people is the obvious but under-emphasized fact that the poor have very low purchasing power. Designing a business model to serve the poor has to start with this basic insight rather than a minor adaptation of the business model successful in affluent markets. Firms must shift from creating needs in existing markets to creating markets out of unmet needs.

If there is no great fortune to be harvested from the people at the base of the pyramid, marketing beneficial products to them does offer some limited business opportunities. It is the companies that make the relevant trade-offs that will profit from seizing these opportunities. The current situation of businesses selling to the poor might be analogous to the "New Economy" fad in the late 1990s, when many dot.com gurus were calling for a change in the business paradigm, and myriad start-up firms launched "new business models" that denied basic economic principles. After the bubble burst, a few winners did emerge, such as Amazon and Google. Tomorrow's champions in markets of the poor are probably hidden somewhere in today's current experiments. Firms must recognize and overcome the challenges of providing low-cost products the poor actually need and can afford.

CHAPTER 6

Employment Is the Solution

Give a man a fish, you feed him for a day; teach him how to fish, and he will not be hungry for life. That is an old cliché, and like all clichés, it has an element of wisdom. But, it does not go far enough. A fisherman with a simple rod and a canoe will not be hungry, but he will still be poor. For him to rise above poverty, he needs steady employment at reasonable wages in a commercial fishing company. Now, his daughter might go on to become an engineer and move up the development ladder.

T he starting point for addressing the challenge of poverty is the simple and obvious observation that the primary problem of the poor is that they have a low income. As the above parable indicates, the best way to alleviate poverty is to increase the income of the poor by providing productive employment. It is necessary to view the poor as producers, and emphasize buying from them. Many of the current approaches to poverty alleviation miss this simple point.

The advocates of foreign aid believe that poor countries are caught in a poverty trap and need major injections of aid to trigger economic development.[1] The critics argue that foreign aid has failed to reduce poverty because it has emphasized big objectives, big projects, top-down planning, and one-size-fits-all approaches.[2] William Easterly instead advocates bottom-up solutions tailored to the local context. Another criticism is that very little aid actually goes to stimulate enterprise development, even though private enterprise is well established as the best path out of poverty. Foreign aid is also accused of creating continuing dependency and fostering corruption.

The advocates of the Washington Consensus believe that free and open markets are the only vehicle for growing a nation out of poverty, and that the trickle down effect will lead to poverty reduction.[3] In fact, globalization has not brought the promised economic benefits to many poor people in the developing world.[4] The problem with the libertarian free-market approach is that it grossly underestimates the role of the government in economic development and poverty reduction. Ha-Joon Chang argues that today's economic powers from the United States to Britain to South Korea all attained prosperity through some government intervention in industry.

We have seen that the foreign aid approach sees the poor as passive recipients of charity; the Washington Consensus views the poor as automatic beneficiaries of a trickle-down effect; and the BOP approach envisions the poor primarily as consumers. None of these poverty reduction approaches emphasize directly increasing the productive capacity of the poor, that is, increasing their earning power. To alleviate poverty it is necessary to focus on the poor as producers and to emphasize buying from the poor, not selling to them.

To escape from poverty, the poor need productive jobs and higher incomes. As we saw in Chapter 1, the United Nations' MDGs outline international goals for eradicating poverty and hunger. By 2006, there was widespread conviction that poverty can only be reduced if people have a decent and productive job, and a new target was added under MDG 1: *Reaching full and productive employment and decent work for all, including women and young people.* The 2006 United Nations Conference on Trade and Development argues that poverty reduction in the least developed countries requires a "paradigm shift" so that national and international policies focus on developing productive capacities and creating productive jobs.[5] The International Labor Organization states "nothing is more fundamental to poverty reduction than employment," and then goes further and argues vigorously for "decent employment"—work that offers a worker a good income, security, flexibility, protection and a voice at work.[6] Employment is not only the key source of income, it also enhances other dimensions of well-being by increasing the individual's skills, physical abilities, and self-respect.

Increasing employment in poor countries requires three major thrusts: (1) the generation of new jobs; (2) increasing the employability of workers; and (3) making the labor markets more efficient. The first thrust works on the demand side of the labor market by creating job opportunities appropriate to the skills of the poor. The second thrust works on the supply side of the labor market by increasing the employability of the poor through education and vocational training programs. Labor markets, especially in developing countries, have much friction due to a lack of both information and labor mobility. The third thrust would include programs such as job matching and placement services, which help to improve labor market efficiency .

Increasing employment opportunities, employability, and labor-market efficiency means, of course, confronting complex challenges, and there is no magic solution for achieving these goals. A broad range of public policies and private strategies are needed to generate employment for the poor. It is too ambitious and perhaps futile to try to develop a holistic theoretical framework or a comprehensive action program to increase employment for the poor. It is better to make well-targeted and practical interventions supported by conceptual logic and empirical evidence. As we saw in Chapter 5, rather than trying to find the optimal, large-scale solution to poverty, it is preferable to choose a "good enough" starting point, an effective and feasible place to begin, and then take some action. It is worth sacrificing breadth for focus, comprehensive theory for pragmatic action.

Even though the private sector is primarily responsible for job creation, governments, international organizations, and NGOs can and should facilitate this process. Generating employment requires regulatory policies that facilitate the creation and growth of private businesses. The World Bank's Doing Business project provides a useful basis for understanding and improving the regulatory environment for business.[7] In this chapter, I advocate for focusing on the SME sector as the major driver of job creation, looking at TechnoServe's success at revitalizing the cashew nut industry in Mozambique. I will also focus on increasing the employment of the poor youth. This approach is illustrated using the case study of Employment Generation and Marketing Mission (EGMM), organized by the government of Andhra Pradesh state in India to identify, train, and link unemployed rural youth to jobs in the private sector.

Employment

In development economics, there is much theoretical and empirical support for the increasing preponderance of wage labor in a developing economy. The ILO divides the labor force into four categories: (1) *employees* are paid wages or salaries based on an explicit or implicit contract; (2) *employers* are self-employed and have engaged one or more employees; (3) *own-account workers*, alone or with one or more partners, are self-employed and have not engaged employees; and (4) *contributing family workers* are employed on an informal basis in an establishment operated by a relative living in the same household. Own-account workers in developing economies are associated with subsistence agriculture and other low value-added activities (such as petty trade), often providing low and irregular income. Contributing family work is often unpaid, though family workers are often compensated indirectly in the form of family income; it is particularly common among women in developing countries. The share of "vulnerable" employment is defined as the sum of contributing family workers and own-account workers divided by total employment. A high proportion of vulnerable workers is an indication of a large subsistence agricultural sector, lack of growth in the formal economy, and widespread poverty. Empirical research by the ILO confirms a positive relationship between the incidence of poverty and vulnerable employment.[8] Poverty reduction is linked to an increase in employment and a reduction in vulnerable employment.

Growing Employment

No country has significantly reduced poverty without experiencing economic growth. Economic growth, however, has had widely different impact on poverty reduction across countries. For example, a 1 percent increase in per capita GDP can reduce income poverty by as much as 4 percent or as little as 1 percent.[9] The link between economic growth and poverty reduction is mediated by job creation. It is possible to have economic development without significant job creation, but this has a lesser impact on poverty reduction. In recent years, many of the least-developed countries have achieved higher rates of economic growth than in the past, and an even higher growth of exports, yet there is a widespread sense that this is not translating effectively into poverty reduction and improved human well-being.[10] Analyzing the recent economic history of Mexico, Zepeda concludes that, "mainstream policies managed to generate growth that proved neither pro-poor nor sustainable. The Mexican experience shows the need to leave behind the blind faith in market forces and embrace employment-based policies."[11] In a similar vein, Amartya Sen recently recommended that Indian leaders pay more attention to reducing chronic undernourishment among the poor than pursuing ever higher economic growth rates.[12]

For example, the Indian economy has experienced rapid economic growth for several years, especially since the process of economic reforms was initiated in 1991. Despite this growth, unemployment and underemployment are still a major problem. Open unemployment—about 8 percent in 2007—is not a true indicator of the gravity of the unemployment problem. Sixty percent of India's workforce is self-employed, and many remain very poor. Nearly 30 percent are casual workers (i.e., they work only when they are able to get jobs and remain unpaid for the rest of the days). Only about 10 percent are regular employees, and two-fifths of these work in the public sector. India's jobless growth is the result of a distorted emphasis on a capital-intensive and skill-intensive development path.[13] Capital-intensive sectors, such as heavy manufacturing, and skill-intensive sectors, such as information technology, will not resolve India's poverty problem. Rajat Gupta, former managing director of the consulting firm McKinsey, says, "There's much talk in India about the knowledge worker and the knowledge economy. Yet they are sideshows to getting the basics right. India needs more jobs in sectors such as manufacturing, construction, and agribusiness, where it isn't necessary to be a knowledge worker to make a living."[14]

There is growing concern about the need to ensure "pro-poor" growth. The last decade has witnessed a global decline in the working-age population (aged 15 years and older) that is employed. It stood at 61.4 percent in 2006, which was 1.2 percentage points lower than ten years earlier. The decrease was larger among the youngest segment of this group (ages 15 to 24); within this group, the ratio decreased from 51 percent in 1996 to 46.8 percent in 2006.[15]

In developing countries, the problem is not only underemployment and unemployment, but also conditions among those who are employed. In 2006, 1.3 billion people worked but were still unable to lift themselves and their families above the $2/day poverty line. In addition, account must be taken of the unemployed people looking for work but unable to find it, and people so discouraged that they have given up looking for work. That is a very large deficit of decent employment.

Development expert S.R. Osmani examines the employment nexus between economic growth and poverty in five countries: Armenia, Uzbekistan, Vietnam, Bangladesh, and Indonesia.[16] He demonstrates that poverty reduction is linked to both the rate of economic growth and the extent to which poverty is responsive to growth. Two factors determine this responsiveness. The first is the *elasticity factor*, which determines the impact of economic growth on improving the quantity and quality of employment. The second is the *integrability factor*, which determines whether the poor are actually able to seize the employment opportunities created by the growth process.

Free-market advocates often assume that economic growth will automatically lead to job creation that in turn will lead to poverty reduction.[17] The problem is that the trickle-down effects of general economic growth are too little, too slow, and too uneven. There is a need to target programs at poverty reduction rather than just wait for the general growth effect to kick in. The recent political changes—disillusionment with market liberalization and a drift to the populist left—in several South American countries (such as Venezuela, Bolivia, Ecuador, and Nicaragua) support such a direct emphasis on poverty reduction. Developing countries need to emphasize growth in labor-intensive, low-skill sectors such as agriculture, light manufacturing, garments, and tourism, generating employment targeted at the poor. Unfortunately, many poor countries have not generated adequate employment, and as a result, have not made much progress on poverty reduction. Some combination of inappropriate government policies and market failures leads to inadequate job creation.

This is not to advocate a return to statist policies that stifled economic growth for decades in countries such as India and China. There is much ideological debate about the roles of the free markets and the state in achieving overall economic growth.[18] Regardless of one's position on this ideological debate, it is clear that contemporary history shows that the private sector is the best engine of job creation. For example, China's success over the last three decades in achieving poverty reduction began with reforms in 1978 that led to tremendous growth in the private sector, at 20 percent per year for the last 25 years, more than double the economy's average. Since 1992, the private sector has created three quarters of all jobs created in China, according to the IFC.[19]

Doing Business

There is no point in asking business to create jobs to reduce poverty. Business is motivated by self-interest and is responsible for creating value for its owners and shareholders. Business will create jobs without being asked if it is in its self-interest to do so, especially in developing countries with low labor costs. If government rules discourage business growth or distort the market incentives to employ labor, then business is less likely to create jobs. The solution then is for the government to facilitate business growth and job creation by designing appropriate rules.

A thriving business sector is absolutely essential for job creation. The World Bank's Doing Business project measures the ease of doing business in 183 countries based on indicators in ten different areas, which helps us understand how various policies, laws, and regulations can facilitate the growth of the private sector.[20]

1. **Starting a Business**: Procedures, time, cost, and paid-in minimum capital to open a new business.
2. **Dealing with Permits**: Procedures, time, and cost to obtain construction permits, inspections and utility connections.
3. **Employment**: Difficulty of hiring index, rigidity of hours index, difficulty of redundancy index, as well as redundancy cost.
4. **Registering Property**: Procedures, time, and cost to transfer commercial real estate.

5. **Getting Credit:** Strength of legal rights index, depth of credit information index.
6. **Protecting Investors:** Strength of investor protection index, extent of disclosure index, extent of director liability index, and ease of shareholder suits.
7. **Paying Taxes:** Number of tax payments, time to prepare and file tax returns and to pay taxes, total taxes as a share of profits before all taxes borne.
8. **Cross-border Trading:** Documents, time, and cost to export and import.
9. **Enforcing Contracts:** Procedures, time, and cost to resolve a commercial dispute.
10. **Closing a Business:** Recovery rate in bankruptcy.

The Doing Business project collects data on these ten topics in a standardized way. "The indicators presented and analyzed measure business regulation and protection of property rights—and their effect on businesses, especially small and medium-sized domestic firms."[21]

Hubbard and Duggan, in their book *The Aid Trap,* view the World Bank's ten indicators as the "key elements that make local business thrive." It is not a perfect or a comprehensive list of policies that lead to significant economic growth and employment. There are anomalies. Some countries rank high but are not that business friendly; for example, Saudi Arabia is ranked number 13 out of 183 countries, whereas Costa Rica, where business is doing well, is ranked 121 on the list. Nonetheless, the Doing Business project offers a good overall picture of regulatory obstacles to business and offers some guidance on potential reforms. It is a good starting point.

"A fundamental premise of Doing Business is that economic activity requires good rules."[22] The emphasis in the Doing Business project is on regulatory policies, and, at least implicitly, on deregulation. Other factors that influence business growth and job creation might include access to capital, financial system, pool of entrepreneurial talent, macroeconomic stability, infrastructure, and public services. To facilitate business growth, the government also needs to emphasize providing infrastructure (such as electricity) and developing supporting institutions (such as capital markets). This is particularly true in the context of facilitating the growth of SMEs. Larger companies can often develop their own infrastructure. For example, large firms can invest in stand-by electricity generators or in co-generation; SMEs have to rely on public utilities. Large firms can provide their employees with in-house transportation to and from work; SME employees have to rely on public transportation.

Large firms have relatively easy access to capital; microenterprises have access to microcredit. SMEs need financing options—both debt and equity—in the range of $10,000 to $1 million, which are almost nonexistent in most developing countries.[23] Traditional banks often view SME financing as too risky because entrepreneurs lack business experience and acumen and have little collateral. There is a clear need to develop financial institutions to provide "mesofinance."

For business firms to grow and create jobs, even low-skilled jobs, they need a pool of potential workers who have access to basic health care and education—services that are in the domain of the public sector. China and India have both been moving towards market-oriented economies, but with differing results. Amartya Sen concludes that, "while Indian efforts have slowly met with some success, the kind of massive results that China has seen have failed to occur in India.... When China turned to marketization in 1979, it already had a highly literate people, especially the young, with good schooling facilities across the bulk of the country.... In contrast, India had a half-literate adult population when it turned to marketization in 1991, and the situation is not much improved today.... The health conditions in China were also much better than in India because of the social commitment of the pre-reform regime to health care as well as education."[24] Even in 2003, the adult literacy rate in India was only 61 percent (compared to 91 percent for China in 2000), and gender bias makes the situation even worse for Indian women. Yet, even this may understate the problem in India. *The Economist* argues, "the official national literacy rate of 61 percent includes many who are able to write their names but are functionally illiterate."[25]

Despite the relatively small impact of foreign aid on development and poverty reduction, it is important to point out that such aid is not *necessarily* harmful or useless. The challenge is how to make aid part of the solution, not part of the problem. One way is to devote more aid resources to facilitating the growth of private enterprises, especially SMEs, and to emphasize job creation. Kurt Hoffman, former director of the Shell Foundation, argues that only job-creating businesses can really make poverty history, which requires two things: economic growth and growth of private sector enterprises, especially SMEs.[26] His "admittedly rough calculations suggest that enterprise has attracted much less than 10 percent of all official and private aid flows of the past decade." It is necessary to reprioritize both foreign aid and resources of local governments to emphasize private enterprise, especially SMEs, and job creation.

Small- and Medium-Sized Enterprises

Which sector of the economy is likely to be a good target for job creation? The nongovernment economy can be divided into three sectors: the informal sector, SMEs, and large enterprises. The informal sector covers all economic activities for which income is not reported for tax purposes, and which are not covered or are insufficiently covered by formal arrangements and generally operate outside the formal reach of the law. Definitions of SMEs vary by country, although most sources define SMEs in terms of numbers of employees. There is, however, rough agreement about the cut-off points: Microenterprises have fewer than 10 employees; small enterprises, fewer than 50 employees; and medium enterprises, fewer than 250 employees. SMEs are defined as formal enterprises. In practice, especially in developing countries, most microenterprises operate in the informal economy. Virtually all the vulnerable employment discussed above takes place in the informal sector.

Ayyagari, Beck, and Demirguc-Kunt provide a database containing comprehensive statistics on the contribution of SMEs and the informal sector to the total GDP across a broad spectrum of countries (see figure 6.1).[27] The SME sector generates a higher fraction of GDP in high-income countries compared to low-income countries. The size of the informal sector has a negative relationship with the country's income level. Interestingly, the joint contribution of the informal and SME sectors to GDP remains approximately constant across income groups at about 65 to 70 percent. However, as income increases, there is a marked shift from the informal to the SME sector.

The economic structure in low-income countries is polarized, with the informal and large enterprises playing the primary roles and the SME sector being too small—the so-called *missing middle*. The path to economic development is clearly associated with a growing SME sector.[28] Indeed, a World Bank study using cross-country data finds a "strong association between the importance of SMEs and GDP per capita growth. This relationship, however, is not robust to controlling for simultaneity bias."[29] Thus, while

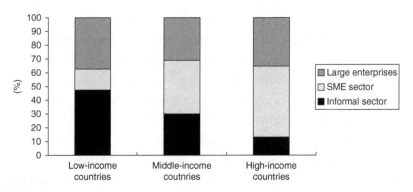

Figure 6.1 Contribution of different sectors to total GDP

Source: Meghana Ayyagari, Thorsten Beck, and Asli Demirguc-Kunt. Small and Medium Enterprises across the Globe: A New Database. Policy Research Working Paper 3127, The World Bank, August 2003.

a large SME sector is a characteristic of successful economies, there is not enough empirical evidence to prove that SME growth causes economic growth. It is plausible that the direction of causality flows in both directions.

Nevertheless, most governments have programs to support the development of the SME sector; for example, in Pakistan, the promotion of SMEs has been the "center piece of Government's strategy for economic revival, poverty alleviation, and employment generation."[30] The World Bank and other international aid agencies provide targeted assistance to SMEs in developing countries. The World Bank, for example, approved $1.5 billion for SME support programs in 2002.[31] Several NGOs also focus their efforts on the SME sector. One example is the Washington-based NGO TechnoServe, which is discussed in-depth later in the chapter. Another example is ApproTEC, a small NGO that aims to promote economic growth and employment creation in Kenya and other countries by developing and promoting technologies that can be used by entrepreneurs to establish and run profitable small-scale enterprises.

The ILO argues that SMEs are the major creators of employment opportunities and therefore hold an important key to employment and poverty reduction.[32] SME expansion boosts employment more than large firms because SMEs are more labor intensive, less skill intensive, and less capital intensive—creating jobs better suited to the poor and appropriate for developing countries with an abundance of labor and a relative shortage of capital. SMEs contribute to a more equitable income distribution because they tend to be more widely dispersed geographically than larger enterprises, thus helping to reduce economic disparities between urban and rural areas. The presence of SMEs in the economy tends to increase competition, which promotes greater economic dynamism. SMEs are often the source of economic growth and innovation, and support the development and diffusion of skills and entrepreneurial talent in the economy.

In developed countries, some microenterprises are successful and grow into SMEs over time. This is much less common in developing countries. The self-employed poor, that is, the microentrepreneurs in developing countries, usually have no specialized skills and often practice multiple occupations, and rarely progress into SMEs.[33]

It is interesting to compare China and India in this regard. In the last two decades, China has reduced poverty significantly more than India because China has created a large number of jobs that pay enough to lift people out of poverty. This has been possible because in China there has been much faster growth of low-skill employment in the manufacturing sector.[34] The industry structure in manufacturing in China is dramatically different than in India. In India, about 87 percent of manufacturing employment is in microenterprises with fewer than 10 employees, a smallness of scale that is unmatched in any emerging country.[35] The corresponding number in China is less than 5 percent. About 5 percent of manufacturing employment in India is in the SME sector, compared to 40 percent in China.

Vulnerable Employment

To eliminate poverty, it is not enough to increase employment; it is also necessary to reduce vulnerable employment. It is instructive to consider the pattern of poverty and vulnerable employment over time in East Asia, South Asia and sub-Saharan Africa, three regions which together account for about three-quarters of the poor in the world.[36]

In East Asia (largely, China), where the incidence of poverty has declined significantly (see figure 6.2), the share of vulnerable employment is relatively small and shrinking (see figure 6.3). In South Asia (largely, India) and sub-Saharan Africa, where the incidence of poverty has declined much more slowly, the share of vulnerable employment is significantly larger and shrinking only slowly. By way of comparison, the share of vulnerable employment in developed economies is dramatically smaller. Vulnerable employment, most of which takes place in microenterprises, is not effective in reducing poverty.

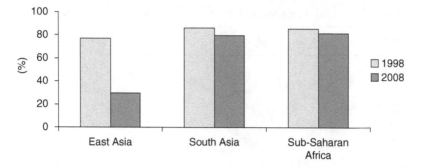

Figure 6.2 Working poor[37] ($2/day) as a fraction of total employment

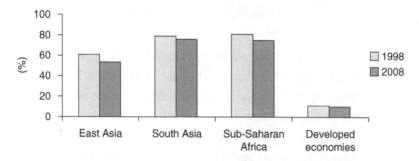

Figure 6.3 Vulnerable employment as a percentage of total employment

Source: International Labor Organization. *Global Employment Trends*. 2010.

Economies of Scale

Research confirms that there is a positive relationship between firm size and labor productivity. Evidence from India shows that total factor productivity is about twice as high in firms with more than 250 employees than in those with only up to 10 employees, with progressive increases in scale yielding considerable gains in productivity (table 6.1).[38]

This problem is particularly acute for microenterprises with fewer than 10 employees. Many of these businesses operate at too small a scale, and their low productivity leads to meager earnings that cannot lift their owners out of poverty. Daniels, in his study

Table 6.1   Gains in productivity from larger firm size in India

Firm size: Number of employees	Productivity multiple
1–10	1.0
10–20	1.25
20–50	1.5
50–100	1.7
100–250	1.8
250+	2.1

Note: Total factor productivity in a given firm size relative to a firm with 1 to 10 employees. *Source*: Sean M. Dougherty, Richard Herd, Thomas Chalaux, and Abdul Azeez Erumban. India's Growth Pattern and Obstacles to Higher Growth. Working Paper No. 62, OECD, Paris, 2008.

of microenterprises in Kenya, found that only 26 percent of these owners earned an income above the minimum wage.[39]

The productivity of SMEs lies somewhere between that of microenterprises and large firms.[40] SMEs concentrate on activities for which the scale economies are not so significant, and their relative disadvantage compared to large firms is minimal (e.g., labor-intensive industries, such as light manufacturing, and service industries, such as restaurants and vehicle repair). Another strategy is to avoid direct competition with large firms by focusing on specialized and niche markets. Small firms also have the advantage of greater flexibility and agility.[41] Small firms can also try to gain economies of scale through strategic alliances and outsourcing. SMEs in developing countries need to better practice these strategies in order to achieve growth—this is exactly how TechnoServe helps small enterprises in developing countries to thrive and grow.

TechnoServe

While it is the primary responsibility of the government to facilitate business growth, civil society can play some useful role too.

Although civil society does not have the power to change the rules for doing business, it can intervene on a case-by-case basis and have a positive effect.

TechnoServe is a midsized NGO (annual budget of about $50 million) based in Washington D.C. that generates jobs by facilitating the growth of SMEs in many poor countries, especially Africa and Latin America.[42] Its mission is to help entrepreneurial men and women in poor areas of the developing world to build businesses that create income and employment. Adopting a market-oriented approach, TechnoServe identifies high-potential but underperforming economic subsectors, and seeks to resolve the identified market failures that constrain their development. In 2008, TechnoServe helped 1,348 businesses to achieve total sales of $149 million and profits of $16 million; these businesses paid $9 million in wages to 32,600 employees. TechnoServe's approach can be summarized as follows:

- Emphasize job creation to reduce poverty. Focus on SMEs as the engine of job creation.
- Emphasize a market-oriented approach with private businesses as the drivers of economic growth and job creation; involve multiple players, including government and trade organizations. TechnoServe acts as a facilitator.
- Emphasize appropriate technology to balance labor intensity with productivity. Competitive advantages of SMEs include an appropriate balance between labor and capital intensity, flexibility, speed, and "localization."
- Support local entrepreneurs, who play a critical role in this process. The business has to succeed in a competitive environment by emphasizing cost competitiveness and being responsive to customer needs.

To see this approach in action, we look at one of TechnoServe's success stories: the revitalization of the cashew nut industry in Mozambique.

Cashew Industry in Mozambique

The cashew nut industry in East Africa was once a driving economic force. Mozambique was the leading producer in the world, achieving its peak in 1973, accounting for 240,000 tons of raw cashew nuts, of which 210,000 tons were processed in Mozambique.

After Mozambique gained independence in 1975, its government planners ignored cashew nut production, and the industry started to decline. This trend was aggravated by years of disruption in agricultural marketing, initially stemming from the government's interventionist approach to national resource allocation (a centrally planned economy) and later by the devastating and prolonged civil war. Unable to pay attention to their trees, the farmers left them untreated for years, causing the spread of pests and diseases. Uncontrolled forest fires affected important parts of the cashew orchards. Processing capacity, too, deteriorated, both physically and in terms of managerial expertise. Total production dropped to as little as 22,000 tons in 1990, recovering only to 50,000 tons in 2002, of which none was processed locally. In 1998, the government lifted an export ban on raw cashew nuts. Exporters could offer higher prices than the struggling domestic factories, and most raw nuts were diverted to India for processing. Factories were shut down, eliminating many jobs and reducing the domestic demand for raw nuts. By 2000, instead of feeding a vibrant domestic industry serving the global market, Mozambique's raw nuts were being sold to Indian processors, effectively exporting a major agroindustrial opportunity.

TechnoServe in Mozambique

TechnoServe's efforts in Mozambigue revitalized the broken industry. In 2005, Mozambique produced 82,000 tons of raw nuts, of which 9,000 tons were processed locally, and exports amounted to $3.6 million, with a strong potential for further growth. By 2008, exports of processed kernels had more than doubled, reaching $10 million and creating over 6,200 formal-sector jobs. A combination of yield improvement and better prices boosted the incomes of about 120,000 small-scale cashew farmers. For 2007 and 2008, price increases attributable to domestic processing resulted in incremental income increases for farmers calculated at just under $2.5 million. The ultimate size of the industry has the potential to grow many times larger, based on gradual replanting and expansion of the nation's overmature cashew orchards.

TechnoServe began by identifying the opportunity and making a business case for the cashew industry in Mozambique. That Mozambique had a progressive government was an important positive factor. TechnoServe wants to work in countries in which entrepreneurs can flourish and regulations are not onerous. Its donors share its organizational skepticism of centrally planned economies. The TechnoServe regional director then wrote an unsolicited proposal to the United States Agency for International Development (USAID), which was funded.

The new TechnoServe director for Mozambique (a seasoned agribusiness professional) teamed up with a volunteer from the Netherlands office of McKinsey & Company, the management consulting firm, to come up with a competitive strategy. Working with key stakeholders, they did an extensive industry analysis to identify key drivers of commercial success and decided on an approach involving three major interrelated elements: SMEs, manual shelling, and locating factories near cashew farms. The analysis had revealed that smaller factories in prime production areas had advantages in purchasing raw materials and transportation costs, and that using labor-intensive shelling technologies was superior to mechanical options when workers are properly trained and motivated. The lower investment and operating costs of these smaller plants made them more feasible for local entrepreneurs.

Historically, large-scale domestic processors had dominated the Mozambican cashew industry. The old large-scale plants had 10,000-ton capacities and used mechanical shelling technology;

this yielded a capital cost of $600 per ton and an operating cost of $1.30 per kilogram of output. TechnoServe proposed building small-scale plants with a capacity of 1,000 tons, and using manual shelling technology; the capital cost would be $140 per ton, and the operating cost, $0.56 per kilogram of output. Even the output quality (measured by the percentage of whole nut yield) was better for the small plants. Running large-scale plants successfully required sophisticated managers, not readily available in Mozambique. The smaller plants were seen as much more likely to achieve better capacity utilization. Small, geographically dispersed plants located close to raw nut sources reduce transportation costs and increase supplier loyalty and commitment.

Each small plant would employ 200 workers, for a monthly wage bill of $15,000; the employees would receive an official minimum wage salary, one month paid vacation, all insurance, health and pension entitlements, one meal a day and child care. Each plant would provide a reliable market for the raw cashew nuts of about 10,000 small-scale farmer families and would pay a premium price for quality. They could also promote improved production and husbandry by providing farmers with better seedling varieties, extension training, and other inputs.

TechnoServe then recruited a business advisor, a local industry expert, to establish a one-stop shop for all services to entrepreneurs. In 2001, TechnoServe partnered with a progressive Mozambican entrepreneur, Antonio Miranda, to launch the new enterprise Miranda Caju, a nut processing plant. In the early phase, the business advisor provided intensive support for Miranda Caju: recruiting and hiring supervisors and workers, advising on the compensation system, worker training , plant-layout design, identifying equipment and designing locally fabricated equipment, such as the boiler. After some start-up glitches, the firm was soon profitable. Miranda Caju opened a second 1,000-ton plant in 2004; revenues that year were $1 million.

TechnoServe used Miranda Caju's first plant as a working laboratory for refining the business model and training other interested entrepreneurs. By 2006, TechnoServe was working with nine start-up processing plants, with a total capacity of 11,700 tons. TechnoServe offers a wide range of resources including strategic planning, marketing, technical advice, quality control, supply chain management, and facilitating access to investment and working capital. Volunteer consultants, many with McKinsey & Company, Bain & Company, or other global company backgrounds, supplement TechnoServe skills in Mozambique. Miranda Caju, the initial processing plant paid TechnoServe $5,000 per year for consulting services, a mechanism that ensured TechnoServe was really adding value. That fee was waived for later industry entrants, in exchange for their support of the industry trade associations, Association of Agribusiness Industries (AIA) and AICAJU.

Marketing Cashew Nuts

Although small-scale rural plants are efficient processors, they lack both the know-how and resources to market their products, which involves developing and maintaining communications and commercial relationships with foreign buyers, as well as branding, promoting, and advertising efforts. Export markets require container-size shipments of uniformly graded and sorted cashew nuts, which is easier to do on a large scale. TechnoServe took the lead in developing AIA, a service company privately owned by some of the cashew processing companies. Located in the northern port city Nacala on Africa's eastern coast, AIA is the primary marketer of the processed cashew nuts of its owners, as well as some non-owners. It acts as a final quality-control agent and exporter, organizes bulk purchases of equipment and consumables, and offers limited training and technical assistance to its members. With "pro bono" assistance from the advertising agency Young & Rubicam, AIA has developed a brand, Zambique, to communicate the superior qualities of AIA-branded cashew nuts and to control product quality. AIA is also assuming from TechnoServe the leading role in negotiating with the government policies that affect the industry. AIA has begun to provide on a for-profit basis many of the services that TechnoServe provided in the first several years.

TechnoServe has also worked with the industry to resuscitate the trade association AICAJU as a broad industry advocate. It released a key staff member to work as a private consultant to assist the government of Mozambique in strategic planning for INCAJU, the government agency responsible for promoting the cashew nut industry. With TechnoServe's guidance, AIA is working with the government to design and implement policies favorable to the cashew industry (e.g., by advocating a gradual reduction of the protective export tax on raw nuts, which penalizes the farmers and undermines real long-term industry competitiveness). When the processors needed working capital to purchase their year's supply of raw material during the brief harvest season, TechnoServe worked with INCAJU to design a loan guarantee program supported by the government. Needs rapidly expanded beyond INCAJU's resources. USAID then supported a loan guarantee program offered by the Ministry of Industry and Commerce. In 2009, efforts began to have a local commercial bank take over the loan program without a guarantee.

In 2008, the factories in Mozambique processed 23,700 tons of cashews. TechnoServe's 16 client cashew-processing plants bought nuts from over 100,000 small-scale producers and had total sales revenues of $12 million, employing over 4,700 people and paying $1.6 million in wages.

In 2008, TechnoServe, having achieved its original intention of reviving the domestic processing industry in Mozambique, ceased its direct support. Having subsequently spread some of the lessons learned in Mozambique into its cashew sector work in Tanzania, Kenya, and South Africa, TechnoServe is now replicating the approach through a large program working with West African cashew processors in Benin, Burkina Faso, Cote d'Ivoire, and Ghana.

Fostering Employment

Contemporary economic history supports the view that the government should intervene in the market only when there is sound justification to do so, and then, with a light hand. Governments that have tried to pick "winners and losers" and to implement heavy-handed industrial policies have often done more harm than good. That said, governments can sometimes play a positive role by actively fostering a particular sector or industry, such as in countries where free markets are severely damaged. For example, since the end of the civil war, the government in Rwanda has successfully fostered the growth of the tourism industry.

Rwanda's gorilla-viewing opportunities drew 22,000 visitors to the country in 1990. The number of foreign visitors dropped to zero in 1994, when civil war and genocide swept through the country. In 1999, a slowly recovering industry plunged again after eight tourists were murdered in Uganda by Rwandan Hutu rebels. Since then, the government has been strongly committed to revitalizing the tourism industry and has succeeded to a significant extent.[43] Tourism has helped Rwanda to recover from economic collapse; the tourism industry generated revenues of $42 million and attracted 43,000 visitors in 2007 and was the top foreign-currency earner, ahead of coffee and tea. The tourism industry employed 34,000 people, about 2 percent of the country's workforce.

It made sense for the Rwandan government to focus on the tourism industry. Tourism is labor intensive and provides a wide range of employment opportunities, including flexible and part-time jobs, which require relatively low-level skills and little training, and are well suited to women and youths. Given the growing global interest in wildlife tourism, Rwanda, with its large gorilla population, has a comparative advantage in tourism. Tourism creates opportunities for small enterprises in both the formal and informal economy. The infrastructure it requires, such as transportation and communications, water supply and sanitation, public security, and health services, can also benefit poor communities. And besides the material benefits, it also is a source of cultural and national pride.

Recognizing these benefits, the Rwandan government took several steps to actively develop the tourism industry. Its first step was to safeguard the gorillas from poachers, treat the sick animals, and then to protect the Virunga National Park, part of the Virunga Gorilla Conservation Area in Africa's only rain forest, home to many mountain gorillas. Squatters were removed from the park, and the facilities were cleaned up. Since 2002, Rwanda's Office of Tourism and National Parks has been the guardian of a tourism strategy targeting upscale tourists who spend over $200 per day. High-profile visits, such as those by Bill Gates and Bill Clinton, helped with these marketing efforts. In the Rwandan case, government involvement has been necessary because of a shortage of private sector leadership to take on these tasks.

The government has also significantly improved security in the country, which is critical to attracting international tourists, so much so that in a recent travel survey, Rwanda was rated as the safest destination in East Africa. The government offers a package of incentives to attract investment. The number of high-end boutique hotels charging $350 to $600 per night has grown significantly, with 346 rooms built or renovated between 2002 and 2007. The restaurant business, too, is booming and offers very attractive returns on investment. Ancillary businesses such as handicrafts and transportation are also doing well. There are now 15 high-end tour operators in Rwanda. Goverment officials are starting to consider diversifying the tourism industry to include exotic birds, cave exploration, and water tourism. In October 2007, the real estate firm Dubai World announced it would invest $230 million in eight tourism facilities in Rwanda including luxury hotels, a golf course, and high-end eco lodges. The hope is that the government will take a less active role in the future in activities that should be driven by the private sector, and at the same time remain actively involved in public issues such as conservation, the environment, and linkages to local communities.

Rwanda serves as a good example of what can happen when the free markets in a country are severely damaged, governments can actively foster employment generation.

Employability

Of course, job creation goes hand in hand with the need to increase the employability of the poor. Thus it is necessary to increase educational opportunities for the poor, although education alone will not solve unemployment. In fact, in developing countries, the supply of educated people has often outpaced the supply of jobs to accommodate them, and unemployment rates tend to be higher among better-educated young people. This is certainly true in India, where "there is a widening chasm between students' qualifications and employability. It sweeps the country, particularly its non-metropolitan regions."[44] Data from EGMM, for example, indicates the magnitude of the problem in the state of Andhra Pradesh (see table 6.2). The official unemployment rate among the educated was 7.3 percent, six points higher than the state's overall unemployment rate of 6.7 percent. Educated people who cannot find employment are probably even more frustrated than less educated people.

Table 6.2   Education level and unemployment in Andhra Pradesh

Level of Education	Employed	Unemployed
10th grade	300,000	Not available
Intermediate (Equivalent to 12th grade)	170,000	50,000
Vocational training; polytechnic; industrial training institute	20,000	20,000
University graduate	350,000	50,000
Engineering graduate	95,000	20,000

Even when economic growth generates employment opportunities, the problem is that these potential jobs might go unfilled because of friction in labor markets. The educational system sometimes graduates students without all the appropriate skills required by the employers. There is a mismatch between the curricula adopted by the schools and the requirements of the marketplace. There is a need for job training, or vocational training, especially for the poor. Companies have job openings and there are people with the right or almost right qualifications who need jobs, and yet the jobs and people do not get linked together. The poor may not be motivated to look for a job, and there are also the problems of lack of both information and labor mobility. Even if they are motivated, the poor often do not know where and how to search for a job. The transition too might be problematic, if, for example, it is the poor person's first job, and/or the job is located in a geographically, socially, and culturally unfamiliar place.

Youth Unemployment Crisis

How well poor youths make the transition from school to work, from childhood to adult life, can determine both their and their family's—and collectively, their community's—chances of escaping poverty. When they themselves become parents, having a history of good and steady employment is likely to lead to a significant and sustained reduction in poverty. Young people are among the world's greatest assets; youth unemployment is a tremendous waste of opportunity. And yet the global deficit of employment opportunities has resulted in a situation in which one out of every three young people is seeking but unable to find work, has given up the job search entirely, or is working but still living below the $2/day poverty line. Youths are more than three times as likely as adults to be unemployed. "The world is facing a growing youth employment crisis.... In recent years slowing global employment growth, and increasing unemployment, underemployment and disillusionment have hit young people the hardest."[45] The world's demographics are such that 89 percent of the world's youth live in developing economies, where the employment deficit is worse.

There is growing evidence that being unemployed at an early age has a direct and negative impact on future income streams. Research has shown that unemployed youths suffer a permanent decrease in their lifetime earning profile; one study suggests an income penalty from early unemployment in the magnitude of 13 to 21 percent at age 42.[46] Youth unemployment results in reduced investment in human capital, depriving the young of work experience during that portion of the lifecycle when such experience yields the highest return, and frequently leading to unsuitable labor behavior patterns that last a lifetime.

Without the proper foothold from which to start out right in the labor market, young people are less likely to make choices that improve their own job prospects as well as those of their future dependents, thus perpetuating the cycle of insufficient education, low productivity, and poverty from one generation to the next. Youth unemployment is costly, not only in terms of economic development, but also in terms of social development. There is a proven link between youth unemployment and social exclusion.[47] An inability to find employment creates a sense of vulnerability, uselessness, and idleness among young people. Youth unemployment is associated with high levels of crime, violence, substance abuse, and the rise of political extremism. In some countries, virtually the only paid occupation open to many young men is with the various armed groups involved in civil conflict. For young women, the danger of entrapment in the sex industry is widespread.[48]

Christoph Ernst of the International Labor Organization calls for special youth employment programs, arguing that a job-creation strategy needs to cover both labor demand and supply, combined with well-targeted and structured interventions.[49] Many governments all over the world have developed initiatives targeted at youth employment. Even in a rich country like Canada, the government created the Youth Employment Strategy to help young people, particularly those facing barriers to employment, get the information and gain the skills they need to make a successful transition from school to the workplace.[50] Recognizing the risk of falling behind on the target of achieving decent employment, and youth employment in particular, the government of Tanzania has introduced an employment-creation program.[51] NGOs, too, have entered this arena; the Youth Entrepreneurship and Sustainability (YES) campaign was launched in 2002 to promote youth employability and employment creation.[52] The YES networks in 83 countries bring together diverse stakeholders including governments, companies, banks, and NGOs.

The EGMM is a good example of what Ernst advocates: a well-targeted intervention focused on youth employment.

Employment Generation and Marketing Mission

The Employment Generation and Marketing Mission is an innovative and effective organization that addresses the issue of employment among underprivileged rural youth in Andhra Pradesh in India.[53] EGMM does not help create jobs; rather it facilitates employment for the state's rural poor youths by reducing friction in the labor markets.[54] It was launched in October 2005 as an autonomous body under the Rural Development Department of the state government of Andhra Pradesh in Hyderabad. It is a government organization that works closely with the private sector and with rural communities. The program works on a large scale: 101,000 youth were trained in 2009, with 73 percent placed in organized-sector jobs. EGMM first identifies and motivates the poor unemployed youths, and then provides them with brief training. It then works with companies to match these young people to jobs, and finally to make the transition to a job in the urban environment.

Andhra Pradesh

Andhra Pradesh is the fourth largest state in India, with a population of about 80 million. Its per capita income is about the same as for the whole of India. The state's annual economic growth rate was 5.5 percent during the last two decades. Andhra Pradesh is a major producer of agricultural products; it is also home to many industrial and information technology (IT) companies. As is the case throughout India, unemployment is a major problem in the state; in fact, its unemployment rate is slightly higher than the overall rate in India, and higher still in the state's rural areas than in urban areas. In a typical village of 500 households (about 2,500 people), there will be 50 to 60 unemployed people, of which five are university graduates, and seven are graduates from an industrial training institute. Fortunately, the state's rapid economic growth in recent years has created many low-skilled jobs, such as security guard, retail assistant, construction worker and garment factory worker.

Identifying and Motivating

Identifying unemployed rural youths in interior areas is the first challenge since remote areas like tribal hamlets have limited connectivity. EGMM has trained a cadre of workers from among the community, known as "job resource persons" (JRPs). The JRPs travel to the villages, going from house to house and also participating in village meetings to gather the information needed to create a database of the unemployed youths.

The next step is motivation. The youths in remote areas who have managed to receive education and training are often frustrated because their education has not resulted in jobs, and previous government programs have not been effective. They easily fall prey to the temptations of drugs and "naxalism" (a radical, often violent, revolutionary communist movement in India). These youths constantly challenge the JRPs to explain why they should enroll in EGMM training programs. The JRPs sponsor talks at which youths are addressed by an employed youth who benefited from the training or by his/her mother, whose life has been improved by the sustained income flow. Attendees are shown the basket of training options, according to their aspirations and qualifications.

The government of Andhra Pradesh has also facilitated the creation of a large network of self-help groups (SHGs) of rural women. These are basically thrift and credit groups who meet regularly and use their collective savings to leverage bank loans for income generation and consumption purposes. EGMM works with the SHG leaders, who are opinion makers in the community, to discuss unemployment and jobs issues in their monthly meetings and participate in the valedictory functions. They take the SHG leaders on trips to visit the companies in which youths from their villages may be placed. This helps to create a grassroots feeling of ownership of the work and makes them stakeholders in the process. SHG leaders and monthly meetings influence the mothers of unemployed youths, who in turn motivate their children.

Training

EGMM has set up 280 no-frills training academies linked to emerging growth sectors of the economy. These include the Rural Retail Academy, Rural Security Academy, Rural English and Soft Skills, Work Readiness and Computer Academy, Construction Training Center and Textile Training Center. To achieve acceptance and scale, the unemployed youths are channeled into a training program appropriate to their qualifications and aspirations. Those who are illiterate and want to remain in the villages are advised to enroll in the construction or textile industry training programs. Those who are literate (10th grade and upward) and willing to relocate enroll in the retail, security, English, and work-readiness academies.

The security services industry, for example, is growing rapidly in India, at the rate of 35 percent a year. There are 800 companies or contractors in this sector in Andhra Pradesh alone. Many of them are disreputable, exploitative operators who hire young people from the villages and often do not pay them their entitled wages. These are the youths who end up returning to their villages after just a few months, disenchanted with the system. To combat this, EGMM formed an alliance with G4S (formerly G-4 Securicor), a $2 billion Danish company and the world's leading security solutions group, with operations in over 100 countries. G4S is the largest security services company in India, with 130,000 employees. Entry-level security guards earn reasonable wages, Rs. 48,000 annually (equivalent to about $1,066 at market exchange rate of $1=Rs. 45, and about $3,270 at PPP exchange rate of $1=Rs. 14.67) and receive fringe benefits, such as a retirement fund and medical reimbursement, which compares to the per capita income in India of Rs. 38,084 in 2009. Before the alliance with EGMM was formed, G4S interviewed 200 youths, and less than 10 percent passed the company's screening tests. EGMM then did an analysis of the company's recruiting needs and, with G4S's help, developed a 15-day training module that taught the young people basic conversational English, grooming, and goal-setting skills. EGMM spent $82 on each candidate in the training program. After the training, 70 to 80 percent of the youths passed the company's screening tests. "The quality of manpower provided by EGMM is really good and we plan to recruit 5,000 persons in 2006–07," said P.V. Sudarshan, the G4S general manager in Andhra Pradesh.[55]

Buoyed by the G4S success, other security services companies, such as Protex, have also approached EGMM seeking skilled manpower. EGMM trained and placed 15,000 youths in security agencies in 2007.

Surveys have indicated that, in response to India's booming retail market, 500,000 entry-level retail jobs would be created in the southern states of India alone. EGMM thus set up Rural Retail Academies, which offer a 45-day training program. The course modules were developed with industry help. Besides emphasizing customer relations management, the program also teaches simple spoken English, life skills, and personality skills. This included lessons on body language, grooming, etiquette, time management, conflict management, and leadership qualities. Students are taught how to write their resumes, interviewing skills, and job search skills. Local teachers were recruited through written tests and interviews and groomed to be trainers rather than teachers. In the schools in rural India, classes tend to be nonparticipatory and to emphasize rote learning. In contrast, EGMM trainers were groomed to emphasize active, participative learning and market-oriented skills. Besides learning pedagogical approaches such as role playing, the trainers were taken through an immersion process. They accompanied the JRP to the villages for three days and worked on identifying youths for their first class. The trainers also sat through company interviews to understand the market requirements.

In 2007, 15,000 young people were placed in entry-level jobs in companies such as McDonald's, Wipro, Reliance Retail, and the India Tobacco Company. Their incomes ranged between $533 per year in semiurban locations and $1,333 in major cities. "The results have been very encouraging," says S. Sivakumar, CEO of India Tobacco Company's agribusiness division.[56]

Transition

Going from living with one's family in a rural village to living alone in a big city and working in a large company is a challenging transition. An EGMM survey of companies that had hired rural youth showed high attrition rates during the first month of employment. A significant factor in the attrition was the simple fact that the companies paid their workers only at the end of the first month. But many of the poor young people had often arrived in the cities without any money, which made it difficult for them to survive the first month and resulted in their dropping the job.

EGMM now loans one-month's salary to the newly employed youths, which is repayable in soft installments. EGMM counselors meet the youths when they first migrate to cities and help them to find low-cost hostel accommodations and settle in. Counselors also visit new employees in the workplace to help them deal with any initial challenges. The late Y.S. Rajasekhara Reddy, then chief minister of Andhra Pradesh, announced in 2007 a plan to arrange transit homes in and around Hyderabad, the state's biggest city.[57] Young people are allowed to stay in these homes for three-to-six months until they find other suitable accommodations.

While EGMM does provide training, its success is more due to its role in improving the efficiency of the labor market for rural youths from remote locations. It identifies and motivates young people, and then provides them with appropriate information about job opportunities. Very importantly, it increases labor mobility by facilitating their transition from remote rural locations to an unfamiliar urban environment.

Impact

EGMM was started in 2005 by the state government of Andhra Pradesh with the help of the World Bank and the Indian central government and seed capital of $1.11 million. The results so far have been impressive: In 2007, EGMM trained 38,000 youths; in 2008, 75,000; and in 2009, 101,000. Budgets increased to $4.44 million in 2007, and $24.44 million in 2008. About 80 percent of the trainees were placed in jobs in the private organized sector; recruiting firms include McDonald's, Reliance Fresh, HDFC Bank, Hindustan Unilever, Larsen & Toubro, and Arvind Mills. "We are spending about $222 per student and the target is to train 100,000 rural youth to make them employable in 2007–2008," said rural development minister Chinna Reddy.[58]

The EGMM experience shows that providing a job in the organized sector to just one youth takes the entire family out of poverty in a sustained manner. India's rural poor are mostly agricultural laborers with erratic incomes of barely $266 a year. Youths who work in the cities often send money back to their families. One small survey conducted by EGMM showed average remittances of $533 a year. The survey also showed that 38 percent of the families use the remittances to pay off debts; 19 percent, to purchase assets; 12 percent, to fund their education; 23 percent put theirs in savings, and 8 percent use the money for other reasons.

Many anecdotes suggest a significant increase in the self-confidence and self-esteem of the youths. For example, Gonela Swamy, a 20-year-old from Veldanda village in Warangal was clueless about what he wanted to do after graduating from school.[59] He became depressed when he failed to get a job because of his lack of fluency in English and poor communication skills. But Swamy completed the 45-day training program at the Rural English and Soft Skills Academy and is now working as a customer support associate in Hometown, a shopping mall in Hyderabad. "It is the turning point in my life. From loitering around in my village, today I am working in the capital," a beaming Swamy said.

Interestingly, aspirations soar even in seemingly low-level entry jobs in which the youths are placed. Several youths who worked as security guards in IT companies have enrolled in computer classes; they now have higher aspirations of working "from outside to inside an IT company." An EGMM executive recounted the story of a manager at IBM who was amazed to hear a security guard tell him it was his last day on the job, as he had learned computer programming in his spare time and was now switching careers.

Employment opportunities in India are highly discriminatory against women.[60] EGMM also helps to overcome this imbalance: 40 percent of their trainees are women.

Government's Role

A major reason for the EGMM's success is that it combines the market-oriented approach of the private sector with the economies of scale provided by the government and grassroot community commitment. It is an excellent example of a government-managed program strongly linked to private-sector needs. EGMM is incorporated as a society by the Rural Development Department of the Andhra Pradesh state government, and its institutional framework departs from existing governmental norms. The executive committee is chaired by the state's minister of rural development, and its members comprise senior government officers and top executives from the private sector. EGMM's top managers, headed by the executive director, are a private-sector team, and are responsible for strategy development and implementation. Aiding the top management team are senior government officers and, in the field, an implementation team of professionals and members of community organizations. State-level ministers participate in activities such as graduation ceremonies from the training academies, which helps to achieve political support. The program and its targets are monitored by the chief minister, which also results in an enabling political environment. This institutional framework allows the strengths of the private sector to be complemented by the large-scale organization of the government and the commitment from the grassroots communities.

The Rural Development Department of Andhra Pradesh consciously decided that the government should fund EGMM budgets, without any contribution from private companies, to achieve the scale needed. The funding was justified partly on the basis that the program reduces social tensions created by unemployed youth. And, it does so at the reasonable cost of $222 per employed youth. The impact is measurable and can be achieved in a short period of just two to three months, which is the length of the training courses. Government participation also helps reduce costs. For example, unused government schools were converted into training academies.

According to TeamLease, a temporary staffing company in Bangalore, India, 58 percent of India's youths are not prepared for work or suffer from some kind of skill deprivation.[61] While around 14 million people enter the workforce every year, only 7 percent work in the organized sector. While privatization of skill development is possible to some extent, significant government intervention in training delivery and financing is needed with regard to poor people. Manish Sabharwal, chairman of TeamLease, says companies are not ready to pay for training potential recruits, and candidates are unable to pay for training or placement services. Much then depends on programs like EGMM. "We are not a human resources outfit. Our agenda is to take people out of poverty and provide jobs to first-generation workers," says Meera Shenoy, executive director of EGMM.

Private-Sector Network

The management team of EGMM has cultivated a network of linkages with companies in rapidly growing industries with large demand-supply gaps for entry-level manpower, such as services, textiles, and construction. Corporate participants in the network range from CEOs of companies to the regional manager of human resources. EGMM does not base its appeals for corporate involvement on social responsibility. Rather, the companies participate in the network because it is in their self-interest to do so, and because the rapid growth in the Indian economy in recent years has created a demand for qualified labor. EGMM works on the supply side of the labor market, and this puts EGMM and the network companies on an equal footing, which helps them in negotiating better work conditions for these young people. For example, in the retail sector, companies recruiting for entry-level positions used to require candidates to have passed 12th grade. Now, they are recruiting youths who have passed only 10th grade but have been trained by EGMM.

Young people are encouraged by EGMM to work in the companies for at least one year, which reduces the attrition level for the benefit of the companies. Recruiting from the rural academies also reduces recruiting costs for companies since the candidates have been pre-screened by EGMM. The network companies tend to come back regularly to the rural academies to fulfill their entry-level manpower needs.

Company participation in the design of training programs ensures that they are market-oriented and deepens the companies' commitment to the program. In order to recruit from the rural academies, company executives quite often have to spend a night in (or near) a village. This gives them a chance to interact with the young people. Hearing their stories of poverty and struggle helps the executives to better understand the context and have a deeper interface with the community. It also sensitizes companies to the passion and vision of EGMM. Subsequently, executives often volunteer to participate in training modules and give guest lectures.

Conclusions

Poverty reduction efforts should focus on increasing employment. Such a focus on employment assumes a reasonably pro-business environment within a country, but this is a low threshold requirement. Although this approach might not work in collapsing economies in failed states such as in Sudan, Myanmar, and Somalia, it would work in a large number of emerging economies. The two countries discussed above, Mozambique and India, are far from ideal environments. On the World Bank's Doing Business index, Mozambique ranks 135 and India ranks 133 out of 183 countries. On the Corruption Perception Index, Mozambique ranks 126 and India ranks 85 out of 180 countries. However, it must be noted that, within India, Andhra Pradesh ranks near the top in terms of pro-business environment and lack of corruption. In that sense, our two case studies are set in environments that are similar to those of many emerging economies.

At a conceptual level, both the TechnoServe and EGMM interventions are consistent with and illustrate the central thesis of this chapter: The best way to reduce poverty is to emphasize creating opportunities for steady employment at reasonable wages. The labor market involves employers (the demand side) and employees (the supply side). It is a good idea to target employers in the SME sector, which is the major creator of employment opportunities and is underdeveloped in poor countries—exactly what TechnoServe does. It is a good idea to target youths as employees because they experience higher unemployment than adults and would benefit more from increased employment—exactly what EGMM does. These ideas, illustrated in practice by TechnoServe and EGMM, have broad generalizability: initiatives that focus on increasing employment, and targeting the SME sector or youths would be useful in most developing countries.

Piecemeal Reform

Aside from the above focus on employment, there is another reason the TechnoServe and EGMM examples were chosen. TechnoServe and EGMM share a common approach to social reform that is effective in the context of poverty reduction.

To return to William Easterly's distinction between planners and searchers that we discussed in Chapter 1, planners set out a large goal and determine what to supply; searchers find out what is in demand. Planners apply global blueprints; searchers adapt to local conditions.[62] Global poverty is a big problem, but it is a fallacy to believe that big problems need big plans. Easterly makes the case that the planners have had mostly failures, and that more of the successes have been attributable to the searchers.

The two case studies described above are clearly examples of searchers implementing piecemeal reform, not planners with a utopian vision. Both TechnoServe and EGMM adopt a problem-solving, pragmatic approach, and both implement well-targeted interventions supported by conceptual logic and empirical evidence. These interventions are suited to their own local settings; they cannot be blindly imposed in different contexts and expected to work as well. For example, the EGMM approach would work only in an environment in which there is significant economic growth, large firms are creating employment opportunities, and the government is providing basic education (10th grade) to rural youth. There are many places, besides Andhra Pradesh state, characterized by such an environment, and a similar program might work there. According to one consultant: "If other states are able to replicate the model, there could be enough ammunition [to] handle India's rural employment dilemma."[63] At the same time, this intervention probably would not work as well in other parts of India (such as Bihar) nor other countries (such as Mozambique) with lower economic growth, less employment creation, and fewer large, high-growth companies.

Both TechnoServe and EGMM implement goal-oriented piecemeal reforms that require only a few changes to make a difference. This approach leverages the positive factors in the environment, and intervenes in a targeted manner only where there is some identifiable and relatively narrow market or government failure. There is no systemic failure and there is no need for wholesale reform. What is needed is a "nudge" to make the system perform better and increase employment; TechnoServe and EGMM focus on providing this nudge.[64]

EGMM does not create jobs—the economic growth in Andhra Pradesh is already doing that; EGMM does not provide basic schooling either—the Andhra Pradesh government is already doing that. EGMM leverages these positive developments and intervenes in a targeted manner to reduce the friction in the labor market by connecting the rural youths to urban employment opportunities. It is true that the state's educational system is flawed: Classes tend to be nonparticipatory and to emphasize rote learning. Trying to reform the entire school system managed by the ministry of education would require systemic change and "utopian reform." EGMM chooses the more effective approach of piecemeal reform by grooming trainers to emphasize active, participative learning and market-oriented skills, and designing short supplementary vocational training programs.

Similarly, TechnoServe leveraged the comparative advantage of Mozambique in the cashew nut industry, and the government in the year 2000 was receptive to an alternative solution after its earlier policies failed. Some of the needed infrastructure and skills for the cashew industry already existed in Mozambique. TechnoServe helped correct a relatively narrow market failure by intervening to facilitate the creation and growth of SME firms in the cashew industry. After just a few years, the market seems to be functioning well, and TechnoServe has concluded its program of subsidized assistance. There is, of course, no assurance that the enterprises TechnoServe helped to start and grow will continue at the same level of success. The future of these enterprises and the structure of the cashew industry in Mozambique will be determined by market forces, and appropriately so.

CHAPTER 7

Government Intervention

There is ideological debate in economics and the political realm over the role of business versus government, with the political right preferring free markets and a minimal role for the state, and the political left preferring a much larger role for the state. The political right appears to have a blind spot about market failure in public goods and in achieving equity; the political left appears to have a blind spot about the need for reforms in the public sector given the way it has performed in most developing countries. The right is blind to market failure; the left is blind to government failure. Rather than engaging in this debate, it is more useful to discuss the roles for business and government in a particular context.

This chapter discusses the basic logic for the roles of business and government in general. This logic is then applied in the context of poverty reduction. Government must regulate markets to protect poor vulnerable consumers. More importantly, the government has a major responsibility to ensure that the poor have access to various public services such as education, public health, sanitation and infrastructure. Two cases of successful government involvement are medicated bed nets in Africa and rural sanitation in India. Some development experts argue that governments should just give money to the poor as a direct way to reduce poverty. More than 45 developing countries have adopted some variant of this approach in recent years. Two examples are described here: the conditional cash transfer program in Mexico, Oportunidades, and the workfare program in India, National Rural Employment Guarantee Scheme (NREGS). Clearly government intervention is required to achieve poverty reduction and many avenues are currently being explored to change the existing socioeconomic conditions.

Government 101

Society uses three types of organizations to manage resources to meet its needs: for-profit businesses, public organizations, and not-for-profit organizations. Contemporary history proves the critical role markets play in creating value for society, and it is impossible to be against markets in general. Markets are basically about exchange; freedom of exchange is both desirable in and of itself and also value enhancing. As Amartya Sen puts it, being generically against markets is as odd as being against conversations between people.

Social Value and Markets

An organization, be it for-profit, public, or not-for-profit, consumes resources—labor, materials, and capital—to provide goods to its clients. The social value created by the organization is equal to the value of the output as determined by the customers minus the value of the inputs. The goods are sold to the customers at a certain price. If this is a business organization, the market determines the price of the goods traded. When public and not-for-profit organizations provide the goods, they determine the price for the goods; this price is usually lower than what the market price would have been if this were a for-profit firm.

As figure 7.1 illustrates, the value of outputs minus the firm's revenues is *consumer surplus,* and the revenues minus the cost of inputs are profits or, what the economists call, *producer surplus.* Social value created is equal to consumer surplus plus profits. Profits accrue to individuals, yet they are part of the social value created—individuals, after all, are part of society. In a public or not-for-profit organization, revenues are usually not adequate to cover costs, and the economic loss has to be subsidized by taxes or philanthropy.

In this discussion it is necessary to take into account the cost of capital used by the organization. The logic for determining the cost of capital is the opportunity cost of foregoing other alternative investments, adjusted for risk. The objective of private firms

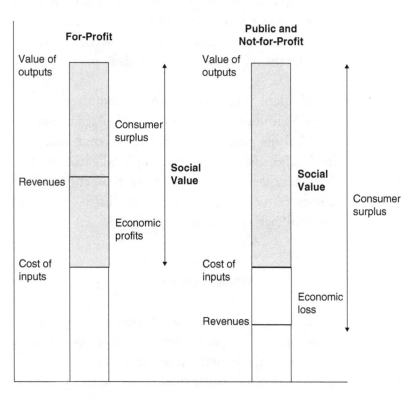

Figure 7.1   Social value created

is not just accounting profits, but rather economic profits, defined as accounting profits minus the opportunity cost of capital. The ability to generate accounting profits is not enough; economic profitability is necessary for the long-term viability of business. The rest of the chapter refers to economic profits, not accounting profits.

If markets are working well, then private profits and social value are aligned, and firms acting in their own self-interest will lead to a socially optimal outcome. Adam Smith wrote in *The Wealth of Nations* more than two hundred years ago,

> every individual necessarily labours to render the annual revenue of the society as great as he can. He generally, indeed, neither intends to promote the public interest, nor knows how much he is promoting it...He intends only his own gain, and he is in this, as in many other cases, led by an invisible hand to promote an end which was no part of his intention. By pursuing his own interest he frequently promotes that of the society more effectually then when he really intends to promote it.[1]

The genius of Adam Smith was his understanding of the harmony between private interest and social value. Guided by Smith's "invisible hand," firms pursuing rational self-interest maximize social welfare. It is because this insight is empirically true that free market capitalism is the best path to economic prosperity, and the political ideology of the world has decisively shifted in the last thirty years toward market-oriented economics.

Market Failure

Adam Smith's invisible hand argument, of course, depends on the efficiency of markets, as Joseph Stiglitz has pointed out, "Smith was far more aware of the limitations of the market than his latter-day followers. Today, we realize that the reason that the invisible hand often seems invisible is that it is not there."[2] If markets worked perfectly for all social needs—an unrealistically rosy picture—there would be no need for public or not-for-profit organizations (leaving aside the issue of equity). In fact, markets often do fail because of externalities, monopoly power, and imperfect information. It then becomes the role of the government to step in to provide a solution.

A common reason for market failure is externalities, whereby the organization and its customers do not bear all the costs (such as pollution—negative externalities), or do not capture all the benefits (such as spillovers from research and development [R&D]—positive externalities) related to the goods produced. The social value created in this case is equal to consumer surplus plus economic profits, minus negative externalities and plus positive externalities. Government regulation is then needed to try to fix the market failure, essentially by internalizing the externalities. Governments may prohibit or mandate some activities (such as banning fluorocarbons or requiring catalytic converters in cars), impose taxes on organizations to compensate for the negative externalities (such as a carbon tax), or reward firms for positive externalities (such as subsidizing R&D). At times, the state chooses to have public organizations directly provide the goods, such as government-owned research facilities.

In some industries, such as electricity, where scale economies are very large, one or a few firms might dominate the market and could exploit market power to the detriment of social value. In the case of such natural monopolies, the government can address the market failure either through regulation (e.g., the government-regulated private utilities in the United States) or through public organizations that provide the goods and services directly to consumers (e.g., government-owned utilities in most countries).

The third reason for market failure is imperfect information. If consumers are ill-informed, firms can exploit them and reduce the social value created. Governments usually address this market failure through regulation. For example, in regard to the pharmaceutical industry, most patients and even some doctors lack the knowledge and expertise to assess the safety and efficacy of drugs, and the government in every country requires all prescription drugs to be approved by a public agency (e.g., the United States Food and Drug Administration) before they are allowed into the market.

Based on some combination of externalities, public goods, and the monopoly power argument, the government is responsible for providing basic public services such as education, public health, water, sanitation, electricity, and infrastructure. The unregulated market is not an effective way to meet these social needs. There is much debate about whether the actual production of these services should be privatized or outsourced. A recent United Nations Development Programme (UNDP)–supported book *Privatization and Alternative Public Sector Reform in Sub-Saharan Africa* comes to the conclusion that privatization has been a widespread failure.[3] The focus of investors on cost recovery has not promoted social objectives, such as reducing poverty and promoting equity.

Consider the example of the urban water sector in Zambia.[4] Zambia's central government had historically provided urban water delivery services, except in the Copperbelt. Water tariffs were subsidized. The government then decided to privatize the water sector starting in the early 1990s, and by 2006, ten private water companies were supplying urban centers. Commercialization led to rate increases of up to 600 percent in real terms, and the proportion of the population with access to safe water declined from 72 percent to 57 percent between 1992 and 2002. Zambia's privatization strategy emphasizes tariff rationalization, but this has failed to ensure full cost recovery and further constrained affordability and accessibility. According to current estimates, the MDG of halving the number of people without access to safe drinking water will be achieved only in 2040, long after the 2015 target, especially in sub-Saharan Africa. The report concludes that in many developing countries, privatization has resulted in "spectacular failures." A better approach would be up-front public investment to renew and extend the infrastructure. This would reduce unit costs, and affordable tariffs would improve equitable access.

Even when the government privatizes these services, it still plays a role by regulating or financing them. For example, if the water supply is privatized, the government needs to regulate the rates the company charges its customers; or the government can choose to finance the water supply but outsource the management. Few would argue that the state could totally avoid all responsibility for such public services. The governments in almost every developing country certainly profess to accept responsibility for these traditional functions. Regardless of the debate about privatization, public organizations are the dominant providers of these services and will remain so for the foreseeable future. It is critical that we ensure that the government has the financial resources, human capital, and organizational capabilities to effectively deliver basic services.

Equity

Even if there is no market failure, society might prefer the government to fulfill a particular social need. Social welfare is determined not just by the total amount of value produced, but also by the "distribution" of this value. Markets driven by efficiency often produce more inequality than society considers desirable. Citizens often desire a more egalitarian society than what free markets produce, and they express this desire for social justice through the political process. For example, there is arguably no market failure in the case of the food industry, and accordingly, the need for food is satisfied largely by for-profit businesses. Yet many poor people, even in affluent countries, cannot afford adequate nutrition. In many countries (especially in affluent ones), public agencies provide food assistance to the needy. The same argument could be made for other societal needs such as housing and health care. Many societies consider basic nutrition, health, and education to be fundamental human rights, and require the state to be responsible for fulfilling these social needs.

This is especially true for services targeted toward children. Social justice requires attenuation of the effects of the "lottery of birth": Children born to poor parents tend to grow up to be poor adults and to pass on the disadvantage to their children in turn. Being born into a poor household significantly raises the risk of deprivation. In the Philippines, there is a four-year education gap between the richest and poorest households. The gap in India is seven years.[5] Social justice and equality of opportunity requires that all children have access to a certain level of education. (Another argument for state intervention in education is that there are spillover effects here, a positive externality.) Even Milton Friedman, Nobel Laureate in Economics, advocated the school voucher system, and not for the state to withdraw totally from the field of education. Education is a function that should not be left to free markets.

Haiti, one of the poorest countries in the world, is an uncommon example of a country that does not follow this prescription. The Haitian state's role in primary education is uniquely low, which has a negative impact on its poor population. Of the world's 20 poorest countries, Haiti is the only one in which more than 50 percent of children are enrolled in private (for profit and not-for-profit) schools. In fact, 82 percent of all primary and secondary school students attend private, fee-based schools.[6] School fees are estimated to account for 15 to 25 percent of rural households' expenditures. This privatization has created a great deal of educational disparity based on income and location. School attendance by 7- to 14-year-old children was 87.2 percent for the richest quintile of the population, and only 73.6 percent for the poorest quintile. School attendance in urban areas was 84.8 percent, compared to only 73.3 percent in rural locations. Problems of access are exacerbated by issues of quality. There is a small elite category of expensive, private, not-for-profit schools at the top catering only to the wealthiest Haitians. These are followed by a large group of public schools that occupy the middle segment. The vast majority of private schools are at the bottom, catering to the poor, and these are for-profit schools. According to some studies, 60 percent of teachers in these private for-profit schools are unqualified, and many informal, disreputable educational establishments operate without licenses in inadequate environments. For-profit schools targeting the poor is consistent with the BOP premise, but it is certainly not beneficial for the poor. This is a major problem, since "education is the single most important determinant of an individual's potential to escape poverty in Haiti." Haiti under-invests in human capital and the quality of education is "alarmingly low."

It is encouraging that India is trying to move in the opposite direction. With the Right to Education Act enacted in 2009, India has made education free and mandatory for children aged 6 to 14. The challenge, of course, will be to enforce the law and to deliver on the promise, and it will require both financial resources and institutional capacity. In fact, 135 countries already have constitutional provisions for free and non-discriminatory education for children. However, despite legal guarantees, 72 million children of primary school age and 71 million adolescents do not attend school.[7] Other factors such as gender, location, and ethnicity interact with poverty to make education access even worse for some people. For example, in Nigeria, the average youth aged 17 to 22 has received seven years of education. For poor rural Hausa females, that figure drops to less than six months.

The citizens in most modern societies desire equality and fairness on several dimensions such as gender, race, ethnicity, religion, and geographic location. It is the responsibility of the government to try to achieve this equality, an essential element of poverty reduction. In many countries the government has intervened in or constrained markets to achieve some larger social goal along these lines, such as affirmative action policies.

Three Sectors

The three types of organizations, for-profit, public, and not-for-profit, are very different. Public and not-for-profit organizations usually incur an economic loss, not because they are inefficient, but because they intervene in cases of market failure or to cater to people who cannot afford market prices. Therefore, these organizations need to find sources of funds to cover this loss. Governments have the legitimate power to impose taxes on citizens to fund public activities. Not-for-profit organizations rely on donors motivated by altruism.

Contemporary economic history clearly demonstrates that the market system is the best way to allocate resources and achieve overall growth. The first choice for fulfilling a societal need is free markets. The invisible hand ensures that social value is optimized, assuming the market is functioning well. However, if there is a market problem—market failure or a concern for equity—then the government should step in and either regulate the market or ensure that public agencies directly or indirectly satisfy the societal need. In a well-functioning democracy, the political process—the counterpart of the invisible hand in the public context—ensures that the government creates social value consistent with the values of its citizens. In an ideal world, for-profit and public organizations would fulfill all societal needs and there would be no need for civil society. (We would still need civil society for other reasons, such as fulfilling spiritual needs.) Unfortunately the world is far from ideal. There is a useful role for civil society, as discussed in Chapter 8. Like the invisible hand, the political process too is at times flawed, and governments often fail due to inefficiency, incompetence, and corruption.

Government and Poverty

To summarize, the government has a role only when there is a market problem—market failure or a concern for equity. In that case, the government should either regulate the market, or ensure that public agencies directly or indirectly provide the public service. These governmental responsibilities are magnified in the case of the poor because markets for the poor fail more often and the poor are critically dependent on the public services.

Public Services

To achieve a more egalitarian society, the government is responsible for providing additional services to the poor, services that it might not provide to affluent people, such as basic health care and basic nutrition. In India there is a political movement to make the right to food a legal entitlement. The Congress Party election manifesto for 2009 included a promise to enact a right to food act, and the government is working on it now. Finance minister Pranab Mukherjee said in June 2010, "Earlier, we felt development will take place due to trickling down effect, but now the focus is on empowering people by giving them entitlements backed by legal enactment."[8] There have even been demands that the right to food should be extended to include safe drinking water and other health concerns.

Providing access to the basic public services is an essential part of poverty reduction. Amartya Sen says, "Social and economic factors such as basic education, elementary health care, and secure employment are important not only in their own right, but also for the role they can play in giving people opportunity to approach the world with courage and freedom."[9] The most important role of the government in poverty reduction is providing basic public services to the poor. Yet the governments in most developing countries have failed dismally to provide these basic services. Whereas the rich often purchase these services from private enterprises, it is the middle class that is the main beneficiary of the public service expenditures. The poor have no or little access to these services, or get very low-quality public services, or pay very high prices for private services. For example, the rich go to world-class private hospitals and clinics. The middle class has access to reasonable public health facilities. While public health centers do exist to serve rural and poor areas, these centers are grossly underfunded and understaffed. Even worse, the staff may not be qualified, and are often absent.

The children of the rich go to exclusive private schools. The middle class uses a mix of private and public schools. Children of the poor often do not go to school or go to low-quality public schools. In one survey, a quarter of the teachers were absent and another quarter was present but not teaching. Absentee rates for teachers and health workers are higher in poorer regions. The rich hire private guards. The middle class lives in reasonably well-policed neighborhoods. The poor have little protection from thugs and criminals. The rich have ample access to clean water; they purchase bottled-drinking water, drill private tube wells, and use booster pumps. The middle class settles for piped water, even if only for a few hours a day, and often must boil the water to make it potable. The poor have no or little access to a clean public water supply, and often drink polluted water. In a "tragedy of the commons," the drilling of private wells by the rich probably depletes the water table, reducing the water supply for others.

The burden of the failure of public services is also borne disproportionably by women, which exacerbates gender inequality. Lack of access to toilets poses a bigger problem for women because of anatomy, modesty, and susceptibility to attack. Women often lose much time to hauling buckets of water over long distances. They are more likely than men to need medical care; they are expected to care for sick family members, especially children. Girls also attend school less often, especially in poor families.

Regulation

Markets for the poor fail more often than markets for affluent people because two causes of market failure are exacerbated: imperfect information and monopoly power. Compared to affluent people, the poor are ill informed, less educated (often illiterate), and disadvantaged due to various social, cultural, and political deprivations, which makes them vulnerable consumers.

Every government regulates alcohol and tobacco markets to protect consumers. The need for protection is even greater for poor people. For example, package-label warnings about the hazards of smoking are useless if consumers can't read them. Pictorial warnings are far preferable, but the tobacco industry opposes these. The retail banking industry is regulated to protect affluent consumers. The financially less literate clients of microcredit need even more protection; yet, perversely, this market for the poor is less, not more, regulated. Any regulations that do exist are often less enforced in the context of the poor. For example, restrictions on the sale of alcohol are enforced less in poor villages than in cities. This is not to argue that all markets for the poor should be heavily regulated. The government needs to be vigilant in regulating markets for the poor using standard economic theory and the *empirical* characteristics of the poor as consumers rather than making an ideological assumption that the poor are perfectly rational economic actors. There are discussions earlier in the book about the need for greater regulation in cases of alcohol (Chapter 4), microcredit (Chapter 2), and other questionable products (Chapter 4). Government regulation to protect vulnerable consumers is critical for products in the *cigarettes quadrant* in figure 5.1.

The second reason market failures are more common for the poor is monopoly power. Markets for the poor are often small and isolated due to geographic distance and bad infrastructure, which leads to minimal competition. For example, the market for financial services in urban affluent locations is competitive, which is not the case in poor rural locations. Another example is retail distribution in villages. The Indian subsidiary of Unilever has created a rural direct-distribution system called Shakti to sell its consumer packaged goods in villages; at the outset, the vision was that the project would cover one million entrepreneurs by 2005.[10] With 45,000 entrepreneurs thus far, it has fallen far short of that goal.[11] At the same time, if the Shakti distribution channel were to grow much larger, there would be concern about Unilever earning monopoly rents. There is minimal competition in rural distribution channels, and not surprisingly Unilever does not allow its Shakti saleswomen to sell competing products.

Government as the Problem

Just as there are examples of market failure, there are many examples of government failure.[12] Regulation can end up making situations worse and reducing public welfare. When, for example, the government overestimates the extent of a market failure, its regulatory policy could end up forcing the economy to incur unnecessary costs and reducing public welfare. Another cause of government failure could be shortsighted, inflexible, and contradictory policies of government agencies. A flawed political system might allow certain interest groups to influence government intervention to accrue economic rents at the expense of social welfare. The industry that the government is trying to regulate might capture the regulatory process to its own benefit. The theory of regulatory capture has demonstrated that regulation designed to protect consumers often ends up benefiting the industry to the detriment of consumers.[13] Public choice theory demonstrates that some costs (i.e., failures) are characteristic of a democratic system of government. The problems of government failure are exacerbated when the government lacks the resources and competence to design and administer appropriate regulations and to manage public services, which is particularly true in complex environments requiring much specialized knowledge. If there is corruption in government, the situation is even worse.

India provides an example of the failure of public services. The Indian economy is growing rapidly, the stock market is doing well, Indian companies are expanding abroad, and a large middle class is emerging. Economically, it is the best of times. Contrast this with the other side of India, characterized by persistent gender and caste inequality, and growing income inequality. Fifteen percent of boys and 19 percent of girls do not attend even primary school. Seventy-nine percent of rural households and 46 percent or urban households do not have adequate sanitation. India is not alone in this failure of the state; it is easy to cite similar statistics for many other developing countries. About 884 million people in developing countries do not have adequate access to clean drinking water, while 2.6 billion lack basic sanitation. Nearly 1 billion people are illiterate and 101 million children of primary school age are not in school. The boom in the private sector has been accompanied by a significant failure by the state to provide basic public services.

Government as the Solution

There is no magic solution to these failures of the state, but we certainly should not accept them as inevitable. Giving the poor a voice is vital to the development process. Yet, in many developing countries, an autocratic government has stifled them. Even in developing countries with representative democracies, the political process has been hijacked: The business community, bureaucrats, politicians, and the media are full of self-congratulation about the booming private sector (e.g., on the increased penetration of cell phones). However, the image that is emblematic of many developing countries is not the cell phone, but human beings defecating in the open.

An intriguing possibility for empowering the poor can be seen in the recent rights-based approach to development in India. The coalition government led by the Congress Party has passed into law rights to information, education, and employment. There is much talk of extending this movement to cover other societal needs such as nutrition, health care, public health, and environment. Enacting a law, of course, does not automatically lead to the fulfilment of a societal need. But, it might serve to give a voice to the poor and make the government more accountable. It makes clear that public services are a universal entitlement, not a privilege to be dispensed at the government's discretion. Once the citizens, especially the poor, understand this, they will demand these services and hold the government accountable at the local, state, and federal levels. This will force the government to deliver on its promises, which it has failed to do in the past. "The ambition goes beyond poverty alleviation to the cleansing and improvement of a rotten administrative and social system."[14] Even if the ambition is not fully realized, the rights-based movement has already focused attention on and injected urgency into India's poverty reduction efforts.

Although government is the solution when markets fail, the reverse is not true. When the state fails, the market may be a partial complement to, but cannot be a total substitute for, government. There is no alternative viable mechanism for fulfilling its responsibilities. Only the government has the legitimate power to enforce regulation and to impose taxes to fund public services. When governments fail, the only solution is to fix them.

That said, state failure is not inevitable. We need to get away from the stereotype that governments are always bureaucratic, wasteful, and corrupt. Economist Amil Petrin argues that, while the popular stereotype is that decision making in public organizations is rigid and bureaucratic, they still allow room for flexibility and entrepreneurship.[15] Several case studies demonstrate that government agencies and departments can, in fact, be creative in addressing problems.[16] The challenge is to build the institutional capacity to make governments more efficient, responsive, and even entrepreneurial. The existence of some strong examples of well-run, efficient public services means governments can perform better.

The government of Singapore, for example, effectively and efficiently delivers a wide range of public services, from "basics," such as public health and infrastructure, to "frills," such as public libraries and public recreational facilities. Another example is the British government's launch of a wide-ranging regulatory reform program in 2005, based on its belief that "effective and evidence-based regulations can play a critical role in correcting market failures, and provide essential protections for the general public...The Government is focused on striking the right balance between guaranteeing essential protections and rights are upheld and recognizing the impact of excessive regulations on businesses..."[17] The effort focuses on five characteristics of good regulation: It is transparent, accountable, proportionate, consistent, and targeted. A new, independent Regulatory Policy Committee has been set up whose role is to advise the government on whether it is doing all it can to accurately assess the costs and benefits of regulation. The government claims, "We are on target to cut the administrative burden of existing regulation by 25 percent by 2010."

Positive examples of government performance are not confined to developed countries. The metro system in Delhi, India, has received much praise for excellent management. The first phase of the project was completed in 2006 on budget and ahead of schedule. The system continues to be well run. *Bloomberg Businessweek* describes it as "nothing short of a miracle." The EGMM program described in Chapter 6 is an innovative and effective program run by the state government of Andhra Pradesh, India.

Consider the examples of Kerala and Uttar Pradesh, two states in India, functioning under the same constitution, laws, and political system. Yet, Kerala is far ahead of Uttar Pradesh in its ability to deliver various public services (see table 7.1). Economists Jean Dreze and Amartya Sen suggest that Kerala's success is the result of public action that promoted extensive social opportunities and the widespread equitable provision of basic public services.[18]

Effective Government

Like business success, government effectiveness requires four elements: good strategic planning, financial resources, organizational effectiveness to execute the strategy, and accountability. It is fruitless to contrast private organizations with public organizations and debate their comparative performance. The challenge is to discern the characteristics of an effective organization, and determine how to move any organization, private or public, toward greater effectiveness.

Table 7.1 Public services in Kerala and Uttar Pradesh

	Kerala	Uttar Pradesh
Literacy rate: male	94.2%	68.8%
Literacy rate: female	87.7%	42.2%
School enrollment: male	91.0%	77.3%
School enrollment: female	90.8%	61.4%
Sex ratio women/men	105.8%	89.8%
Immunization coverage rate	75.3%	23.0%
Skilled delivery care % of births	99.4%	27.2%
Life expectance at birth: male	71.4 years	60.3 years
Life expectancy at birth: female	76.3 years	59.5 years
Households with electricity	70.2%	31.9%
Households with bathroom inside: rural	42.3%	15.9%
Households with bathroom inside: urban	19.8%	12.8%

Note: Data for varying years during 2000 to 2006.

Source: National Health Profile of India—2009.

Strategic Choices

Developing strategies, of course, requires domain knowledge, analytical skills, and a capability to make significant choices that drive organizational performance. This involves making difficult trade-offs in a complex environment under uncertain conditions, and these choices are necessarily controversial.[19] If the correct choices were obvious, all organizations would be successful. Albert Einstein is said to have defined insanity as doing the same thing and expecting a different result.

Vision statements of companies are often trite and full of platitudes, generic and exchangeable, not controversial, and hence, not strategic! This is also true, maybe even truer, of public organizations, which often loudly proclaim politically correct platitudes. Successful organizations, private and public, go beyond these platitudinous vision statements to make real strategic choices.

An effective strategic planning process must be capable of dealing with controversy and the inherent conflict that arises. Given the complexity of the choices, managers may come to different conclusions based on their diverse perspectives, backgrounds, competencies, and access to information. The best way to deal with this issue is to make the strategic planning process as participative, explicit, and transparent as possible. This is an idealistic view of the process and it will never be so perfect due to hidden assumptions and biases, vested interests, and personal agendas. The challenge is to at least move in that direction.

Confronting differences is the key. We need to bring conflict out into the open. This is how wise trade-offs among competing alternatives can be made. Intellectual debate among managers with divergent views is a vital source of creative and innovative solutions within the organization. Conflict is the source of creativity; dissent is the source of learning. Conflict, of course, needs to be managed such that it is constructive and intellectual, as opposed to personal, politicized, and destructive. Organizations, whether public or private, structured in rigid, tiered bureaucracies suppress conflict rather than mange conflict constructively.

Financial Resources

Private companies acquire financial resources in capital markets from investors motivated by potential profits. Public organizations acquire finances from the government treasury, which raises resources from taxes and foreign aid. Even though foreign aid has often not had a positive impact in the past, it might be a critically useful source of money in many cases. Foreign aid per se is not the problem. The delivery and use of foreign aid needs to be improved, not eliminated. The challenge is to structure the other three elements (strategy, organizational effectiveness, and accountability) such that the money is used appropriately and with good effect. Regardless of the source of the money, the government needs to allocate it to the right priorities.

Consider the case of public expenditure on education in Mexico. Mexico, like many developing countries, especially in

Latin America, has been characterized by high income inequality. Recently, there has been a decline in inequality, as reflected in the Gini coefficient falling from 0.543 in 1996 to 0.498 in 2006.[20] A partial reason for this improvement was increased government spending on basic education that helped to correct an existing deficit. "Public spending on education in the 1970s and 1980s was heavily biased towards higher education. In the 1970s, the share of educational spending allocated to upper secondary and tertiary education grew from 20 percent to 42 percent while the share of spending on basic education declined by an equivalent amount, despite an expansion in enrollment in public basic education from 9.7 to 16.5 million students." This bias was subsequently reversed. Between 1992 and 2002, spending per student in primary education increased by 63 percent. The distribution of educational spending in Mexico changed qualitatively over the decade from slightly regressive to progressive. In 1992, the poorest decile of the population received 7 percent of educational spending, while the richest decile received 10 percent. In 2006, the poorest decile received 12 percent of educational spending, while the richest decile received 6 percent.

Organizational Effectiveness

Many organizations, private and public, have great strategies but still fail because they cannot execute the strategies. A good strategy poorly implemented is still a failure. As Will Rogers wisecracked, "Even if you are on the right track, you will get run over if you just sit there." The challenge is how to get large organizations to get up and move fast. Success stories, particularly from the business world, suggest three key elements for organizational effectiveness: empowerment, developing human capital, and appropriate incentives. These lessons are just as applicable to public organizations.

The trend toward empowerment goes by different names: decentralization, delegation, and delayering. Organizations in which power has been pushed down to lower levels are more responsive, flexible, and customer oriented. The flow of information and directives is faster and less distorted in flat organizations. Employees are more committed and satisfied. Decisions are made quicker and closer to the ground, where the appropriate knowledge resides. Table 7.2 lists the characteristics of an empowered organization contrasted with a "command and control" organization.

Few public organizations are as bad as the command and control stereotype; few private organizations are as good as the empowerment ideal. The challenge for any organization, private or public, is to move along the continuum toward the empowerment ideal. Public organizations tend to be large and often cite that as an excuse for being rigidly bureaucratic. Consider Walmart, the world's largest retailer, which has 2.1 million employees and yet is a very well-managed company.

Empowerment only works if the people in the organization have the right capabilities—hence the emphasis on cultivating human capital. This starts with recruiting the right people. Successful organizations invest effort in developing their employees by offering them educational programs, in-house training, job rotation, mentoring, and managing their career paths.

Table 7.2 Organizational effectiveness

Command and Control	Empowerment
Power concentrated at top	Power pushed down
Rigid structure	Fluid organization
Steep hierarchy, many layers	Flat hierarchy, few layers
Formal power	Informal influence
Vertical, authoritarian relationships	Horizontal, collaborative processes
Low employee commitment	Employees engaged, high job satisfaction
Suppress dissent	Constructive conflict
Inflexible	Responsive, customer driven
Rule-bound	Take initiative, action oriented

Employees, like all people, respond to incentives, both financial and nonfinancial. Successful organizations carefully design performance measurement and reward systems, and link them. Public organizations often cannot match the compensation levels of private companies. Even though this may not be easy to change, it is possible to narrow the gap to some extent by increasing the compensation of government officials. At a minimum, public organizations can design systems with a positive alignment between performance and rewards. In many public organizations, rewards are not linked to performance and are instead driven by other factors, such as seniority and patronage, and even outright corruption. Public organizations can also usefully further emphasize nonfinancial incentives, especially given the idealism of many employees. Having a greater social impact might be a reward in itself. Incentive systems should include not only "carrots" but also "sticks." The ultimate penalty is dismissal from the organization. Public organizations must have the freedom to fire employees to prevent public employment becoming a sinecure.

Accountability

In any organization, the top management must be held accountable for the company's performance. Goodwill alone is not enough. A firm is accountable to both its shareholders (or owners) and its customers. Corporate governance tries to ensure that managers act in the interests of the shareholders. A quicker and more direct route of accountability is customers leaving the company. By analogy, we need to bring both types of accountability to bear on public organizations.

A government "for the people" is ultimately accountable to its citizens, who are the counterpart of the private sector's shareholders. Clearly, democracy is essential for creating this accountability. Shifting power to local levels, that is, from federal to state to provincial to city/town/village, would help increase accountability by giving citizens a greater voice. We also need a quicker and more direct route of accountability that gives a greater voice to public-service customers, especially the poor at the local level. Just as all citizens should demand adequate education for all at a national and state level, poor people in a particular neighborhood should be able to voice their discontent with inadequate education in that neighborhood.

Of course, customers who are not happy with the performance of a public service organization most of the time don't have the option of taking their business to an alternative service provider. One way to give a public service customers a voice may be to require public organizations to do regular customer surveys at a local level. Affluent people often voice their opinions as "education consumers" through organizations such as parent-teacher associations. Unfortunately, the poor often do not even understand that it is legitimate to voice their opinions, or, they have no venue for communicating their ideas. This is how the rights-based approach to development described earlier could help—by highlighting the responsibilities of the government to deliver basic services to all people, especially the poor. Another possibility is civil society acting as a watchdog, which is discussed in the Chapter 8.

Below are two case studies of public intervention that are works-in-progress but seem to be achieving some success: medicated bed nets in Africa and rural sanitation in India.

Bed Nets in Africa

Malaria kills nearly one million people every year, mostly in Africa. Eighty-five percent of the deaths are children under five years of age. This is particularly tragic and reprehensible since malaria is preventable and treatable. The World Health Organization (WHO) recommends three primary interventions to control malaria:[21]

- Diagnosis and treatment
- Distribution of long-lasting insecticide-treated bed nets (ITNs), which repel and kill mosquitoes
- Indoor residual spraying to kill mosquitoes

There is a long-standing debate in the malaria-control field over how to distribute ITNs: via free markets, subsidized social-marketing programs, or by giving them away for free.[22] The free-market approach was abandoned a long time ago. An ITN costs about $5 to $7 to produce. Add to this distribution costs, and ITNs are far too expensive for most poor people to buy. In 2002 in Kenya, the only ITNs available were those for sale in small shops, and the penetration rate was only 7 percent.

Social Marketing

Africa next tried a social marketing approach, whereby ITNs were distributed at a heavily subsidized price. USAID and Population Services International, a health NGO targeting malaria, among other international health issues, were among the many organizations involved in social marketing of the ITNs. The Acumen Fund, a proponent of "social entrepreneurship," is an investor in A to Z Textile Mills in Tanzania, which manufactures ITNs.[23] The Acumen Fund also works with the company to develop private-sector distribution channels for the ITNs, such as by hiring women sales agents, who earn a commission by selling the nets in their villages.

The theory behind social marketing is that the poor see more value in brand-name goods they pay for than handouts they get free, and that the trade creates small entrepreneurs. Price can be used to target the product at people who will value it rather than waste it. A higher price might encourage usage if it is interpreted as a signal of quality. The poor are more likely to use the nets if they have to pay for them. The social marketing argument is that bringing businesses into the mix improves efficiency and adds economic incentives and benefits to doing good. This is still somewhat consistent with the libertarian logic, although watered down since it is not a real free market because of the subsidy involved. The Acumen Fund advocates a "market-based approach to nurture small businesses that are able to deliver goods and services to the world's poor on a sustainable basis... The difference to hand-ing out charity is simple: while the recipient of a gift won't speak of its shortcomings, the paying consumer will have an opinion as to the product's quality and usefulness."[24]

Unfortunately, social marketing has not worked in the case of ITNs. In 2007, the WHO put out a new position paper strongly advocating free distribution of ITNs. Arata Kochi, the head of WHO's antimalaria operation, said in an article in the *New York Times*, "the debate is at an end... The time for social marketing of bed nets in a big way is over. It can become a supplemental strategy for urban areas and middle-income countries."[25] Peter Olumese, a WHO officer, tells of a study in Kenya that showed that social marketing had increased the penetration of ITNs from 7 percent to only 21 percent after five years. The "richest of the poor" had 38 percent coverage while the "poorest of the poor" had only 15 percent coverage.[26]

Free Nets

In 2006, the health ministry in Kenya got a big grant from the Global Fund to Fight AIDS, Tuberculosis, and Malaria that enabled it to hand out 3.4 million free ITNs in two weeks. The coverage rose immediately to 67 percent and became more equi-table; deaths of children eventually dropped by 44 percent.

Data from Ethiopia, Rwanda, and Zambia replicate the Kenya results. Within two years of the implementation of a similar mass-distribution program in Ethiopia, the number of childhood malaria cases dropped by 60 percent, and the death rate dropped by 50 percent. In Rwanda, both incidence and deaths dropped by two thirds within one year. In Zambia, cases and deaths dropped by one-third. A key feature of these programs was giving away bed nets for free.[27]

ITNs are characterized by a significant externality, and should not be left to free markets. When used by more than 80 percent of the people in a village, ITNs provide effective vector control and protect everyone in the village, including those who do not use them. On the other hand, sporadic individual use of nets tends to just drive mosquitoes elsewhere in the village. ITNs should be viewed as a public good and reside in the public domain. It is the government's responsibility to provide ITNs to everyone, perhaps with the help of foreign aid and NGOs.

Vaccines for measles and polio are distributed free to the poor on the grounds they a provide public good. Similarly, the Indian government distributes free condoms to the poor. ITNs, too, should be provided for free. Social marketing is also more expensive than free distribution due to costs such as advertising, according to Olumese. Additional support for free ITNs comes from a recent research study using the rigorous methodology of randomized control trials in rural Kenya.[28] The empirical evidence shows that even a low price for ITNs significantly dampens demand. Uptake of bed nets drops by 75 percent when the price increases from zero to just $0.75. There is no support for the argument that free ITNs will lead to increased wastage or reduced usage. "Overall, our results suggest that free distribution of ITNs could save many more lives than cost-sharing programs have achieved so far, and, given the large positive externality associated with widespread usage of ITNs, it would likely do so at a lesser cost per life saved." Population Services International, which used to be a proponent of social marketing is now involved in mass campaigns to distribute free ITNs.

Given the significant benefits to the user of ITNs, the price elasticity observed in the above study is larger in magnitude than expected on the basis of economic rationality. This suggests that pregnant women (the subjects in that study) either have very little money or are very "present-biased," or both. It is not easy for affluent people to really understand how poor the poor are. A village elder confirmed that price was a major impediment: "Our people are poor, and very few could afford to buy a mosquito net even for 50 shillings [$0.75]. We are happy that the nets are free."[29] Olumese puts it this way: "Asking a mother to make a decision to feed her child or buy a net is not fair." It is also possible that the poor are in general very present-biased. The debilitating effect of poverty makes it difficult to be hopeful about the future, and it is understandable that the poor are very short-term oriented.

Recent Progress

Kochi estimates that a campaign costing about $10 billion would be enough to bring malaria under control in most of Africa, and reduce the death rate to a few thousand per year from the current one million.[30] Inventing a vaccine that totally eradicates malaria would be better. That is a good long-term solution, but it does not seem to be feasible in the near future. The Bill and Melinda Gates Foundation, which is supporting the development of a vaccine, states, "Our goal is to ensure the development and launch of a safe, effective, and affordable vaccine against malaria by 2025." Meanwhile, we must do what we can to control the disease. Fortunately, many African countries are launching programs emphasizing free ITNs using their own resources, or with the help of foreign aid and organizations such as the Global Fund and the World Bank. Funding from international donors for malaria control increased from $50 million in 1997 to $800 million in 2007 to $1.7 billion in 2009.[31] The percentage of African households owning at least one ITN went from 9 percent to 31 percent between 2005 and 2008. In some countries, the progress has been even more significant. In Rwanda, the household ITN ownership has grown from 6 percent to 61 percent between 2005 and 2008; in Zambia, it grew from 7 percent to 70 percent in the same period. In countries that have achieved high coverage of their populations with bed nets and treatment programs, malaria cases and deaths have dropped by more than 50 percent. Government intervention is critical to sustain this progress.

Rural Sanitation in India

The practice of open defecation by 1.1 billion people in the world is an affront to human dignity. Moreover, indiscriminate defecation is a major cause of fecal-oral transmission of disease, which has lethal consequences for young children. Water-related illnesses account for about 5 percent of the global burden of diseases. About 2 million children die every year of diarrhea and related waterborne diseases; persistent diarrheal disease radically impairs gut function, which is the single greatest contributor to child malnutrition and growth retardation. Apart from health outcomes, sanitation has a bearing on education and gender equality. One of the reasons for high school drop-out rates among adolescent girls is the lack of sanitation facilities at school. Lack of sanitation has a significant effect on the privacy, dignity, safety, and health of women.

Jawaharlal Nehru, the first Prime Minister of India, once said: "The day everyone of us gets a toilet to use, I shall know that our country has reached the pinnacle of progress." Unfortunately, that day is still far off. About 665 million people in India defecate in the open. Mahatma Gandhi said that "sanitation is more important than independence." India achieved independence in 1947; sanitation remains a distant goal. The good news is that rural India is making progress, driven by a national-level government initiative, Nirmal Gram Puraskar (NGP), meaning "Clean Village Prize," launched in 2003.

Traditionally, sanitation programs in India have focused on subsidizing the construction of toilets in rural areas, with little emphasis on motivating their usage. Many toilets were constructed, but evaluation showed that over 50 percent were unused or used for other purposes, such as storage. Evidence now overwhelmingly shows that providing subsidized toilets does not lead to enough usage or ensure behavioral change for the entire community. Positive public health outcomes can be achieved only when the entire community (village) adopts improved sanitation behavior, the area is free of open defecation, and excreta are safely and hygienically confined. If a significant segment of the population continues to practice open defecation, the risk of bacteriological contamination and disease transmission may continue to be high. In effect, there is an externality here and sanitation is a public good, which requires government intervention, ideally at the local level. Rather than being driven by targets for the construction of toilets in individual households, as in traditional programs, the government decided to adopt the community-led total sanitation approach, which emphasizes stimulation of effective demand in the community as a whole.[32]

Incentive Scheme

The Indian government launched the national-level fiscal program NGP to provide local governments with various incentives to sustain their sanitation initiatives.

The local-level government in India, known as Panchayati Raj Institutions (PRI), is a three-tier system structured as follows. The modern Indian government has decentralized several administrative functions to the *gram panchayats* (GPs), which are village-level elected councils. A GP can be set in a village with a minimum population of 300; sometimes two or more villages are combined to form a GP. The responsibilities of the GP include infrastructure, public health, water, sanitation, education, development schemes, record-keeping, and social-event planning. The GP derives income mostly from property taxes and grants from the state government. One level above the GP is an Intermediate Panchayat, and above that is a District Panchayat.

All PRI, that is, the three tiers of local government described above, are eligible for NGP awards if they have achieved four key criteria as part of a total sanitation program, as follws:

1. All households in the PRI have access to, and all members are using, individual or community toilets, and there is no open defecation.

2. All schools have sanitation facilities that are used for their intended purpose; co-educational schools have separate toilets for boys and girls.
3. All child-care centers must have sanitation facilities; and
4. General cleanliness in the community must be maintained.

The NGP provides incentives to local governments that satisfy the award conditions based on population according to table 7.3.

Recognizing the externalities involved in sanitation and that it is a public good, the initiative accordingly tries to mobilize the community rather than the household. The program understands the power of incentives and correctly focuses on outcomes rather than on inputs, hence the emphasis in the key criteria on behavioral change rather than hardware. The program also provides nonfinancial incentives (citations and mementos) to officials and NGOs that help local governments in their efforts. The president of India hands out the NGP awards at an annual function; local government officials value this recognition. There is a healthy competition among PRI for these awards. Field verification of award applications is carried out by independent research agencies and NGOs to make it transparent and avoid politicizing the awards.

The NGP initiative exploits the benefits of decentralization and empowerment. The choice of methods and technologies with which to achieve the sanitation objectives is left to village-level governments. Since the villages are different in terms of topography, geography, and availability of skills, it is best to let each one decide on which solution to adopt. The state and central governments do provide technological assistance. Behavioral change, which involves social and cultural factors, is critical to achieving sanitation goals. The local community, rather than a distant government, is best suited to take the lead. Local involvement is also critical in sustaining the efforts. The central government provides the financial resources and policy direction to scale up the program to a national level.

Table 7.3 Nirmal Gram Puraskar (NGP) incentives

	Population								
	Gram Panchayat					Intermediate Panchayat		District Panchayat	
Criteria Amount	Less than 1000	1000 to 1999	2000 to 4999	5000 to 9999	10,000 and above	Up to 50,000	50,000 and above	Up to 1,000,000	More than 1,000,000
Incentive (Rs. in thousands)	50	100	200	400	500	1,000	2,000	3,000	5,000

Note: $1 is worth about Rs. 45 at market exchange rates.
Nimral Gram Puraskar ("clean-village prize")

Results

While the results have been positive, there are shortcomings to the program, too, according to an independent assessment done for UNICEF that studied 162 GPs that won the award.[33] About 81 percent of households have access to individual household toilets, 4 percent have access to community or shared toilets, and 15 percent had no access to toilets. Of the household toilets, only 63 percent are functional and being used; the remaining toilets are either not functional or are used for some other purpose, such as storage or as cattle sheds. Overall, only 64 percent of the people reported using household toilets, 6 percent used community toilets, and 30 percent resorted to open defecation. The reasons toilets weren't used included poor/unfinished installation (31 percent), poor maintenance (26 percent), lack of behavioral change (18 percent), and no super structure (14 percent). The motivational factors for constructing toilets were safety and security for women/girls (35 percent), privacy (17 percent), peer pressure by PRI members (28 percent), and health benefits (14 percent). Of the household toilets, about 26 percent had been completely financed by the households themselves; the rest had received some assistance from local credit organizations or the local government. Analysis suggested no relationship between the financing mechanism and whether the toilets were functional and used. As for schools, 96 percent had toilets; 20 percent of which were nonfunctional, mostly due to poor maintenance.

In villages that have won the NGP award, 30 percent of the people still practice open defecation; this is probably the reason only 40 percent of the households report a decrease in waterborne diseases. The battle against open defecation is not over even in these villages. The government needs to improve the supply chain affecting the postconstruction operation and the maintenance of the toilets. The program needs to further emphasize the usage and sustainability of the toilets. The verification process needs to be strengthened, otherwise the awards will lose credibility. It is possible that some of these problems are due to a very rapid scaling up of the program.

Overall, the NGP initiative is working. About 23,000 GPs have won the award during the 2005–2009 period. According to Vijay Bhaskar, joint secretary in the Ministry of Rural Development, investment in rural sanitation increased from $45 million in 2003 to $280 million in 2008. Rural sanitation coverage has gone up from 23 percent to 57 percent during the same period. At the current rate of growth in coverage, India is well poised to meet the MDG for sanitation by 2012, ahead of the target year 2015.

Bangladesh has adopted a parallel scheme to promote sanitation by offering incentives to local governments. In 2004, the government of Bangladesh made a marked shift in policy by allocating 20 percent of its annual budget to local governments for the promotion of sanitation. With over 70 percent coverage in 2007, Bangladesh has already met the MDG for sanitation.

Proponents of market-based solutions to poverty are also trying to solve the problem of sanitation. The NGO World Toilet Organization and the Asian Development Bank organized the World Toilet Summit and Expo in December 2009. According to the Summit's website, "the new paradigm and approach to the 2.5 billion people who are still living without proper access to sanitation is to change the mindset and to consider sanitation as an emerging market worth US$1 trillion dollars. The World Toilet Summit and Expo 2009 continues to explore the use of conventional marketing wisdom and creative approaches to tap into this sunrise market."[34] This approach is unlikely to work because it grossly overestimates the purchasing power of the poor. But government intervention has resulted in progress in some cases.

Cash Transfers

Arguing for a more direct role for the government in poverty reduction, some development experts advocate that the government should "just give money to the poor."[35] In a cash transfer program, the government gives money to the poor directly, as an entitlement, not as charity, and guaranteed for a period of time. Many countries have adopted this approach in recent years; at least 45 countries now give cash transfers to 110 million families. South Africa, Brazil, and Mexico were early adopters of cash transfer on a significant scale.

Cash transfers directly raise the income of the poor and immediately reduce poverty. Many proponents support cash transfers on ethical and moral grounds as promoting fairness and equity. This view is well aligned with the rights-based perspective that an adequate standard of living is a basic human right. People on the political left like this argument, while the political right does not favor such large-scale direct income redistribution.

An intriguing idea, a sort of middle ground, which is attracting people from different parts of the political spectrum, is to require something in return for the cash transfers. One possibility is conditional cash transfers: Give the poor money that will make them less poor today, but condition the money on behaviors that will give their children a better start in life. Typically these conditions involve providing health care, education, and nutrition for the children. Morally the most disturbing aspect of poverty is that children born into poor families start off with a major handicap. Conditional cash transfers try to break the intergenerational cycle of poverty by stipulating that the money is used to invest in the human capital of the children and help them climb out of poverty. A second possibility is "workfare," which provides the cash transfers to the poor in exchange for some type of work, usually manual labor. This satisfies the conservatives who believe that the poor should work for their money.

Linking the cash transfer to either some conditions or to manual work makes the programs politically viable to both the right and the left. "Liberals have largely abandoned entitlements—the so-called nanny state—that took care of people with welfare and other payments while demanding little or nothing on their part. And most conservatives now acknowledge that government must play a role in fighting poverty."[36] The old paternalism offered *unconditional* love; the new "soft paternalism" offers *tough* love. There is an old ideological debate in which liberals argue that the capitalistic system is the cause of poverty, and conservatives argue that it is the fault of the poor that they are poor. Conditional cash transfers and workfare are ways to move beyond this fruitless debate, to a "postideological" solution. Even the market-oriented *The Economist* magazine favors conditional cash transfers. "The programmes have spread because they work. They cut poverty. They improve income distribution. And they do so cheaply."[37]

Conditional Cash Transfers

Nonetheless, imposing conditions on cash transfers remains to some a controversial issue. The recent book *Just Give Money to the Poor* does a good job of laying out the arguments on both sides of this controversy.[38] The neoclassical economics view is that the poor are rational actors, will act in the best interests of their children on their own, and can make decisions regarding their children better than a government bureaucracy. Imposing conditions on them is not only demeaning to them, but there may also be wastage due to distortions in resource allocation caused by the conditions, and finally, there is a cost to administering the conditions. According to one study, eliminating these conditions would reduce the administrative costs of the Mexican program by 25 percent.

On the opposite side, the growing field of behavioral economics demonstrates that, like more affluent people, the poor are not always rational (as discussed in Chapter 4). There is empirical evidence that the poor tend to underinvest in their future well-being, particularly in human capital, and that they do not spend enough on nutrition, health care, or education. For example, as we saw with ITNs in Africa, 75 percent of poor pregnant women were not willing to spend $0.75 to buy the nets to reduce the chances of their child contracting malaria. In that case, imposing conditions on parents' behavior is in the best interests of both the children and society. Governments may perceive the need for certain actions or behaviors better than the poor do themselves. For example, governments may value female education more than families do. Conditioning may also help a government overcome information asymmetries. For example, governments may understand the public health benefits of immunization better than individuals do. Making payments conditional may help to overcome the stigma associated with welfare when program beneficiaries feel they are "earning" the cash transfers because they are required to do something in return. Conditioning can also strengthen the bargaining position of women whose preferences are aligned with those of the government, but who lack bargaining power within the household. One study on the Mexican program found that conditioning increased school enrollment by 7.2 percent compared to beneficiaries who received unconditional cash transfers.[39]

A different argument in favor of conditionality is that some of the services that improve the children's welfare are characterized by externalities. In that case, achieving wide adoption requires conditionality rather than individual choice. For example, as noted earlier, ITNs are effective only if they are used by most of the people in a village. Giving each family a cash transfer and giving them the choice of whether or not to buy bed nets does not result in adequate coverage. Similarly, vaccines have a positive externality. Education has positive spillover benefits in the community and society, and as such is a public good warranting government intervention.

Conditional cash transfers are becoming increasingly popular. The World Bank is promoting them heavily.[40] At least 30 countries have now adopted conditional cash transfer programs often modeled on the pioneering Mexican program, Oportunidades, described later. So far, these countries are mostly in Latin America, but there are also programs in Turkey, Cambodia, and Bangladesh. Even New York City has piloted a privately funded program, Opportunity NYC, initiated by Mayor Michael Bloomberg to alleviate poverty in the city. This program goes further than imposing conditions and makes cash payments for educational results achieved, such as passing an exam.

Oportunidades

In 1997, the Mexican government launched a cash transfer program, Progresa, to give money to 300,000 families living below the poverty line. It was expanded in 2002 and renamed Oportunidades. It provides cash payments to families in exchange for regular school attendance, health clinic visits, and nutritional support. By the end of 2005, the program had granted benefits to 5 million families (about 24 percent of the Mexican population), and in Mexico's three poorest states, the program reached more than half the families. The average monthly transfer was about $38, amounting to 27 percent of eligible rural household's average monthly income, and 20 percent of that for the urban poor. The budget for Oportunidades in 2008 was about $4 billion, and equaled 0.3 percent of GDP.

Poor households qualify for the grant based on a complex point system (called a proxy means test), based on the age, gender, and education of each family member; on whether the house has electricity and tap water; and whether the household has assets, such as a television and bicycle. The educational component is conditioned on school attendance. The health component is conditioned on regular visits to a clinic. Payments are made to the female head of the family. Families also receive food supplements and free medicine. Participation in regular meetings where hygiene and nutrition are taught is required. The maximum cash transfer per family is $153 per month. There are no restrictions on how the money is spent.

Oportunidades was designed as a centrally administered program. It has been criticized for its very top-down approach. Santiago Levy, the main architect of the program and a former undersecretary in the Finance Ministry, argues to the contrary that the lack of community participation in the identification of beneficiaries and the allocation of funding help to limit the opportunities for corruption at the local level.[41] The federal government transfers money directly to beneficiaries via a bankcard, eliminating the need for intermediaries. To avoid politicizing the program and to prevent using the program to buy votes, officials are prohibited from signing up new beneficiaries within six months of national elections. The budget explicitly provides for direct communication with beneficiaries to educate them about their rights and responsibilities under the program. Since 2006, the public profile of the program has been raised significantly through extensive radio and television advertising.

Given the size and ambitions of Oportunidades, its officials emphasize the importance of accurate, credible data measuring the program's effectiveness and to help ensure that the program will survive changes in government. The government hired the International Food Policy Research Institute (IFPRI), along with some academic economists, to conduct the evaluation.[42] Oportunidades became the first social program in Mexico to carry out a rigorous independent evaluation that included randomly assigned treatment and control groups. The program also has its own research unit and publishes all the data it generates. This has made the credibility of the results difficult to question and increased the political legitimacy of the program.

Impact

Oportunidades has had a measurable positive impact on household consumption, thus reducing poverty and inequality. In 1994, before Mexico's peso crisis, 21.2 percent of Mexicans lived below the poverty line. This figure had dropped to 13.8 percent in 2006. In 2004, the incidence of poverty among the program's participants had fallen by 9.7 percent in rural areas and 2.6 percent in urban areas compared to nonparticipants. More importantly, numerous studies have demonstrated the impact of the program on children's health, nutrition, and education.[43] There has been an increase of 8 percent in the number of calories consumed, and diets have become more varied and balanced, with an increase in vegetables, fruit, and meat. Children in the Oportunidades program have 12 percent lower incidence of illnesses than non-participants. Children who received treatment between 12 and 36 months of age exhibit a 16 percent increase in mean growth rate per year, corresponding to 0.4 inches (1 cm) taller. Teenagers are 33 percent more likely to be enrolled in school. In rural areas, high school enrollment has doubled. Infant mortality has been reduced by 11 percent.

The program does have its problems and critics. Oportunidades does not have as much positive impact in urban areas as it does in rural areas. This could be because both the higher cost of living in urban areas and the program has been implemented in urban areas for a shorter period of time. More importantly, the program works on the demand side of the equation; it does nothing to directly increase the quantity or quality of services provided. Students go to school, but the program cannot ensure that they get a good education. For this reason, conditional cash transfers might not work in all countries, especially the poorest ones. Conditioning cash transfers on school attendance or health check-ups is inappropriate in places where these services are either absent or of dismal quality. In many poor countries, public funds and efforts should be devoted not only to increasing the demand for social services but also to expanding their supply.

However, the biggest issue is that this program cannot by itself reduce poverty, nor should it be expected to do so. Health and education can only take people so far. Few jobs in the formal sector await even educated young Mexicans. "Youths leaving school are not in general finding substantially better paid employment opportunities than their parents due to the sluggish growth of employment."[44] Job opportunities in many parts of Mexico have been declining for 25 years, which has increasingly forced people to accept subsistence living in the informal sector, or migrate to the cities or to the United States. In a 2008 *New York Times* article, Santiago Levy made it clear that "creating formal-sector jobs is Mexico's central challenge."[45] Without that "it is as if Oportunidades were financing an improved labor force for the United States."

As discussed in Chapter 6 on employment, reducing poverty through employment requires three major thrusts: (1) generate employment; (2) increase employability; and (3) make the labor markets more efficient. The Oportunidades program is targeted only at increasing the employability of poor children as they grow up to be the youth of tomorrow. More action is needed on the other dimensions. Levy, now with the Inter-American Development Bank, agrees with this view. As the same *New York Times* article states, "this is Levy's latest crusade—to get Mexico to channel poor people into productive jobs in Mexico's legal labor market." On the whole, Oportunidades has been a successful program.

Workfare

Conditional cash transfers link to the *supply side* of the employment equation by trying to improve the employability of the poor. Workfare programs link the cash transfer to the *demand side* of the employment equation by generating employment for the poor; their primary benefit is the creation of wage employment. This, of course, provides increased and steady income to the poor, leading to an immediate reduction in poverty. It also leads to all the benefits that go along with increased income: improved nutrition, health care, and education, and asset accumulation. An auxiliary benefit of workfare is the undertaking of public works programs that can improve the welfare of the poor, such as water management (such as conservation and irrigation), land management (such as reducing deforestation and soil erosion), sanitation, and other infrastructure. Increased employment could also lead to strengthening the grassroots processes of democracy and empowerment.

Cash transfer programs incur administrative costs for targeting, to ensure that the recipients are truly poor, and monitoring, to ensure that the recipients satisfy the conditions set. These costs are eliminated in workfare. There is no need for targeting because workfare programs are self-targeting; the nonpoor are unlikely to accept jobs doing manual labor that pay low wages. The cost reduction is significant. According to IFPRI research, dropping both targeting and conditioning would reduce the administrative costs of the Oportunidades program by 56 percent.

There are, of course, problems associated with workfare. Workfare programs tend to incur very high costs for design, administration, and supervision. The very nature of these programs implies widely-dispersed operations, creating the potential for wastage and corruption. Second, some people argue that public workfare could crowd out private employment, leading to labor shortages. Although this is a possibility, the more persuasive counterargument is that it probably is not a major concern given the significant unemployment and underemployment in most developing countries. An intermediate possibility is that workfare leads to labor shortages in localized areas and at certain times of the year because of the seasonal nature of agricultural work.[46] A related concern is that the workfare wage rates are too high relative to market wages leading to upward pressure on wages. This in turn could lead to price inflation, which hurts the poor.

National Rural Employment Guarantee Scheme

The Indian government launched NREGS in 2006.[47] The program guarantees each rural household access to 100 days of unskilled wage employment per year. Seeking high labor intensity, NREGS stipulates that unskilled labor wages will constitute at least 60 percent of its total expenditures. NREGS is the largest workfare program in any developing country; it is also the largest cash transfer program. It involved 45 million households at a total cost of $5.7 billion in 2008–2009 (see table 7.4).

Three-quarters of India's poor live in rural areas. The main reason for the deep-rootedness of rural poverty lies in the still

Table 7.4 Performance of National Rural Employment Guarantee Scheme (NREGS)

	2006–7	*2007–8*	*2008–9*
Total expenditures (billion $)	1.96	3.52	5.71
• Expenditures on wages (billion $)	1.29	2.39	3.83
Districts under the program	200	330	615
Employed households (million)	21.0	33.9	45.1
Working days (million)	905	1,436	2,163
• Women	40%	43%	48%
• Scheduled castes and tribes	61%	56%	54%
Average salary per day ($)	1.44	1.67	1.87
Projects completed (millions)	0.39	0.82	1.21
• Water conservation and irrigation	64%	64%	66%
• Rural connectivity	21%	17%	18%
• Land development	11%	16%	15%
• Other activity	4%	3%	1%

Note: Exchange rate used: $1 = Rs. 45.

Source: *Mahatma Gandhi National Rural Employment Guarantee Act 2005, Report to the People*, Ministry of Rural Development, Government of India, 2010.

largely agrarian economy. There is high unemployment and underemployment. Most of the rural poor are self-employed or employed in the informal agricultural sector, with low productivity. Agriculture absorbs 52 percent of India's labor force but contributes less than 20 percent of the country's GDP. People resort to agricultural work because in India there has been very little growth in labor-intensive, low-skilled manufacturing jobs. Despite economic growth rates of almost 9 percent in recent years, the manufacturing-sector employment is less than 20 percent. The manufacturing sector has not been able to absorb the workforce surplus from the agricultural sector.

The long-run solution to this, of course, is to create low-skill jobs suited to the poor, in the formal labor-intensive sectors of the economy. As discussed in Chapter 6, the private sector must be the primary engine of this job creation. But this has not happened in

India for decades due to a variety of policy and institutional failures. The focus of poverty reduction strategies for the future must be on correcting these failures and on job creation. Meanwhile, some other action is needed to fill the gap. NREGS is a promising initiative for poverty reduction; it is encouraging that NREGS has been expanded rapidly since its launch in February 2006 (see table 7.4).

Impact

There has been little empirical research on NREGS and its impact. A good exception is a recent working paper by Shamika Ravi and Monika Engler.[48] As shown in the Chapter 2 discussion of microcredit research, simply comparing program participants with nonparticipants is problematic due to self-selection biases, and we see the same problem here. Ravi and Engler use *propensity score matching* and *natural randomization* methodologies to overcome these biases. Among NREGS participants, there has been a decline in the incidence of poverty, as measured by the official poverty line, from 44 percent to 37 percent. The main result is that NREGS improves food security and reduces anxiety levels among participating households: Monthly per capita expenditure on food increases by Rs. 35.4 (about $2.41 at PPP rates), on nonfood consumables by Rs. 11.4, and on clothing by Rs. 11.2. The increase in food expenditure amounts to 7 percent of the preintervention level for all participants, and 15 percent for the poorest group. Emotional distress and anxiety decreased by 25 percent. NREGS serves a useful insurance function, enabling the poor to cope with income fluctuations. This could lead to greater future orientation among participants and thus more willingness to invest in human capital, such as children's education. Ninety-six percent of participating households think the program is useful. For 67 percent of households, NREGS provided employment when no other work was available; another 12 percent reported that it increased their household income as additional members got employment. The biggest complaint from the participants about the program was delay in receiving payment.

Besides the immediate benefits to the program participants, it is likely that the work projects, such as irrigation and land management, will lead to higher agricultural productivity in the future. NREGS involves the local government organizations (especially the Gram Panchayats) in selection and execution of the work projects, hoping that the resources will be directed to projects with the highest social benefits.

Criticism

Nonetheless, there has been no shortage of critics and criticism of NREGS. From the political left, the criticism is that the scheme does not go far enough, that the fixed minimum wage makes for poor subsistence and the 100-day employment guarantee is inadequate. Moreover, the program's range is restricted: Many rural districts and all urban districts are not covered. It is also likely to create resentment and tension within families. Typically, many rural households consist of several adults—which one will get the employment? From the political right, the criticism is that NREGS is just an income redistribution scheme, a meaningless palliative wasting its time on rural development and burdening the fiscal deficit instead of focusing on industrialization and urbanization.

Some critics argue for direct cash transfers, without the complications of NREGS. The size and complexity of the scheme poses major practical challenges in managing the implementation. Given the lack of financial infrastructure and the scale of the scheme, there have been many reports of delayed payments, sometimes by as much as four months. There is a trade-off that must be made between responding quickly to the demand for jobs and selecting projects to create sustainable value, and managing this trade-off requires planning and organizational skills that are often missing. One assessment study found that lower-income states with limited organizational capacities tend to lag in the implementation of the scheme.

One field assessment in a district in Tamil Nadu found a "good deal of confusion if not chaos" in the procedural aspects of NREGS.[49] The process of work application and demand-driven employment was nonexistent. A social audit revealed other problems: "low productivity levels, inadequate worksite facilities, and lack of transparency." On the other hand, there were real achievements. Employment levels in the district have shot up. Most workers were earning the full minimum wage and getting paid within 15 days. "In house after house, workers express great happiness with the new opportunities, and a keen hope that the program will continue for many years." One female participant in the NREGS program said, "When we work as agricultural laborers, we earn thirty rupees every day but it doesn't seem to get us anywhere. Since we started working on NREGS, we have been earning Rs. 400 at the end of the week—for the first time we are able to save." Another female participant agreed, "Now we have the confidence to take loans because we know we will be able to repay."

The most vociferous criticism of NREGS has been rampant corruption. There clearly is much room for embezzlement of funds, and there have been many media reports of corruption and fraud. Given the stakes involved, the battle has at times even turned violent. There were widespread reports that several NREGS activists were beaten up, threatened, and abused. In May 2008, Lalit Mehta, a social activist, was murdered, allegedly because he had been helping with a social audit of NREGS in Jharkand. Whistle blowers have also been targeted.[50]

Development economist Jean Dreze, who was significantly involved in designing NREGS, has conducted audits of it in several states.[51] He and his colleagues did find evidence of corruption, but not enough to justify the claim that the bulk of NREGS funds fail to reach the poor. Since the most common method of corruption is the fudging of muster rolls, the survey teams conducted "muster roll verification exercises," which involved interviewing laborers to confirm the number of days worked and wages received. In many districts, the "leakages" of funds were estimated to be about 5 percent, with two major exceptions: In the state of Jharkand, the results suggested leakages of around 33 percent, but there was also evidence of a gradual retreat of corruption. In Orissa, a state that had barely begun to transition away from the traditional system of public works corruption, the leakages seemed to absorb about 22 percent of NREGS funds. To combat this problem, the state of Andhra Pradesh has taken the bold step of paying all NREGS wages through the post office. This is an example of "separation of payment agencies from implementing agencies," as recommended in the NREGS guidelines, which significantly reduces corruption. On the whole, the researchers conclude that corruption can be eradicated from NREGS, and that the "best weapon against corruption is strict enforcement of the transparency safeguards" that are already part of the NREGS guidelines.[52]

The success of NREGS varies significantly from one state to another, and has been exemplary in the state of Andhra Pradesh.[53] First, the program has received much support from the top echelons of the state's political and government leadership. Second, the government in Andhra Pradesh has made extensive use of information technology. "All stages of NREGS work, from registration of workers to issue of job cards, preparation of work estimates, muster rolls and payments to workers have been computerized." A common complaint from all over India has been delayed wage payments to the workers. By contrast, in Andhra Pradesh payments are made within a week. Since the computer system is tightly integrated end-to-end, a delay at any stage is instantly noticed and can be fixed. The third reason is the innovative role of civil society in conducting social audits of NREGS, which enhances transparency and accountability—described in Chapter 8.

India (like other developing countries) needs to create employment in the manufacturing and service sectors to absorb the surplus labor from the lower productivity agricultural sector. This requires both generating employment opportunities and improving the employability of the labor force. There is a danger that by readily providing rural employment related to the agricultural sector, NREGS might discourage rural workers from moving to areas of higher productivity where skills for better employment can be obtained, and thus retard the process of long-term economic development. NREGS, in its current form, cannot be the long-term solution for India. This is a significant issue, though it is rarely voiced by the program's critics. The World Bank in its *World Development Report 2009* criticizes NREGS as a policy barrier to "internal mobility." However, given the amount of unemployment and underemployment in the rural areas, and the slow pace of job creation in the formal sector in India, NREGS is a useful initiative for the near term.

Right to Work

NREGS supporters argue that the program has monumental significance and reinforces the rights-based approach to development. Social rights, including the right to work, are provided for in the Indian Constitution but have not been legally enforceable. Recently, there has been a movement to make these rights legally enforceable, such as the Right to Education Act and NREGS. Political Scientist Rajeev Bhargava sees it as significant that NREGS was enacted in a "climate of hyper-antistatism … where state intervention in the economy is routinely scoffed at—where the welfare state is widely subjected to moral and economic critique and the market reigns supreme, expected to address even the basic subsistence needs of the people."[54] It is pressure from below that led the government to enact NREGS. "No form of accountability is more direct than elections." Aruna Roy, social activist and member of the NREGS Council, argues that one of the major benefits of NREGS is that it has strengthened the democratic system at the grassroots level and increased the bargaining power of the poor. NREGS could mark a pivotal turning point for a new regime of social policy. Many social activists "look at NREGS as not merely giving rise to wage employment but leading to equity, food self-sufficiency, and sustainable livelihoods in rural India. We believe that NREGS affords an unprecedented opportunity for governance reform at grass roots."[55] This is consistent with the discussion in Chapter 4 that giving a voice to the poor is a central aspect of the development process.

When evaluating the impact of NREGS, one should also put expectations into perspective. Even though it is a large program, its budget accounts for less than 0.5 percent of India's GDP. It alone should not be expected to cure the problem of rural poverty in India. Even *The Economist* writes, "Despite such flaws, the NREGS is winning praise from unexpected quarters." The magazine *Foreign Policy* concludes that "the program isn't simply extraordinary because of its scale—though incredibly, it could affect 70 percent of India's 1.1 billion citizens. What makes the program truly exceptional is its transparency." On the whole, NREGS seems to be effective and has the potential to have greater impact in the future.

In Conclusion

Business must play a large role in poverty reduction by providing beneficial products to the poor and by creating employment opportunities. But, markets occasionally fail and sometimes produce more inequality than society considers desirable. These two reasons provide a strong rationale for the role of the government in poverty reduction. First, government must regulate markets to protect vulnerable consumers, especially the poor. Second, more importantly, the government has a major responsibility to ensure that the poor have access to various public services such as education, public health, sanitation, and infrastructure. Finally, cash transfers linked either to some conditions or to manual work are gaining support from different parts of the political spectrum, and becoming increasingly popular in many countries.

CHAPTER 8

Civil Society

A s we have seen, in the popular stereotype, public organizations are unresponsive, bureaucratic, inefficient, and corrupt. For-profit businesses are criticized for being exploitative, rewarding greed, lacking in human compassion, and producing socially unjust outcomes. Whether true or not, these perceptions have led to an increasingly passionate search for a new approach and a proliferation of new buzzwords: "third way," "new middle," "social innovation," and "social entrepreneurship." It is essentially a hope that social entrepreneurship will occupy the space between the market and the state, offering an effective combination of private structure and public purpose.[1] A vast array of organizations—hospitals, universities, professional organizations, development organizations, environmental groups, community associations, soup kitchens, and many more—do try to fulfill societal needs.

Social entrepreneurship has been attracting increasing attention from philanthropists, donor organizations, the not-for-profit sector, international organizations, academia, the media, and the public at large. Business schools, in particular, find the concept of social entrepreneurship appealing for the way it combines social virtue and the business approach. Numerous business schools have established centers dedicated to social entrepreneurship (perhaps using alternative names, such as "social innovation"), including Stanford, Harvard, University of California, Duke University, University of British Columbia, INSEAD, Oxford, and National University of Singapore. And there is a much longer list of business schools that lack a dedicated center but offer research or teaching on social entrepreneurship.[2] This popularity has brought significant and growing resources to social entrepreneurship: talent and money.

Social entrepreneurship is simply old-fashioned not-for-profit organizations trying to use modern management processes. Improving efficiency is a good idea, but this does not change the nature of the organization. Many not-for-profits certainly are well managed. The term "entrepreneurship" has been extended, especially by Peter Drucker, to include social and political activities that create value for society.[3] Drucker argues that one of the best examples of entrepreneurship is the modern university, and especially the modern American university (which are mostly public or not-for-profit organizations). Drucker also cites the example of the Girl Scouts, which introduced innovations affecting membership, programs, and volunteers and reversed the downward trend in enrollment of both children and volunteers.

Distinctly Different Sectors

Much of the literature on social entrepreneurship suggests that the boundaries between the three sectors, public, for-profit and not-for-profit, are blurring. More interestingly, many proponents of social entrepreneurship advocate "dismantling the barriers between the sectors."[4] To the contrary, it is far better to sustain clear boundaries between these sectors. Public, for-profit, and not-for-profit organizations are fundamentally different in terms of their ability to scale up operations and how they allocate their output, and more importantly, play different roles in fulfilling societal needs (see table 8.1). The motives and governance mechanisms of these organizations are not only different but also incompatible.

Scaling Up

Modern financial markets can provide virtually unlimited quantities of capital, provided a venture is expected to earn positive economic profits, thus making it fairly easy for for-profit organizations to scale up. Public organizations enjoy the privilege of access to the government treasury for the resources needed to scale up, subject to approval from the political process. Not-for-profit organizations, on the other hand, find it challenging to scale up the activities and at the same time satisfy social needs.[5] Not-for-profit organizations have neither the legal power to regulate markets, nor adequate resources to substitute for the market or government. And, with few exceptions, such as the Bill & Melinda Gates Foundation, not-for-profits have not been able to attract the capital needed to significantly scale up their activities

Table 8.1 Characteristics of the three sectors

	For-Profit	*Public*	*Not-for-Profit*
Mechanism to ensure creation of social value	Invisible hand	Political process	Wisdom of the donors
Products/services allocation driven by	Price mechanism	Citizen rights; political power	Preferences of the donors
Providers of funds driven by	Self-interest	Coercion: taxation	Altruism
Governance mechanism	Shareholder rights	Citizen rights	Self-governed
Ability to scale up	High	Varies	Low

so that they can directly provide a service. What not-for-profits can do is act as catalysts, advocates, and watchdogs to prod business and public organizations to better fulfill their responsibilities to satisfy societal needs.

Even though the not-for-profit sector has been attracting increasing attention, there has been a lack of even the most basic information about these organizations. The best source of empirical data is the Johns Hopkins Comparative Nonprofit Sector Project, which provides portraits of the sector in 35 countries, including 16 advanced industrial countries, 14 developing countries, and 5 transitional countries of Central and Eastern Europe.[6] The not-for-profit sector (including religious congregations) represents 5.1 percent of the GDP of these countries. The not-for-profit sector in developed countries is proportionally more than three times larger than that in developing countries (7.4 percent vs. 1.9 percent). By comparison, government revenues account for 27 percent of the world GDP, according to World Bank data.[7] These data reinforce the view that it is unlikely that not-for-profit organizations can directly satisfy social needs on a large scale. This is even truer in developing countries, where the not-for-profit sector is smaller, and the scale of unfulfilled social needs is much larger.

In developed countries, for example, there are always some poor people who cannot afford adequate nutrition. Government food assistance programs do not cater to all the needy, and not-for-profits, such as religious groups and various community organizations, do an admirable job of filling in the gap. This is possible because the gap is relatively small. But in India, 230 million people are undernourished, and 43 percent of children under five years old are underweight.[8] It is difficult to imagine that not-for-profits will directly fill this enormous gap. The Right to Food Campaign in India, is an advocacy network of not-for-profit organizations and activist individuals that has been gathering momentum.[9] "The campaign believes that the primary responsibility for guaranteeing basic entitlements rests with the state," and has been agitating for an act of parliament to increase food assistance to the needy.[10]

The government sometimes lacks the resources it needs to fulfill its responsibilities. For example, the governments in many countries in Africa do not have the financial and organizational resources to fulfill their public responsibilities. At a minimum, foreign aid is a source of money and can help to close some of this gap.

Social Value

All three types of organizations, for-profit, public, and not-for-profit, can and should create social value. The market mechanism and government regulation ensure that private for-profit firms create value. A well-functioning political system ensures that public organizations create social value. Not-for-profit organizations can usefully supplement the political system to ensure that for-profit and public organizations create social value. However, there is no well-defined mechanism to ensure that not-for-profits create social value. Fortunately, most philanthropists are good people with values congruent to those of society at large. Still, we have to rely on the benevolence and wisdom of the donors and/or the managers of the not-for-profit organizations to create social value.

Just as education should not be left to free markets, it should not be left to civil society catering to the differing values of philanthropists. For example, consider schools that teach extremist religion and even preach violence, such as the *madrassas* in some countries. This too is civil society, unfortunately. A less extreme example might be a Christian school teaching creationism instead of evolution. Especially given the ambiguous governance process, society should not solely rely on not-for-profits to satisfy societal needs on a large scale. Civil society cannot substitute for the government because of lack of accountability to a democratic polity.

Allocating the Output

The three types of organizations use very different mechanisms to allocate the goods they produce. For-profit companies allocate goods based on market prices. If there is a shortage of goods, public organizations do not use price to clear the market, they allocate the goods on some other basis. In a perfect democracy, all citizens are politically equal and public organizations allocate goods on the basis of citizen rights. Unfortunately, many governments are not democracies, and many democracies are far from perfect. In those cases, public organizations often allocate goods on the basis of political power and patronage. For example, personal and property security is a public good, and markets cannot fulfill this societal need. Therefore, police protection is a public activity. On the logic that all citizens are equal, the government claims to provide equal police protection to everybody. However, it is not accidental that rich neighborhoods tend to be better patrolled than poor neighborhoods.

Free markets allocate business resources across different social needs, such as food, shelter, and health care. The political process helps governments prioritize different needs. In principle, the political process should reflect the collective desires of the citizens. In practice, vested interests and the self-interest of public officials also play a large role.

Not-for-profit organizations allocate goods to clients in accordance with the preferences of donors. There is no counterpart of the invisible hand or the political process to ensure that social value is optimized. We have to rely on the wisdom and competence of philanthropic donors. For example, the Boy Scouts of America is one of the largest youth organizations in the United States, yet it excludes atheists, agnostics, and avowed homosexuals. Many people consider its membership policies unjust, and these policies have attracted a great deal of criticism. At the same time, many individuals and groups support the Boy Scouts. Assessing the social value created by the Boy Scouts is clearly a controversial proposition.

Governance

Another significant difference across the three types of organizations is the governance mechanism, especially to correct organizational failure. In efficient markets and in well-regulated markets, the interests of the shareholders and social welfare are aligned. If a firm does not serve the interests of the shareholders, they can exercise their right to fire the managers. The corporate governance movement in recent years in the United States and other countries seeks to strengthen shareholder rights. If public officials do not create social value, citizens in a democracy can exercise their rights to change the government. In practice, of course, markets and regulation are rarely "perfect," and the democratic process is often not effective, and at times totally absent. At least in principle, there is a governance mechanism for businesses and governments.

In the case of not-for-profits, the governance mechanism, even in principle, is rather ambiguous. Donors cannot easily change the management or the policies of a not-for-profit. They, of course, can choose not to donate to that organization, but that is not a governance mechanism. Shareholders elect a board of directors, and citizens elect government officials, but donors do not get to elect the managers of a not-for-profit. In practice, however, most not-for-profits function quite well given the altruistic idealism of the staff and donors.

Boundaries

The three types of organizations, of course, interact with each other. When their interests are aligned together, there is potential for useful cooperation, but without blurring the organizational boundaries. Effective partnerships are more like "project alliances" than hybrid organizations. The problem with hybrid organizations is the potential for "privatizing the gains, and socializing the losses" to the detriment of the citizens. Hybrid organizations suffer from tension between the mission and the bottom line.[11] It is critical for the not-for-profit organizations to maintain their legitimacy by preserving their independence and capacity to criticize. The two examples below illustrate the problems caused by blurred boundaries.

Social-entrepreneurship organizations such as the Acumen Fund contribute to the confusion by claiming they offer *patient capital*. It is a fallacy to believe that capital markets are short-term oriented or impatient. Investors are long-term oriented and patient provided they are compensated for the time value of money and the risks involved, which is what drives the concept of cost of capital. Capital markets fund investments in ventures such as biotechnology that are not expected to pay off for 15 years or more. The phrase "patient capital" is just a euphemism for low-cost capital subsidized by philanthropy. An individual providing financial resources to a venture and expecting to earn a return lower than the cost of capital is behaving as a philanthropist, not an investor. This individual is, in effect, making a donation equal to the difference between the cost of capital and the expected return. This is not to suggest that philanthropists are irrational; just that there is a critical difference between a philanthropist and an investor. Investors expect to earn more than the cost of capital, and philanthropists expect to earn less than the cost of capital. This is an either-or distinction; there is no blurring of boundaries and no hybrids. Expected returns are, of course, impossible to determine accurately ex ante. The actual returns earned ex post might, and do differ considerably from the expected returns. The cost of capital is very difficult to calculate accurately in practice—much research in the field of finance is devoted to this issue. The fact that both the expected return and the cost of capital are difficult to assess accurately does not invalidate the conceptual distinction between philanthropy and investment.

Contrast the approach to philanthropy by the Acumen Fund and ExxonMobil. The Acumen Fund made a low-cost loan of $1 million to A to Z Textile Mills, a Tanzanian manufacturer of insecticide-treated bed nets used in combating malaria;[12] in effect, the Acumen Fund is subsidizing A to Z. It is not transparent how this benefits the poor in Africa. "Anuj Shah, who runs the company is no do-gooder. He is in it for profit and is determined that net making in Africa is a seriously commercial activity."[13] There are three major players in the commercial industry for manufacturing insecticide-treated nets: BASF, Sumitomo, and Vestergaard Frandsen. They all sell bed nets to various NGOs, international organizations, and local governments, which distribute them either free or at heavily subsidized prices. A to Z participates in this market and accounts for less than one-tenth of Africa's need for bed nets. There is a market price for the nets the manufacturers sell to governments and not-for-profit intermediaries; however, there is no market price for the nets sold to the end users. Providing subsidized capital to A to Z certainly benefits the company; it is ambiguous how it benefits the poor. By contrast, ExxonMobil sells the resin used to manufacture the nets to A to Z at market prices. Driven by philanthropic motives, Exxon is a member of the global partnership "Roll Back Malaria"; the company then donates the money, which it makes from selling the resin, to UNICEF to buy nets to distribute to the poor. The Exxon approach of keeping business and philanthropy transparently separate is more appropriate, thus ensuring that the philanthropy reaches the intended recipients.[14]

In 2001, Project Shakti was initiated by HUL, Unilever's Indian subsidiary, as a multisector partnership to create a direct-to-consumer sales distribution channel to villages. In their research in Andhra Pradesh, where the project was launched, Thekkudan and Tandon find that all the partners by now have withdrawn from the project.[15] While launching the project, HUL sought and received cooperation from NGOs and government officials from the state and district levels. All of the five NGOs who were involved in initiating the project in Andhra Pradesh have discontinued their association, criticizing the assumptions underlying the project. The NGOs have questioned the sustainability of the project since it does not promote the livelihood of the poor. The researchers conclude that "civil society therefore runs the risk of becoming the midwife of market penetration; and in this case, some have disappeared without any accountability to the Shakti Amma [the women entrepreneurs] they were instrumental in creating. Others, questioning their role in the partnership and attempting to resolve it, are left with a sense of helplessness." The government of Andhra Pradesh was keen to participate in Project Shakti at the outset because it expected the benefits to percolate to existing self-help groups. But the government's enthusiasm waned, and it withdrew from the project within three years. HUL has piggybacked on the self-help group network, a system that was promoted and whose investment costs were borne by the government. The researchers conclude: "It seems the government of Andhra Pradesh never questioned the objective of HUL in starting the initiative, but took the philanthropic objectives for granted."

The Role of Civil Society

It is the role of the government to mediate the relationship between markets and society, and to provide goods that cannot be provided by markets. If market failures were infrequent, and were always "corrected" by the government, there would be no need for civil society. Unfortunately, both market failures and government failures are only too common, and even more so in the context of poverty in developing countries. Too much falls through the cracks between the markets and governments. It is the role of civil society to fill this gap. Civil society can be an advocate, and even a catalyst for change, and a watchdog to ensure that both business and government fulfill their respective responsibilities.

Chapter 6 provides an application of this logic in the case of TechnoServe in Mozambique. TechnoServe worked with businesses and the government to stimulate the growth of small- and medium-sized private enterprises in the cashew industry. It did not substitute for business or government; instead it acted as a catalyst. Once the industry was on its feet, there was no longer a need for TechnoServe and it ended its program of subsidized assistance. The NGO has moved on to try to replicate this approach in other countries. Its role in the cashew industry in Mozambique has appropriately morphed into that of a small for-profit consulting firm.

Two positive examples of action by civil society are described below. The first example is civil society playing a critical role as an advocate and more importantly as a watchdog for the NREGS initiative in India. The second example is VisionSpring, which is playing a useful role as a catalyst to try to solve the problem of blurred vision among the poor.

Social Audits of NREGS

Civil society played a major advocacy role in the legal enactment of the NREGS initiative. "The campaign for the right to work was involved in every stage of NREGS formulation." But now that the law has been enacted, civil society needs to play a very different role. Mihir Shah, an economist and member of the Central Employment Guarantee Council, writes, "NGOs cannot also hope to replace the government. One, because it is hard to imagine the voluntary sector being able to upscale operations at the requisite level but even more importantly because of questions of accountability in a democratic polity. Civil society needs to see its primary role as that of ensuring transparency and accountability of state institutions and of empowering the panchayats [village level councils], in close partnership with them."[16]

A grassroots organization called the Mazdoor Kisan Shakti Sanghthana (MKSS), led by activist Aruna Roy (who is also one of the architects of NREGS), introduced the concept of a social audit into the development process in Rajasthan, India nearly twenty years ago. A social audit is a process in which the people work with the government to monitor and evaluate the planning and implementation of a government program.[17] Due to much resistance from vested interests and inadequate support from the state government, the social audit process unfortunately has not gotten very far in Rajasthan. However, the basic logic, that community participation is particularly important for ensuring transparency and accountability, is very promising.

One of the unique features of the NREGS Act as it was passed by the parliament is its insistence on regular social audits. A social audit includes verifying the muster rolls that are the daily attendance registers and evaluating the public work projects undertaken. While the social audit process is working well in Andhra Pradesh, at best it is functioning unevenly across the rest of India.

The government of Andhra Pradesh initiated the process by itself, commissioning civil society organizations to conduct social audits and encouraging them to bring into the open instances of corruption and maladministration in NREGS. This was probably the first time that a state government had asked civil society to take the lead in detecting corruption and mismanagement using the Right to Information Act. MKSS and another NGO Action Aid provided the technical expertise to conduct the social audit.

The state government has set up a social audit team, consisting of state-level resource persons and district resource persons (DRPs), who are independent of the NREGS bureaucracy and enjoy great freedom of action. The social audit process begins with an application for records using the Right to Information Act by the DRPs. The DRPs also identify and recruit a few young people in every village, usually those belonging to families of NREGS workers. These youth are trained to conduct social audits, and in teams they go door-to-door authenticating muster rolls, checking out worksites, and interviewing workers. The village social auditors and the DRPs prepare a report that is placed before a village meeting. The names of people who are supposed to have worked and the amounts ostensibly paid to them are read aloud in public, thus uncovering any fraud. The process then culminates in a massive public meeting at the block level, attended by their elected representatives, the media, NREGS officials, and senior government officers. The results of the village-level social audits are read aloud, and workers voice their complaints. Officials are required to immediately specify remedial actions they will take and the time frame. In most cases, they make decisions on the spot. Corrupt officials often are suspended and monetary recovery proceedings instituted immediately. These meetings, which are typically attended by five to six hundred villagers and last for 10 to 12 hours, have a palpable impact on rural governance. There is a rigorous follow-up process requiring the social-audit teams to go back to their villages 15 days after the block meeting to ensure that the decisions taken are actually enforced.

It is interesting that, after the social audit is finished, corrupt officials in many villages have gone back to the workers and "voluntarily" returned the money. Formal action has been initiated against thousands of officials, and a number of criminal cases have been filed. Another by-product of the process has been a dramatic increase in awareness about NREGS and its provisions. A World Bank study found that awareness had increased from 25 percent before the social audit to 99 percent six months after the audit. This is useful since NREGS is a demand-driven program. The social audit process has increased the bargaining power of the poor, as well as their confidence and self-respect.

This systemic review process does not mean an end to problems. The process is mainly driven top-down by the state government; civil society needs to be more proactively involved. The social audits have focused on verifying muster rolls, and have not paid adequate attention to the quality of assets created, and to the process of selecting, planning, and implementing the work projects. The challenge for the central government of India and for the civil society is to scale up the success from Andhra Pradesh to the rest of the country.

There is an unusual and innovative relationship between civil society and the state government of Andhra Pradesh. The state-level and district-level resource persons are recruited from civil society organizations. The government facilitates the social audit by providing all the relevant information. At the same time, for civil society to be an effective watchdog, it has to be careful not to get co-opted. Worries about becoming rubber stamps could be one reason why relatively few NGOs have come forward to participate in the social audit process. The government does not subcontract NGOs to undertake social audits. This increases the independence of the NGOs, but it requires them to raise funds in other ways. This, too, probably restricts the participation of Indian civil society, especially in light of resource constraints. It is a delicate balance between a partnership and an adversarial relationship.

Better Vision for the Poor[18]

If the NREGS case study illustrates how civil society can be an effective watchdog, the one that follows shows civil society acting as a catalyst. Many poor people with bad eyesight, unfortunately, do not have eyeglasses. The case describes different approaches to provide eyeglasses to the poor that have been attempted, and shows how an NGO, VisionSpring, is acting as a catalyst to solving the problem.

Approximately 517 million people in developing countries are considered visually impaired because they do not have access to eyeglasses.[19] The Centre for Vision in the Developing World at Oxford University has a higher estimate: Over one billion people need but do not get vision correction.[20] For the poor, eyeglasses often are either inaccessible or unaffordable. A variety of approaches have been tried to solve this problem: For-profit business model, innovative technology, and social entrepreneurship. Yet, to date, none have succeeded on a large enough scale.

Challenges

Many challenges confront the provision of eyeglasses to the poor in developing countries. One study in India of poor people with presbyopia found that about 23 percent of the subjects were unaware of the problem, another 29 percent did not assign it a high priority or accepted poor eyesight as a "natural" process of aging, 18 percent did not have the money to afford treatment, and the rest said "other obligations" (such as need for travel and no escort) prevented an eye exam.[21]

Not only do the poor lack information about the importance of vision correction, but they also lack knowledge of how to go about getting eye care. A study in Tanzania found that although the subjects perceived eyeglasses to be useful and affordable, most did not know where to get them.[22] In the developing world, eyeglasses are primarily available in high-priced urban optical shops. For the rural poor, a trip to buy glasses requires travel to an urban center to visit an eye doctor, which is often a day-long trip each way.

In the Tanzania study, 31 percent of the people surveyed were unable to afford eyeglasses at "a price that covered the cost and shipping of the spectacles."[23] A study in East Timor found that 49 percent of rural subjects were unwilling to pay even $1 for eyeglasses, and only 16 percent were willing to pay $3.[24] A recent study in India provided eyeglasses free to the subjects. One month after using the eyeglasses, the subjects were asked how much they would be willing to pay for the eyeglasses; the median answer was about $4.[25] (This is an overestimate of the true willingness to pay because in real markets consumers have to purchase eyeglasses prior to use.)

A major barrier to delivering vision correction is the lack of trained optometrists. Many developing countries have as few as one optometrist for every million people; the figure for the United Kingdom is one per 8,000 people; in Mali, the ratio is one per 8 million.[26]

Business Solutions

Chapter 5 described Essilor's BOP venture to sell eyeglasses to the rural poor in India, which has not succeeded so far. Another approach to solving the vision problem emphasizes technological innovation to provide low-cost self-adjustable eyeglasses, which let untrained wearers set the right focus for the lenses themselves in less than a minute, greatly reducing the need for trained optometrists.[27] The problem is that these eyeglasses now cost more than $15 per pair and are too expensive for the poor. This might be a feasible solution in the future if technological changes and economies of scale can dramatically reduce costs.

VisionSpring

VisionSpring is a good example of social entrepreneurship, and has won several awards for its efforts. VisionSpring was founded in 2001 by Jordan Kassalow and Scott Berrie as a non-profit organization with the mission "to reduce poverty and generate opportunity in the developing world through the sale of affordable eyeglasses." VisionSpring started by providing only ready-made reading glasses to correct farsightedness. This strategy was adopted because of the strong link between poor near vision and economic productivity and the fact that presbyopia represented about 75 percent of the visual impairment problem; this was the simplest "low lying fruit" portion of the overall problem. Its objective was to take reading glasses out of the exclusive hands of eye care professionals and make them a consumer product. In the developed countries, this shift had already happened decades ago and reading glasses are widely available as an over-the-counter product.

To accomplish its mission, VisionSpring developed an innovative business model to provide basic screening services and ready-made reading eyeglasses to people living in rural villages. After assessing multiple suppliers around the world, management decided that China was the most cost-effective source for ready-made reading eyeglasses. To reach people living in rural communities, VisionSpring trains local women as Vision Entrepreneurs, who are independent commissioned sales representatives that go into villages and sell its reading glasses for under $4 a pair. Vision

Entrepreneurs provide basic screenings using distance and near eye charts to determine the appropriate strength of the lenses. VisionSpring provides them with a "business in a bag," a sales kit containing an inventory of reading glasses, screening tools, marketing materials, and a uniform. Vision Entrepreneurs undergo a three-day training program in basic eye care and business management.

To increase its global reach and scale, VisionSpring has also developed a franchise model on a fee-for-service basis. This involves disseminating its sales kits to other nonprofit and for-profit organizations, such as BRAC, a microcredit organization in Bangladesh. Through this franchise model, VisionSpring presently has over 5,000 Vision Entrepreneurs in 11 countries.

Finally, using a wholesale approach, VisionSpring distributes its reading glasses through pharmacies in urban and periurban centers. These retail outlets are expected to help VisionSpring reach a greater breadth of people. They are presently testing this approach with Apollo, one of the largest pharmacy chains in India.

Performance

VisionSpring has operations in eleven countries in Asia, Latin America, and Africa, with its biggest presence in India. In 2008, VisionSpring sold 98,000 pairs of glasses, and 201,000 in 2009, doubling their sales for the fifth straight year. They have the objective of selling one million eyeglasses in 2012. Much of the growth is expected to come from franchising and wholesaling their business model to leverage large distribution networks that already exist in target countries, especially the partnership with BRAC.

In 2009, VisionSpring earned revenues of $0.26 million while its total costs were $1.36 million; the difference was covered by philanthropic donations and grants. The cost of eyeglasses procured was 13 percent of total costs, while field and overhead expenses (e.g., training, marketing, staff salaries, travel, etc.)

accounted for the remainder. This implied that the total cost to deliver a pair of glasses was $6.70.

VisionSpring's budget for the year 2012 anticipates 1 million eyeglasses sold, earned revenues of $1.3 million, and total costs of $2.8 million, requiring philanthropic subsidy of $1.5 million. Overhead and field expenses would account for 71 percent of total costs. Presently, 19 percent of total costs are covered by earned revenue; VisionSpring expects this ratio to reach 46 percent in 2012, and has a long-term goal of 100 percent earned revenue coverage. Though VisionSpring seeks to be self-financing in the long run, at least for the medium term its business model is highly dependent upon "repeatable philanthropy," which is defined as "dollars that are raised using processes that can be reliably repeated from one year to the next, in a sustainable manner."[28] Looking into the future, management believes that VisionSpring will require at least three to five more years of subsidizations before reaching sufficient economies of scale to be self-sustainable. Enterprise break-even point is estimated at 5 million eyeglasses per year.

VisionSpring significantly reduces costs by substituting a low-skilled Vision Entrepreneur instead of a professional optometrist. It also reduces the production costs by centralizing purchasing, sourcing from China, and providing glasses in a few standardized strengths. Overall, its revenues are not high enough to cover its costs, and VisionSpring needs philanthropic subsidies, which limits its ability to achieve scale commensurate with the size of the vision problem. Scaling up their model is also constrained by limited distribution channels that serve the poor, especially in rural areas. At the same time, creating a distribution network dedicated to one product is a very expensive solution. Piggybacking onto an existing distribution network is more cost effective, as VisionSpring is doing in its partnership with BRAC, Women's Development Business, and others. An initial drawback of VisionSpring's approach is that it provided only reading glasses. This left out the significant number of people suffering from myopia, especially children who are much more likely to be myopic.

VisionSpring is trying to scale up its efforts and hopes to sell 1 million pairs of eyeglasses per year by 2012. Even if VisionSpring achieves this goal, however, the impact is arguably too little given that estimates of people needing eyeglasses range from 517 million to 1 billion—and that number too is growing. While VisionSpring is an admirable effort, it is clearly only a small part of the solution.

Proposed Solution

But the situation is not hopeless. The challenge is to move the entire eyeglass business from a low volume, high margin approach to a high volume, low margin emphasis to gain much greater penetration among the poor. The starting point is to reduce costs as much as possible by reducing overall quality, while still providing "acceptable" quality. The proposed solution utilizes a basic screening process that does not require a trained professional, resulting in significant cost reduction. This sacrifices precision, but that is acceptable because medical evidence suggests that the undercorrection of vision does not have significant negative side effects.[29] Overcorrection, however, does have side effects such as headaches and nausea. The screening process needs to avoid overcorrection, which is easy to do using simple techniques.

Self-adjustable glasses rather than becoming the final product could be utilized for determining a patient's prescription without using a high cost technically trained professional. There is some interesting research (not yet published) going on in China that shows self refraction with adjustable lenses results in end points quite similar to the refractions done by an eye doctor for about 90 percent of the children, which is certainly good enough to be a viable solution.

The production costs of eyeglasses can be reduced by manufacturing eyeglasses in a large factory, emphasizing scale economies, centralized sourcing, and standardization.[30] Lenses would be manufactured from the least expensive material, which is probably acrylic; this is the type of plastic that is used in ready-made reading glasses sold in the United States. Lenses would be offered in steps of 0.50 dioptres for reading glasses; in steps of 0.25 dioptres up to -2.00D; and in steps of 0.50 dioptres above this for distance glasses; there would be no correction for astigmatism (which requires customized prescription). Using this approach, about 80 percent of the people who require a distance prescription would be corrected to 20/40 or better.[31] This is a level of vision that is required to drive legally in the United States. A study in India conducted a randomized clinical trial with poor adults to compare ready-made eyeglasses with customized eyeglasses. The results showed that while vision is slightly better with customized glasses, after one month of use, 90 percent of the subjects were satisfied with ready-made eyeglasses and planned to continue wearing them.[32] Another similar study with Chinese school-age children confirms the high level of satisfaction and acceptance of ready-made glasses.[33]

There would be a very limited variety of frame styles carefully selected based on local preferences. The factory cost of producing standardized prescription eyeglasses using simple frames in China is well below $2 per pair. Distribution costs would be reduced by piggybacking onto an existing network such as a microcredit organization, a packaged consumer goods company, or even government offices/agencies. Overhead would be minimized by locating all possible costs in a developing country and restricting the scope to one or a few neighboring countries.

Even after following all these suggestions, it is not certain whether the total costs will be below what the poor are willing to pay for glasses. There are two major sources of uncertainty here. First, what will be the total cost per pair of eyeglasses after following all these suggestions for cost reduction, and assuming a significant scale of operation. Second, how much are the poor willing to pay for such standardized eyeglasses? Clearly, this willingness to pay will vary depending on the country, region, cultural factors, and the income level of the target population. If willingness to pay is high enough to cover the total costs, then there is no need for government intervention. This could be a profitable business for private firms, and consistent with the current vogue of market-based solutions for poverty alleviation.

However, if the costs are still too high compared to the willingness to pay, then the only way to cover the gap is a subsidy. It is important to note that the subsidy does not need to cover the entire cost of the glasses, but rather only the gap between the willingness to pay and the cost. Given the scale of the problem (i.e., at least 500 million people need eyeglasses), the only source for such large subsidies is the government. Governments bear the responsibility, and accept the responsibility for public health. Since the economic and social benefits of solving the blurry vision problem far exceed the costs, this is an area where governments can intervene effectively. Governments can play a key role in building the market for eyeglasses by funding education/awareness campaigns or subsidizing eye care centers. They can also implement targeted policies such as requiring children to get basic eye screening in schools.

The appropriate role for not-for-profit organizations is that of advocate and catalyst to prod governments and companies to solve the problem. If it is profitable to sell eyeglasses to the poor (using the approach proposed above or some other business model), then a not-for-profit organization such as VisionSpring can demonstrate and publicize the economic viability of this approach. The hope is that this profit potential will attract private companies, multinational or domestic, into the market to satisfy the need for eyeglasses. The not-for-profit organization could even morph into a for-profit company in that case. However, if it is not profitable to sell eyeglasses to the poor, then the not-for-profit has to act as an advocate and catalyst to get the government to step in on a large scale. There are only two possible approaches to providing eyeglasses to the poor on a significant scale: profitable companies or government subsidies. The role of NGOs is to act as catalysts and advocates by demonstrating the appropriate approach. VisionSpring has begun pilot projects to provide eyeglasses for myopia to both children and adults somewhat long the lines of the above proposal.

Private companies and government intervention are not mutually exclusive solutions, however. They can coexist side by side. For example, there is a societal need for condoms in less developed countries to prevent sexually transmitted diseases and for birth control. The condom market in India is divided into three segments: sold at market prices by private companies, social marketing programs that sell condoms at low prices due to government subsidies, and condoms distributed free by the government. A similar segmentation might be useful for eyeglasses.

CHAPTER 9

Rage Leading to Action

UNICEF in its 2009 report *The State of the World's Children* states:

- 8.8 million children die every year before their fifth birthday due to poverty.
- 4 million newborns die in the first month of life.
- 22 million infants do not get routine immunizations.
- 101 million children (more girls than boys) are not attending primary school.
- 148 million children under five years of age are underweight.

If you find these facts emotionally distressing, that is good: You have compassion. The high under-age-five mortality rate is particularly disturbing because it is a good measure of poverty and human development.[1] First, it measures an end result of the development process rather than 'inputs,' such as per capita calorie availability or number of doctors. Second, the child mortality rate is a result of a wide variety of factors:

- Nutritional status and health knowledge of mothers
- Level of immunization and oral rehydration therapy

- Availability of public health inputs such as insecticide-treated bed nets
- Availability of health services, especially maternal and child health services
- Income and food availability in the family
- Availability of safe drinking water and basic sanitation
- Overall safety of the environment, especially for children

Emotional distress should not lead to despair and fatalistic acceptance. Poverty is a big and complex problem, but the appropriate reaction is moral rage that it persists despite the fact that the problem is solvable. Poverty exists in the midst of plentitude. The arid desert of poverty is surrounded by an ocean of affluence, and even opulence—that is the injustice that is morally reprehensible. Approximately 1.2 billion people in the world suffer from hunger and malnutrition. At the same time, about 1.2 billion people suffer from obesity. As discussed in Chapter 1, all it would take to eradicate poverty is a 1.3 percent shift in the global income distribution. There is no excuse for persistent global poverty.

The starting point is to highlight the problem. As UNICEF explains this need: "Every day, the equivalent of a major earthquake killing over 30,000 young children occurs to a disturbingly muted response. They die quietly in some of the poorest villages on earth, far removed from the scrutiny and the conscience of the world. Being meek and weak in life makes these dying multitudes even more invisible in death."[2] Poverty and its impact must be made very visible. We need to stop romanticizing poverty, and, instead, highlight its magnitude and inhumanity.

To significantly reduce poverty requires resources. Only the business sector and the government can provide resources on the scale needed, and it is impossible to eradicate poverty without the active involvement of both. Business is driven by the profit motive, and government is driven by political consensus. A public debate is needed to achieve this consensus. One objective of this book is to contribute to and even stimulate such a debate.

Eradicating poverty requires financial resources on a very large scale from the governments of both developing and developed countries. It has been argued that foreign aid in the trillions of dollars has failed to reduce, let alone eradicate, poverty; therefore, foreign aid is not the solution. This is a fallacy; foreign aid can and must play a useful role. Currently, donor countries give aid equivalent to about 0.3 percent of their gross national income, which is significantly less than the 0.7 percent target they had agreed upon at the UN General Assembly in 1970. But the issue is not just the amount of aid but also how it has been used (or misused). Both foreign aid and local government resources need to be targeted to programs that actually help reduce poverty.

Unfortunately, much of the debate about poverty reduction has been ideologically driven. The political right believes the poor are poor because it is their fault; they are not diligent enough to earn more. The political left believes the poor are caught in poverty traps caused by institutional failures. Meanwhile, the poor, especially the children, are caught in the ideological crossfire. It is hard to argue that the poor child dying of diarrhea is to blame for lack of diligence. It does not matter whether the underlying cause of poverty is the poor themselves or the social-political-economic system. There is a moral imperative to reduce poverty. We need to go beyond these ideological battles and adopt an evidence-based, problem-solving approach. All people, whether they work in business, government, or civil society, have a responsibility to help eliminate poverty. More importantly, we as citizens must ensure that our governments fulfill their responsibilities to eradicate poverty. Emotional distress should lead to moral rage, which, in turn, should lead to both private and public action.

Notes

1 Fighting Poverty

1. Amartya Sen. *Development as Freedom*. Anchor Books, New York, 2000.
2. Jeffrey Sachs. *The End of Poverty*. Penguin Books, New York, 2005.
3. Data for 2005 are the most recent available.
4. The poor as a percentage of the population of the developing world has declined from 69.2% to 47.0% between 1981 and 2005. Even here, the bulk of the improvement is due to China. Excluding China, this percentage has declined modestly, from 58.6% to 50.3%.
5. Sabina Alkire and Maria Emma Santos. Acute Multidimensional Poverty: A New Index for Developing Countries. Oxford Poverty & Human Development Initiative, Working Paper No. 38, July 2010.
6. Laura D'Andrea Tyson. It's Time to Step up the Global War on Poverty. *Business Week*, December 3, 2001.
7. Alberto Abadie. Poverty, Political Freedom, and the Roots of Terrorism. *American Economic Review*, 2005, 95(4): 50–56.
8. C.K. Prahalad and Allen Hammond. Serving the World's Poor, Profitably. *Harvard Business Review*, 2002, 80(9): 48–58.
9. Christopher Eppig, Corey Fincher, and Randy Thornhill. Parasite Prevalence and the Worldwide Distribution of Cognitive Ability. *Proceedings of the Royal Society*, 2010.

10. Joseph Stiglitz. *Globalization and Its Discontents*. W.W. Norton, New York, 2002. Ha-Joon Chang. *Bad Samaritans*. Bloomsbury Press, New York, 2008

11. Muhammad Yunus. *Creating a World Without Poverty: Social Business and the Future of Capitalism*. Public Affairs, 2007, p. 55.

12. Hernando de Soto. *The Mystery of Capital: Why Capitalism Triumphs in the West and Fails Everywhere Else*. New York: Basic Books, 2000.

13. C.K. Prahalad. *The Fortune at the Bottom of the Pyramid*. Wharton School Publishing, New Jersey, 2005.

14. William Easterly. *The White Man's Burden*. The Penguin Press, New York, 2006.

2   Microcredit Misses Its Mark

1. This chapter draws heavily on two of my earlier articles: Microfinance Misses its Mark. *Stanford Social Innovation Review,* Summer 2007; Microfinance Needs Regulation. *Stanford Social Innovation Review,* Winter 2011.

2. United Nations. Press Release, November 18, 2004. Available at: http://www.un.org/News/Press/docs/2004/sgsm9601.doc.htm [Accessed 24 December 2010.]

3. Tom Easton. The Hidden Wealth of the Poor. *The Economist,* November 3, 2005.

4. Claire Cane Miller. Microcredit: Why India Is Failing. *Forbes,* November 10, 2006.

5. Microfinance at a Glance—2008. Microfinance Information Exchange. Available at: http://www.themix.org/sites/default/files/Microfinance%20at%20a%20Glance%202009-12-31.pdf. [Accessed April 27, 2010.]

6. Sam-Daley-Harris. State of the Microcredit Summit Campaign Report 2009. Available at: http://www.microcreditsummit.org/uploads/socrs/SOCR2009_English.pdf.

7. Huned Contractor. Let Us Compete in Poverty Eradication: Muhammad Yunus. *One World South Asia,* November 19, 2007. Available at: http://southasia.oneworld.net/Article/let-us-compete-in-poverty-eradication-muhammad-yunus. [Accessed April 17, 2010.] Bangladesh will Send Poverty to Museum by 2030: Yunus.

Financial Express, February 18, 2007. A Partial Marvel. *The Economist,* July 16, 2009.

8. T.W. Dichter. Hype and Hope: The Worrisome State of the Microcredit Movement. Available at: http://www.microfinance-gateway.org/content/article/detail/31747, 2006. Vijay Mahajan. From Microcredit to Livelihood Finance. *Economic and Political Weekly,* October 8, 2005. Robert Pollin. Microcredit: False Hopes and Real Possibilities. *Foreign Policy Focus,* 2007. Available at: http://www.fpif.org/fpiftxt/4323. [Accessed on December. 2, 2008.]

9. See Grameen Bank website http://www.grameen-info.org/index.php?option=com_content&task=view&id=19&Itemid=114. [Accessed July 30, 2010.]

10. Muhammad Yunus. Expanding Microcredit Outreach to Reach the Millennium Development Goals, International Seminar on Attacking Poverty with Microcredit, Dhaka, Bangladesh, January 2003.

11. Geroge Negus. Foreign Correspondent—Interview with Prof. Muhammad Yunus. *ABC Online,* March 25, 1997.

12. Muhammad Yunus. *Creating a World Without Poverty.* Public Affairs, New York, P. 55, 2007.

13. David Roodman and Jonathan Morduch. The Impact of Microcredit on the Poor in Bangladesh: Revisiting the Evidence. Center for Global Development, Working Paper 174, June 2009.

14. Macro Credit. *The Economist,* October 21, 2006

15. Evaluating the Impact of Microfinance. Center for Global Development, 2007. Available at: http://www.cgdev.org/content/article/detail/12338/. [Accessed December 4, 2008.]

16. See Online Extra—Microlending: It's no Cure-all. *Businessweek Online,* December 13, 2007.

17. D. Hulme and P. Mosley. *Finance Against Poverty.* Routledge, 1996.

18. Abhijit Banerjee, Esther Duflo, Rachel Glennerster, and Cynthia Kinnan. The Miracle of Microfinance? Evidence from a Randomised Evaluation. Department of Economics, Massachusetts Institute of Technology, Working Paper, May 2009.

19. Dean Karlan and Jonathan Zinman. Expanding Microenterprise Credit Access: Using Randomized Supply Decisions to Estimate

the Impacts in Manila. Working Paper, Department of Economics, Yale University, New Haven, July 2009.

20. Sarah Glazer. Evaluating Microfinance. *CQ Global Researcher.* 2010, 4(4): 79–104.

21. D. Hulme and P. Mosley. *Finance Against Poverty.* Routledge, 1996.

22. Salil Tripathi. Microcredit Won't Make Poverty History. *Guardian Unlimited,* October 17, 2006.

23. Macro Credit. *The Economist,* October 21, 2006.

24. Anis Chowdhury. Microfinance as a Poverty Reduction Tool—A Critical Assessment. United Nations DESA. Working Paper No. 89, December 2009.

25. Daryl Collins, Jonathan Morduch, Stuart Rutherford, and Orlanda Ruthven. *Portfolios of the Poor,* Princeton University Press, Princeton, New Jersey, 2009.

26. Does Microfinance Need Regulators? Nobel Laureate Yunus Thinks So . . . *Knowledge@Wharton,* December 13, 2007.

27. A. Banerjee and E. Duflo. The Economic Lives of the Poor. *Journal of Economic Perspectives,* 2006.

28. Abraham George. *India Untouched: The Forgotten Face of Rural Poverty.* Writers' Collective, 2005.

29. Daryl Collins, Jonathan Morduch, Stuart Rutherford, and Orlanda Ruthven. *Portfolios of the Poor.* Princeton University Press, Princeton, New Jersey, 2009.

30. Dipak Mazumdar. The Employment Problem in India and the Phenomenon of the Missing Middle. Working Paper, University of Toronto, 2010.

31. L. Daniels. The Role of Small Enterprises in the Household and National Economy in Kenya: A Significant Contribution or Last Resort. *World Development,* 1999, 27(1): 55–65.

32. Milford Bateman and Ha-Joon Chang. The Microfinance Illusion. 2009. Available at: http://www.econ.cam.ac.uk/faculty/chang/pubs/Microfinance.pdf. [Accessed April 24, 2010.]

33. Amar Bhide and Carl Schramm. Phelps's Prize. *The Wall Street Journal,* January 29, 2007.

34. Overview of the Bangladesh garment industry. Available at: http://www.garmentbangladesh.com/overview_bangladesh_garments_industry.php. [Accessed May 26, 2010.]

35. Mohammed Ziaul Haider. Competitiveness of the Bangladesh Ready-made Garment Industry in Major International Markets. *Asia-Pacific Trade and Investment Review*, 2007, 3(1): 3–27.

36. Khandaker Mainuddin. Case of the Garment Industry of Dhaka, Bangladesh. The World Bank, April 2000. Available at: http://www-wds.worldbank.org/external/default/WDSContentServer/WDSP/IB/2003/08/21/000160016_20030821162205/Rendered/PDF/265920NWP0Urba1v0no106garment1dhaka.pdf. [Accessed May 26, 2010.]

37. Bhide and Schramm. Phelps's Prize.

38. Jonathan Morduch. How Can the Poor Afford Microfinance. Financial Access Initiative. Wagner Graduate School, New York University, New York, 2008.

39. J. Morduch. Does Microfinance Really Help the Poor? New Evidence from Flagship Programs in Bangladesh. Harvard Institute of International Development and Hoover Institution, Stanford University. http://www.wws.princeton.edu/~rpds/downloads/morduch_microfinance_poor.pdf. 1998.

40. G. Sabharwal. From the Margin to the Mainstream. Micro-Finance Programmes and Women's Empowerment: The Bangladesh Experience. University of Wales, Swansea. Available at: http://www.gdrc.org/icm/wind/geeta.pdf. 2000.

41. J. Sebstad and G. Chen. Overview of Studies on the Impact of Microenterprise Credit. AIMS, USAID, Washington. 1996.

42. Sarah Glazer. Evaluating Microfinance. *CQ Global Researcher*, 2010, 4(4): 79–104.

43. Keith Epstein and Geri Smith. The Ugly Side of Microlending. *Business Week*, December 13, 2007.

44. Reuters India. Microcredit Lenders Urged to Improve Transparency. July 28, 2008. Available at: http://in.reuters.com/article/domesticNews/idINJAK5066620080728. [Accessed on May 24, 2009.]

45. Online Extra: Yunus Blasts Compartamos. *Business Week*, December 13, 2007. Available at: http://www.businessweek.com/magazine/content/07_52/b4064045920958.htm. [Accessed on May 24, 2009.]

46. Sudhirendar Sharma. Death by Microcredit. *The Times of India*, September 16, 2006.

47. Nimal A. Fernando. Understanding and Dealing with High Interest Rates on Microcredit. Asian Development Bank, May 2006.
48. Amy Kazmin. Cradle of Microfinance Rocked. *Financial Time,* December 11, 2010.
49. Richard Rosenberg, Adrian Gonzalez, and Sushma Narain. The New Moneylenders: Are the Poor Being Exploited by High Microcredit Interest Rates? Occasional Paper 15, Consultative Group to Assist the Poor, Washington D.C., February 2009.
50. Muhammad Yunus: Lifting People Worldwide out of Poverty. *Knowledge@Wharton.* Available at: http://knowledge.wharton. upenn.edu/article.cfm?articleid=2243. [Accessed July 15, 2009.]
51. Carlos Danel and Carlos Labarthe. A Letter to Our Peers. June 2008. Available at: http://www.microfinanceinsights.com/oldsite/ Download/Alettertoourpeers.pdf. [Accessed May 25, 2009.]
52. Rosenberg, Gonzalez, and Narain. The New Moneylenders.
53. Nimal Fernando. Understanding and Dealing with High Interest Rates on Microcredit. Asian Development Bank, Manila, May 2006.
54. Strengthening Consumer Protection. Available at: http://financialstability.gov/docs/regulatoryreform/strengthening_consumer_ protection.pdf. [Accessed June 24, 2009.]
55. Jane Kim. Plain-vanilla Financing Could Melt Bank Profits. *The Wall Street Journal,* June 26, 2009.
56. Education In India, 2007–08: Participation And Expenditure. National Sample Survey Office, Government Of India, May 19, 2010.
57. Akhand Tiwari, Anvesha Khandelwal, and Minakshi Ramji. How Do Microfinance Clients Understand Their Loans? Center for Micro Finance, Institute for Financial Management and Research, Chennai, India, October 2008.
58. Richard Rosenberg, Adrian Gonzalez, and Sushma Narain. The New Moneylenders: Are the Poor Being Exploited by High Microcredit Interest Rates? Occasional Paper 15, Consultative Group to Assist the Poor, Washington D.C., February 2009.
59. See their website http://www.mftransparency.org/about/.
60. Chuck Waterfield. Implementing Pricing Transparency in Microfinance. Available at: http://www.mftransparency.org/ media/pdf/e-mfp-newsletter1.pdf. [Accessed June 25, 2009.]

61. Subrata Kumar Mitra. Exploitative Microfinance Interest Rates. *Asian Social Science*, 2009, 5(5), 87–93.

62. Chuck Waterfield. Explanation of Compartamos Interest Rates. May 19, 2008. Available at: http://www.microfin.com/aprcalculations.htm. [Accessed April 26, 2010.]

63. Daryl Collins, Jonathan Morduch, Stuart Rutherford, and Orlanda Ruthven. *Portfolios of the Poor.* Princeton University Press, Princeton, 2009, p. 143.

64. Rosenberg, Gonzalez, and Narain. The New Moneylenders.

65. Chuck Waterfield. Why We Need Transparent Pricing in Microfinance. Presentation available at: http://www.mftransparency.org/. [Accessed July 15, 2009.]

66. David Porteus. Competition and Microcredit Interest Rates. Occasional Paper 33, Consultative Group to Assist the Poor, Washington D.C., February 2006.

67. Nimal A. Fernando. Understanding and Dealing with High Interest Rates on Microcredit. Asian Development Bank, May 2006.

68. Brigit Helms and Xavier Reille. Interest Rate Ceilings and Microfinance: The Story So Far. Occasional Paper 9, Consultative Group to Assist the Poor, Washington D.C., September 2004.

69. France 24. The Crushing Burden of Microcredit. Available at: http://www.france24.com/en/20080404-bangladesh-burden-microcredit-caring-grameen-bank-mohammed-yunnus. [Accessed July 23, 2008.]

70. Ibid.

71. In the Shadows of India's Loan Boom. *The Wall Street Journal,* January 8, 2008.

72. Keith Epstein and Geri Smith. The Ugly Side of Microlending. *Business Week,* December 13, 2007.

73. Adam Ross and Paula Savanti. Empirical Analysis of the Mechanisms of Group Lending. Center for Micro Finance, Institute for Financial Management and Research, Chennai, India, August 2005.

74. Akhand Tiwari, Anvesha Khandelwal, and Minakshi Ramji. How Do Microfinance Clients Understand Their Loans? Center for Micro Finance, Institute for Financial Management and Research, Chennai, India, October 2008.

75. Jonathan Lewis. Microloan Sharks. *Stanford Social Innovation Review,* Summer 2008.

76. Crook Clive. The Good Company. *The Economist,* January 20, 2005.

77. The Pocantico Declaration is available at http://www.accion.org/ Document.Doc?id=442. [Accessed July 15, 2009.]

78. Alex Counts. Reimagining Microfinance. *Stanford Social Innovation Review,* Summer 2008.

79. Available at: http://www.mfnetwork.org/images/stories/working-groups/proconsumer/MFN%20Pro-consumer%20Pledge%20 English.pdf. [Accessed July 15, 2009.]

80. Patrick Meagher. Microfinance Regulation and Supervision in South Africa. Paper No. 6, IRIS Center, University of Maryland, April 2005.

81. Yunus. Lifting People Worldwide out of Poverty.

82. Available at: http://www.thefinancialexpress-bd.com/2009/04/29/ 65167.html. [Accessed October 28, 2009.]

83. Brigit Helms and Xavier Reille. Interest Rate Ceilings and Microfinance: The Story So Far. Occasional Paper 9, Consultative Group to Assist the Poor, Washington D.C., September 2004.

84. Hernando de Soto. *The Mystery of Capital: Why Capitalism Triumphs in the West and Fails Everywhere Else,* New York: Basic Books, 2000.

85. United Nations. *Rethinking Poverty: Report on the World Social Situation 2010.* United Nations, New York, 2009.

86. Sebastian Galiani and Ernesto Schargrodsky. Property Rights for the Poor: Effects of Land Titling. Ronald Coase Institute, Working Paper Series, January 2009.

87. John Gravois. The de Soto Delusion. *Slate,* January 29, 2005. Available at: http://www.slate.com/id/2112792. [Accessed May 29, 2010.]

88. United Nations. *Rethinking Poverty.*

3   Mirage at the Base of the Pyramid

1. This chapter draws heavily on my earlier article The Mirage of Marketing to the Bottom of the Pyramid, *California Management Review,* 2007, 49 (4): 90–111.

2. C.K. Prahalad, *The Fortune at the Bottom of the Pyramid: Eradicating Poverty through Profit,* Wharton School Publishing, New Jersey, 2005.

3. See http://www.growinginclusivemarkets.org/?page_id=316 [Accessed August 3, 2010.]

4. Erik Simanis, Stuart Hart, and Duncan Duke. The Base of the Pyramid Protocol. *Innovations,* Winter 2008.

5. Prahalad, *The Fortune at the Bottom of the Pyramid,* p. 21.

6. *The Next 4 Billion,* World Resource Institute and International Finance Corporation, Washington DC, 2007.

7. C.K. Prahalad and S.L. Hart. The Fortune at the Bottom of the Pyramid. *Strategy + Business,* 2002.

8. C.K. Prahalad and A. Hammond. Serving the World's Poor Profitably. *Harvard Business Review,* 2002, 80(9): 48–58.

9. For example, Ted London writes about firms seeking growth "opportunities in emerging markets." A Base-of-the-Pyramid Perspective on Poverty Alleviation. William Davidson Institute, University of Michigan, Working Paper, July 2007.

10. Jean-Louis Warnholz. Poverty Reduction for Profit? A Critical Examination of Business Opportunities at the Bottom of the Pyramid. University of Oxford, Working Paper 160, October 2007.

11. Christina Passariello. Danone Expands Its Pantry to Woo the World's Poor. *The Wall Street Journal,* June 29, 2010.

12. Jean-Louis Warnholz. Poverty Reduction for Profit? A Critical Examination of Business Opportunities at the Bottom of the Pyramid. University of Oxford, Working Paper 160, October 2007.

13. Muhammad Yunus. Poverty Alleviation: Is Economics Any Help? Lessons from the Grameen Bank Experience. *Journal of International Affairs,* 1998, 52(1): 47–65.

14. Here, it refers to the tendency of one group to "crowd out" another's ability to benefit from a program.

15. If the poverty line is defined at $3,000 per year, then the number of people in the BOP is about 4 billion.

16. There is controversy in the development field about the exact number of poor people below any given poverty line, but the

disagreements usually are not that big, and the claim usually is that the World Bank is overestimating the extent of poverty. In any case, these technical controversies are not the cause of the BOP's mistaken numbers, which are dramatically *higher* than the World Bank estimates.

17. For example: Profits, a Penny at a Time. *The Washington Post*, July 6, 2005; Profits and Poverty. *The Economist*, August 19, 2004.

18. J. Walsh, J.C. Kress, and K.W. Beyerchen. Book Review Essay: Promises and Perils at the Bottom of the Pyramid. *Administrative Science Quarterly*, 2005, 50(3): 473–482.

19. T. Easton. The Hidden Wealth of the Poor. *The Economist*, November 3, 2005.

20. Prahalad and Hammond. Serving the World's Poor Profitably.

21. Shubhashis Gangopadhyay and Wilima Wadhwa. Changing Pattern of Household Consumption Expenditure. Society for Economic Research & Financial Analysis, New Delhi, The Planning Commission, Government of India, 2004.

22. Sofie Van den Waeyenberg and Luc Hens. Crossing the Bridge to Poverty, with Low-Cost Cars. *Journal of Consumer Marketing*, 2008, 25(7): 439–445.

23. Abhijit Banerjee and Esther Duflo. The Economic Lives of the Poor. Working Paper, MIT Boston, October 2006.

24. Anand Kumar Jaiswal. The Fortune at the Bottom or the Middle of the Pyramid? *Innovations,* Winter 2008.

25. Prahalad, *The Fortune at the Bottom of the Pyramid*, p. 131.

26. Ibid., p. 119.

27. The previous name of the company was Hindustan Lever Limited.

28. V. Sarvani. The Indian Kitchen Salt Market—Brand Wars. ICFAI Center for Management Research, Hyderabad, 2003.

29. Prahalad, *The Fortune at the Bottom of the Pyramid*, p. 181.

30. R. Gopalakrishnan. Unshackling the Rural Markets—for Authentic Engagement, First. *The Hindu Business Line,* October 20, 2004.

31. Hammond and Prahalad. Selling to the Poor.

32. Prahalad and Hart. The Fortune at the Bottom of the Pyramid.

33. Vinay Kamath. HUL Tastes the Cream Finally. *The Hindu Business Line*, August 21, 2002; Sindhu Bhattacharya. The Ice-cream Punch. *The Hindu Business Line*, June 24, 2004.

34. See, for example, *The "Bird of Gold": The Rise of India's Consumer Market*. McKinsey Global Institute, May 2007; and *From "Made in China" to "Sold in China": The Rise of the Chinese Urban Consumer*. McKinsey Global Institute, November 2006.

35. Prahalad, *The Fortune at the Bottom of the Pyramid*, p. 16.

36. S. Dobhal and S.D. Munshi. The New Rural Consumer. *Business Today*, January 30, 2005.

37. Prahalad, *The Fortune at the Bottom of the Pyramid*, p. 186.

38. P&G's Global Target: Shelves of Tiny Stores. *The Wall Street Journal*, July 24, 2007.

39. Prahalad, *The Fortune at the Bottom of the Pyramid*, p. 17.

40. Ibid.

41. K. Yamini Aparna. Casas Bahia. Case study No. 505-039-1, ICFAI Center for Management Research, 2005.

42. Ibid.

43. Prahalad and Hart. The Fortune at the Bottom of the Pyramid.

44. Ibid.

45. Anand Kumar Jaiswal. Fortune at the Bottom of the Pyramid: An Alternate Perspective. Indian Institute of Management, Ahmedabad, Working Paper 2007-07-13, July 2007.

46. Ibid.

47. Prahalad, *The Fortune at the Bottom of the Pyramid*, p.25.

48. Hindustan Lever Takes a Bath. *Business Week*, December 27, 2004.

49. Monitor Group. *Emerging Markets, Emerging Models*, 2009. Available at: http://www.monitor.com/Portals/0/MonitorContent/imported/MonitorUnitedStates/Articles/PDFs/Monitor_Emerging_Markets_NEDS_03_25_09.pdf. [Accessed October 24, 2009.]

50. Prahalad (*The Fortune at the Bottom of the Pyramid*, p. 30) calls for improving price-performance by 30 to 100 times; this is equivalent to reducing price by 97% to 99%.

51. Green revolution involved high yielding varieties of grains, hybridized seeds, irrigation infrastructure, and synthetic fertilizers and pesticides.

52. Prahalad, *The Fortune at the Bottom of the Pyramid*, p. 29.

53. Aman Bhandari, Sandra Dratler, Kristiana Raube, and R.D. Thulasiraj. Specialty Care Systems: A Pioneering Vision for Global Health. *Health Affairs*, 2008, 27(4): 964–976.

54. Prahalad, *The Fortune at the Bottom of the Pyramid*, p. 269.
55. Marcelo, R. India Fosters Growing 'Medical Tourism' Sector. *The Financial Times,* July 2, 2003.
56. N. Puri. FICCI seminar on Medical Tourism. 2003. Available at: http://www.ficci.com/media-room/speeches-presentations/2003/dec/maxhealthcare.pdf. [Accessed August 20, 2006.]
57. S. Miller. McSurgery: A Man Who Saved 2.4 Million Eyes. *The Wall Street Journal,* August 5, 2006.
58. See Amul's website http://www.amul.com/. Also see Chandra (2005).
59. ITC to Invest $1 b in e-Choupal Infrastructure. *The Hindu,* January 4, 2006.
60. Deepa Narayan and Soumya Kapoor. Beyond Ideologies: Creating Wealth for the Poor. Arusha Conference, New Frontiers of Social Policy, December 12–15, 2005.

4 Romanticizing the Poor

1. This chapter draws heavily on my earlier articles Romanticizing the Poor. *Stanford Social Innovation Review*, 2009, 7(1): 38–43; Failure of Libertarian Approach to Reducing Poverty. *Asian Business & Management*, 2010, 9(1): 5–21; and Doing Well By Doing Good. Case Study: 'Fair & Lovely' Whitening Cream. *Strategic Management Journal*, 2007, 28(13): 1351–1357.
2. India in Style. *Vogue India*, August 2008.
3. Pamela Timms. Vogue's India Fashion Shoot Sparks Disgust. *The Independent,* February 21, 2010.
4. Nikhat Kazmi. Slumdog Millionaire. *The Times of India,* January 22, 2009.
5. Anand Giridharadas. Indians Adopt a Vision under Siege in America. *The New York Times,* January 15, 2009.
6. *PovcalNet* database of the World Bank. Available at: http://iresearch.worldbank.org/PovcalNet/povcalSvy.html [Accessed January 3, 2011.]
7. Education In India, 2007–08: Participation And Expenditure. National Sample Survey Office, Government Of India, May 19, 2010. Available at: http://mospi.gov.in/press_note_NSS_%20Report_no_532_19may10.pdf [Accessed January 3, 2011.]

8. India Statistics. United Nations Children's Fund. Available at: http://www.unicef.org/infobycountry/india_statistics.html [Accessed January 3, 2011.]

9. Progress on Sanitation and Drinking Water. World Health Organization/United Nations Children's Fund. 2010. Available at: http://www.wssinfo.org/fileadmin/user_upload/resources/1278061137-JMP_report_2010_en.pdf [Accessed January 3, 2011.]

10. Diarrhoea: Why Children Are Still Dying and What can Be Done. The United Nations Children's Fund/World Health Organization. 2009. Available at: http://whqlibdoc.who.int/publications/2009/9789241598415_eng.pdf [Accessed January 3, 2011.]

11. Joseph Hanlon, Armando Barrientos, and David Hulme. *Just Give Money to the Poor.* Kumarian Press, Sterling, Virginia, 2010.

12. Tom Roston. Slumdog Millionaire Shoot was Rags to Riches. *The Hollywood Reporter,* November 4, 2008.

13. Amelia Gentleman. Slum Tours: A Day Trip Too Far? *The Guardian,* May 7, 2006.

14. Ibid.

15. Voices of the Poor. The World Bank, 2000. Available at: http://go.worldbank.org/IM4HTOJ690. [Accessed June 20, 2010.]

16. Sendhil Mullainathan. Poor Decision Making. Seedmagazine.com, February 3, 2009.

17. Amartya Sen. *Development as Freedom.* Anchor Books, New York, 2000, p. 63.

18. E. Duflo, M. Kremer, and J. Robinson. Understanding Fertilizer Adoption: Evidence from Field Experiments. Mimeo, Massachusetts Institute of Technology, 2006.

19. Another Day, Another $1.08. *The Economist,* April 28, 2007.

20. A. Banerjee and E. Duflo. The Economic Lives of the Poor. *Journal of Economic Perspectives,* 2006, 21(1): 141–167.

21. For example, J. Clay. *Exploring the Links between International Business and Poverty Reduction: A Case Study of Unilever in Indonesia,* Oxfam, Oxford, 2005.

22. Another Day, Another $1.08. *The Economist,* April 28, 2007.

23. Ibid.

24. Amartya Sen. *Development as Freedom.* Anchor Books, New York, 2000, p. 63.

25. Marianne Bertrand, Sendhil Mullainathan, and Eldar Shafir. A Behavioral Economics View of Poverty. *The American Economic Review*, 2004, 94(2): 419–423.

26. A. Banerjee and E. Duflo. The Economic Lives of the Poor. *Journal of Economic Perspectives*, 2006, 21(1): 141–167.

27. A. Banerjee, A. Deaton, and E. Duflo. Wealth, Health and Health Services in Rural Rajasthan. *American Economic Review*, 2004, 94(2): 326–330.

28. J.V. Meenakshi and B. Vishwanathan. Calorie Deprivation in Rural India, 1983–1999/2000. *Economic and Political Weekly*, January 25, 2003.

29. A. Banerjee and E. Duflo. The Economic Lives of the Poor. *Journal of Economic Perspectives*, 2006, 21(1): 141–167.

30. A. Banerjee, E. Duflo, and R. Glennerster. A Snapshot of Micro Enterprises in Hyderabad. Unpublished paper, MIT, 2006.

31. For example, E.F.P. Luttmer. Neighbors as Negatives: Relative Earnings and Well-being. *The Quarterly Journal of Economics*, 2005, 120(3): 963–1002; E. Diener, E.M. Suh, R.E. Lucas, and H.L. Smith. Subjective Well-being: Three Decades of Progress. *Psychology Bulletin*, 1999, 125(2): 276–302.

32. M. Fafchamps and F. Shilpi. Subjective Welfare, Isolation, and Relative Consumption. *Journal of Development Economics*, 2008, 86(1); 43–60.

33. A. Banerjee, A. Deaton, and E. Duflo. Wealth, Health and Health Services in Rural Rajasthan. *American Economic Review*, 2004, 94(2): 326–330.

34. Banerjee and Duflo. The Economic Lives of the Poor.

35. See, for example, John Mirowsky, and Catherine E. Ross. Social Patterns of Distress. *Annual Review of Sociology*, 1986, 12: 23–45; and Alana C. Snibbe and Hazel R. Markus. You Can't Always Get What You Want: Educational Attainment, Agency, and Choice. *Journal of Personality and Social Psychology*, 2005: 703–720.

36. Banerjee and Duflo. The Economic Lives of the Poor.

37. Ibid.

38. Shubhashis Gangopadhyay and Wilima Wadhwa. Changing Pattern of Household Consumption Expenditure. Society for Economic Research & Financial Analysis, New Delhi, The Planning Commission, Government of India, 2004.

39. B. Baklien and D. Samarasinghe. *Alcohol and Poverty in Sri Lanka.* FORUT, Norway, 2004. Report available at http://www.forut.no/index.php/15703-1.

40. D. Efroymson and S. Ahmed. Hungry for Tobacco. PATH Canada, 2001.

41. For example, M. Asunta. Impact of Alcohol Consumption on Asia. *The Globe*, 2001.

42. The Flicker of a Brighter Future. *The Economist*, September 7, 2006.

43. L. Bolin. SABMiller's New Clear Sorghum Beer. *business.iafrica. com*, February 2, 2005.

44. For example, Asunta. Impact of Alcohol Consumption on Asia.

45. Gerard Hastings et al. Failure of Self Regulation of UK Alcohol Advertising. *British Medical Journal,* January 20, 2010.

46. Asunta, Idris, and Hamid. The Alcohol Problem in Malaysia. *The Globe*, 2001.

47. Ibid.

48. This section draws heavily on the Radio Sweden documentary, whose transcript is available at http://sverigesradio.se/sida/artikel.aspx?programid=1316&artikel=2819773. [Accessed June 10, 2010.]

49. N. Leistikow. Indian Women Criticize "Fair & Lovely" Ideal. *Women's eNews*, April 28, 2003.

50. Marketing Practice. February 3, 2006. Available at: http://marketing practice.blogspot.com/2006_02_01_archive.html. [Accessed June 10, 2010.]

51. E. Luce and K. Merchant. India Orders Ban on Advert Saying Fairer Equals Better for Women. *Financial Times*, March 20, 2003.

52. A. Hammond and C.K. Prahalad. Selling to the Poor. *Foreign Policy*, 2004.

53. P. Engardio. Beyond the Green Corporation. *Business Week,* January 29, 2007.

54. S. Ninan. Seeing Red with this Pitch. *The Hindu,* March 16, 2003.

55. K.S. Islam, H.S. Ahmed, E. Karim, and A.M. Amin. Fair Factor. *Star Weekend Magazine*, May 12, 2006.

56. India Debates "Racist" Skin Cream Ads. *BBC News*, July 24, 2003.

57. Ibid.

58. E. Luce and K. Merchant. India Orders Ban on Advert Saying Fairer Equals Better for Women. *Financial Times*, March 20, 2003.

59. V. Doctor and H. Narayanswamy. Ban for the Buck. *The Economic Times*, April 2, 2003.

60. Emily Cook. "Skin-lightening Cream Ad Criticized. *The Daily Mirror,* October 16, 2008.

61. E. Luce and K. Merchant. India Orders Ban on Advert Saying Fairer Equals Better for Women. *Financial Times*, March 20, 2003.

62. R. Chandran. All for Self-control. *Business Line,* April 24, 2003.

63. Luce and Merchant. India Orders Ban on Advert Saying Fairer Equals Better for Women.

64. For example, Thomas Friedman. *The World is Flat*. Farrar, Straus and Giroux, New York, 2005

65. Jean-Louis Warnholz. Poverty Reduction for Profit? A Critical Examination of Business Opportunities at the Bottom of the Pyramid. University of Oxford, Working Paper 160, October 2007.

66. Raghuram Rajan and Luigi Zingales. *Saving Capitalism from the Capitalists*. Crown Business, New York, 2003, p. 293.

67. Amartya Sen. *Development as Freedom*. Anchor Books, New York, 2000, p. 3.

68. Arvind Virmani. Poverty and Hunger in India: What is Needed to Eliminate Them. Working Paper No. 1/2006-PC, Planning Commission, the Government of India, 2006.

69. *In the Public Interest*. Oxfam International, 2006.

70. S.R. Pattnayak. *The Return of the State*. Yash Publications, Delhi, 2006

71. *World Development Indicators 2006*. World Bank, 2006.

72. C.K. Prahalad and A. Hammond. Serving the World's Poor Profitably. *Harvard Business Review*, 2002, 80(9): 48–58.

73. Selling to the Poor. *Time*, April 17, 2005

5   Selling Beneficial Goods to the Poor

1. This chapter draws heavily on my earlier article with Bernard Garrette, Challenges in Marketing Socially Useful Goods to the Poor. *California Management Review*, 2010, 52(4), 29–47.

2. Monitor Group. *Emerging Markets, Emerging Models*, 2009. Available at: http://www.monitor.com/Portals/0/MonitorContent/ imported/MonitorUnitedStates/Articles/PDFs/Monitor_ Emerging_Markets_NEDS_03_25_09.pdf. [Accessed October 24, 2009.]

3. Ian Parker. The Poverty Lab. *The New Yorker,* May 15, 2010.

4. P. Balakrishna and B. Sidharth. "Selling in rural Rural India.' *The Hindu Business Line*, February 16, 2004.

5. Sindhu Bhattacharya. 'Coke's challenge.' *The Hindu Business Line*, July 14, 2005.

6. L. Moses and A. Karnani. Vision Correction in the Developing World. Case study, William Davidson Institute, University of Michigan, 2009.

7. B. Garrette, K. Benkirane, and C. Roger-Machart. Essilor's "Base of the Pyramid" Strategy in India. Case study, HEC Paris, 2008.

8. *Water for Life: Making it Happen.* WHO/UNICEF, 2005. Available at: http://www.who.int/water_sanitation_health/moni-toring/jmp2005/en/. [Accessed October 16, 2009.]

9. M. Hanson and K. Powell. Procter & Gamble PUR Purifier of Water (A) and (B). European Case Clearing House, 2009.

10. M. Hanson. Pure Water. *Management Today*, April 1, 2007.

11. *Monitoring the Situation of Children and Women*. UNICEF, 2009. Available at: http://www.childinfo.org/undernutrition.html. [Accessed October 16, 2009.]

12. *Grameen Danone Foods Ltd, a Social Business in Bangladesh.* Danone Communities, 2009. Available at: http://www.slideshare. net/danonecommunities/grameen-danone-food-ltd-overview-210609. [Accessed February 5, 2010.]

13. Muhammad Yunus. *Creating a World without Poverty: Social Business and the Future of Capitalism.* New York: Public Affairs, 2007.

14. V. Akula. Business Basics at the Base of the Pyramid. *Harvard Business Review*, 2008, 86(6), 53–57.

15. Monitor Group, *Emerging Markets, Emerging Models*, 2009, p. 43. Available at: http://www.monitor.com/Portals/0/MonitorContent/ imported/MonitorUnitedStates/Articles/PDFs/Monitor_ Emerging_Markets_NEDS_03_25_09.pdf. [Accessed October 24, 2009.]

16. J. Ramke, R. du Toil, A. Palagyi, et al. Correction of Refractive Error and Presbyopia in Timor-Leste. *British Journal of Ophthalmology*, 2007, 91(7): 860–866.

17. Shubhashis Gangopadhyay and Wilima Wadhwa. Changing Pattern of Household Consumption Expenditure. Society for Economic Research & Financial Analysis, New Delhi, The Planning Commission, Government of India, 2004.

18. Flocculation refers to the chemical process by which fine particles are caused to clump together into floc, which can then be readily filtered from the liquid.

19. *Household Water Treatment Options in Developing Countries: Household Chlorination.* CDC, 2008. Available at: http://www. ehproject.org/PDF/ehkm/cdc-options_sws.pdf. [Accessed October 24, 2009.]

20. Monitor Group, *Emerging Markets, Emerging Models*, 2009, p. 41. Available at: http://www.monitor.com/Portals/0/MonitorContent/ imported/MonitorUnitedStates/Articles/PDFs/Monitor_ Emerging_Markets_NEDS_03_25_09.pdf. [Accessed October 24, 2009.]

21. S. Vachani and N.C. Smith. Socially Responsible Distribution: Distribution Strategies for Reaching the Bottom of the Pyramid. *California Management Review*, 2008, 52(2): 52–84.

22. *Grameen Danone Foods Ltd, a Social Business in Bangladesh.* Danone Communities, 2009. Available at: http://www.slideshare. net/danonecommunities/grameen-danone-food-ltd-overview-210609. [Accessed February 5, 2010.]

23. Ahmed Rashid and Laurent Elder. Mobile Phones and Development: An Analysis of IDRC-supported Projects. *Electronic Journal of Information Systems in Developing Countries.* 2009, 36(2): 1–16.

24. *Teleuse@BOP3: India's rural millions: Connected?* LIRNEasia, 2009. Available at: http://lirneasia.net/wp-content/uploads/2009/04/ coai-tabop3-mumbai-10feb09_final2.pdf. [Accessed February 4, 2010.]

25. David Lehr. Dialing for Development. *Stanford Social Innovation Review*, 2008, 6(4): 44–49.

26. 'Knocking Down the Affordability Barrier. *Expanding Horizons*, Nokia, 2009. Available at: http://activeark.ipapercms.dk/Nokia/

ExpandingHorizonsQ22009/?Page=9. [Accessed February 4, 2010.]

27. GSMA, 2006. See http://gsmworld.com/newsroom/press-releases/ 2046.htm#nav-6. [Accessed February 4, 2010.]

28. Sunil Jain. Top of the Pyramid. *Business Standard,* January 22, 2009.

29. *Teleuse@BOP3: India's Rural Millions: Connected?* LIRNEasia, 2009. Available at: http://lirneasia.net/wp-content/uploads/2009/04/coai-tabop3-mumbai-10feb09_final2.pdf. [Accessed February 4, 2010.]

30. J. Donner. The Rules of Beeping: Exchanging Messages via Intentional Missed Calls on Mobile Phones. *Journal of Computer-Mediated Communication,* 2007, 13(1).

31. P.S. Ahmad and J. Mead. Hindustan Lever Limited and Project Sting. Case study, Darden Business Publishing, 2004.

32. P.S. Ahmad and J. Mead. Hindustan Lever Limited and Project Sting. Case study, Darden Business Publishing, 2004.

33. David A. Garvin. Competing on the Eight Dimensions of Quality. *Harvard Business Review,* 1987, 65(6).

34. Prahalad (2005), p. 272.

6 Employment Is the Solution

1. Jeffrey Sachs. *The End of Poverty.* New York: Penguin Books, 2005.

2. W. Easterly. *The White Man's Burden.* Oxford University Press, 2006. T.W. Dichter. *Despite Good Intentions.* University of Massachusetts Press, 2003.

3. Thomas Friedman. *The World is Flat.* New York: Farrar, Straus and Giroux, 2005.

4. George Stiglitz. *Globalization and its Discontents.* 2002. Ha-Joon Chang. *Bad Samaritans.* New York: Bloomsbury Press, 2008.

5. United Nations. *The Least Developed Countries Report 2006. Developing Productive Capacities.* United Nations Conference on Trade and Development, 2006.

6. International Labor Organization. *Global Employment Trends Brief.* 2007.

7. See http://www.doingbusiness.org/ [Accessed September 13, 2009.]

8. International Labor Organization. *Key Indicators of the Labor Market*, 5th Edition. 2007.

9. Martin Ravallion. Pro-Poor Growth: A Primer. World Bank, Washington D.C. 2004.

10. United Nations. *The Least Developed Countries Report 2006. Developing Productive Capacities.* United Nations Conference on Trade and Development. 2006.

11. Eduardo Zepeda. Learning from the Past: Mexico's Failed Pro-Market Policy Experience. *Poverty in Focus.* International Poverty Center, Brasilia, December 2008.

12. James Lamont. Nobel Laureate Attacks India on Growth. *Financial Times,* December 21, 2010.

13. K. Kochhar, U. Kumar, R. Rajan, and A. Subramanian. India's Pattern of Development: What Happened, what follows? *Journal of Monetary Economics*, 2006, 53: 981–1019.

14. Rajat Gupta. Fulfilling India's Promise. *McKinsey Quarterly*, Special Edition, 2005.

15. International Labor Organization. *Global Employment Trends Brief.* 2007.

16. S.R. Osmani. The Employment Nexus between Growth and Poverty: An Asian Perspective. United Nations Development Program, New York, 2004.

17. For example: A. Virmani. Poverty and Hunger in India: What is Needed to Eliminate Them. Working Paper No. 1/2006-PC, Planning Commission, the Government of India. 2006.

18. For opposing views on this ideological debate, see, for example, Martin Wolf, *Why Globalization Works,* Yale University Press, New Haven, 2004; and Ha-Joon Chang. *Bad Samaritans.* Bloomsbury Press, New York, 2008.

19. International Finance Corporation. *Scaling up Private Sector Models for Poverty Reduction.* Washington DC. 2004.

20. See http://www.doingbusiness.org/ [Accessed September 13, 2009.]

21. Ibid.

22. Ibid.

23. *Enterprise Solutions to Poverty.* Shell Foundation, March 2005.

24. Amartya Sen. *Development as Freedom.* Anchor Books, New York, 2000, p. 42.

25. Now for the Hard Part. *The Economist*, June 3, 2006.

26. Kurt Hoffman. Placing Enterprise and Business Thinking at the Heart of the War on Poverty. In *Reinventing Foreign Aid*, edited by William Easterly. MIT Press, Cambridge, 2008.

27. Meghana Ayyagari, Thorsten Beck, and Asli Demirguc-Kunt. Small and Medium Enterprises across the Globe: A New Database. Policy Research Working Paper 3127, The World Bank, August 2003.

28. Anne O. Krueger. The Missing Middle. Working Paper No. 20. Indian Council for Research on International Economic Relations, New Delhi, 2009.

29. Thorsten Beck, Asli Demirguc-Kunt, and Ross Levine. Small and Medium Enterprises, Growth, and Poverty: Cross-Country Evidence. Policy Research Working Paper 3178, The World Bank, December 2003.

30. Ministry of Industries, Production & Special Initiatives, Government of Pakistan. SME led Economic Growth —Creating Jobs and Reducing Poverty. Available at http://www.smeda.org/downloads/smepolicy2007.pdf. [Accessed January 8, 2010.]

31. Thorsten Beck, *et al, op cit.*

32. International Labor Organization. *World Employment Report 2004–05.* 2005.

33. A. Banerjee and E. Duflo. The Economic Lives of the Poor. *Journal of Economic Perspectives*, 2006.

34. Anne O. Krueger, *op cit.*

35. Sean M. Dougherty, Richard Herd, Thomas Chalaux, and Abdul Azeez Erumban. India's Growth Pattern and Obstacles to Higher Growth. Working Paper No. 62, OECD, Paris, 2008.

36. Source: International Labor Organization. *Global Employment Trends.* 2010.

37. The working poor do not earn enough to lift themselves and their family above the poverty threshold.

38. Sean M. Dougherty, Richard Herd, Thomas Chalaux, and Abdul Azeez Erumban. India's Growth Pattern and Obstacles to Higher Growth. Working Paper No. 62, OECD, Paris, 2008.

39. L. Daniels. The Role of Small Enterprises in the Household and National Economy in Kenya: A Significant Contribution or Last Resort. *World Development*, 1999, 27(1): 55–65.

40. International Labor Organization. *World Employment Report 2004–05*. 2005.

41. A. Fiegenbaum and A. Karnani. Output Flexibility—A Competitive Advantage for Small Firms. *Strategic Management Journal*, 1991, 12(2): 101–114.

42. I would like to thank Bruce McNamer (CEO), Simon Winter (Senior Vice President), and Steve Londner (Senior Advisor) for much help and access to their organization TechnoServe.

43. Rwanda Tourism Value Chain Case Study. US Aid, micro report 94, January 2008. Hannah Nielsen and Anna Spenceley. The Success of Tourism in Rwanda—Gorillas and More. The World Bank, April 2010.

44. Vishal Krishna. Educated, but Unemployable. Businessworld. Available at http://www.businessworld.in/content/view/2531/2609/1/0/. [Accessed April 28, 2008.]

45. International Labor Organization. *Global Employment Trends for Youth*. 2006.

46. P. Gregg and E. Tominey. The Wage Scar From Male Youth Unemployment. *Labor Economics,* August 2005.

47. P. Ryan. The School-to-Work Transition: As Cross-National Perspective. *Journal of Economic Literature*, 2000, 39: 34–92.

48. International Labor Organization. *Working out of Poverty*. 2003.

49. Christoph Ernst. Promoting Youth Employment. *Poverty in Focus*, International Poverty Center, Brasilia, December 2008.

50. See http://www.servicecanada.gc.ca/eng/epb/yi/yep/newprog/yes programs.shtml. [Accessed January 8, 2010.]

51. See http://webapps01.un.org/nvp/frontend!policy.action?id=462& tab=analysis. [Accessed January 8, 2010.]

52. See http://www.yesweb.org/aboutus.htm. [Accessed January 8, 2010.]

53. I would like to thank Meera Shenoy, Executive Director, Employment Generation & Marketing Mission, for much help and access to the organization.

54. See http://www.egmm.ap.gov.in/. [Accessed January 8, 2010.]

55. Ravi Reddy. Rural Youngsters Fly High with Security Services Jobs. *The Hindu*, September 16, 2006.

56. Malini Goyal. Jobs for Rural Youth. *The Economics Times,* November 7, 2007.

57. Transit Homes for the Rural Youth. *The Hindu,* August 21, 2007.

58. Andhra Charts Plan to train Lakh Rural Youth. *The Economic Times,* November 9, 2007.

59. Ravi Reddy. A Ray of Hope for Rural Youth. *The Hindu,* August 3, 2007.

60. The Mahbub ul Haq Human Development Centre. *op cit.*

61. A Fresh Start. *The Wall Street Journal,* September 17, 2009.

62. William Easterly. *The White Man's Burden.* The Penguin Press, New York, 2006.

63. A Fresh Start. *The Wall Street Journal,* September 17, 2009.

64. There is some parallel between my argument here and use of the word "nudge," and the book by behavioral economists Richard Thaler and Cass Sunstein. *Nudge.* Penguin Books, New York, 2009.

7   Government Intervention

1. Adam Smith. *An Inquiry into the Nature and Causes of the Wealth of Nations.* Methuen, London, 1776, Chapter 2.

2. Joseph Stiglitz. Regulation and Failure. In *New Perspectives on Regulation.* Edited by David Moss and John Cisternino. The Tobin Project, 2009, p. 13.

3. K. Bayliss and B. Fine. *Privatization and Alternative Public Sector Reforms in Sub-Saharan Africa: Delivering on Electricity and Water.* Palgrave Macmillan, London, 2007.

4. Hulya Dagdeviren. Waiting for Miracles: The Commercialisation of Urban Water Services in Zambia. *Development and Change,* 2008, 39(1): 101–121.

5. *Education for All—Global Monitoring Report 2010,* UNESCO, 2010.

6. *Haiti - Social Resilience and State Fragility in Haiti.* The World Bank, Report No. 36069-HT, April 27, 2006.

7. *Education for All—Global Monitoring Report 2010,* UNESCO, 2010.

8. Summit Khanna. India's Economy Must Grow at the Rate of 10%: Pranab Mukherjee. *DNA,* June 17, 2010. Available at: http://www.dnaindia.com/india/report_india-s-economy-must-grow-at-

the-rate-of-10pct-pranab-mukherjee_1397480. [Accessed June 20, 2010.]

9. Amartya Sen. *Development as Freedom.* Anchor Books, New York, 2000.

10. C.K. Prahalad, *The Fortune at the Bottom of the Pyramid,* Wharton School Publishing, New Jersey, 2005, p.67.

11. Nitin Paranjpe, 'Promoting women's economic empowerment,' Case Study, The World Bank Group. Available at http://pslforum. worldbankgroup.org/casestudies/unilever. [Accessed 3 July 2010]

12. Clifford Winston. *Government Failure versus Market Failure.* Brookings Institution Press, Washington, D.C., 2006.

13. E.D. Bo. Regulatory Capture: A Review. *Oxford Review of Economic Policy,* Summer 2006.

14. The Rights Approach. *The Economist,* March 18, 2010.

15. Tea Petrin. Is Entrepreneurship Possible in Public Enterprises?' In *Entrepreneurship Development in Public Enterprises.* Edited by Joseph Prokopenko and Igor Pavlin. International Labor Organization, Geneva, 1981.

16. *Innovation and Entrepreneurship in State and Local Government.* Edited by Michael Harris and Rhonda Kinney, Lexington Books, Oxford, 2003.

17. *Summary of Simplification Plans 2009.* Available at http://www. berr.gov.uk/files/file54013.pdf. [Accessed February 25, 2010.]

18. Jean Dreze and Amartya Sen. *India: Development and Participation.* Oxford University Press, Oxford, 2002.

19. Aneel Karnani. Controversy: The Essence of Strategy. *Business Strategy Review,* 2008, 19(4): 28–34.

20. Gerardo Esquivel, Nora Lustig, and John Scott. A Decade of Falling Inequality in Mexico: Market Forces or State Action. Discussion Paper, United Nations Development Programme, January 2010.

21. Insecticide-Treated Mosquito Nets: A Position Statement. World Health Organization, 2007.

22. Reuben Kyama and Donald McNeil Jr. Distribution of Nets Splits Malaria Fighters. *The New York Times,* October 9, 2007.

23. I discuss the topic of 'social entrepreneurship' in the next chapter.

24. Website: http://www.suite101.com/content/jacqueline-novogratz-and-the-acumen-fund-a210854 [Accessed December 26, 2010]

25. Reuben Kyama and Donald McNeil Jr. Distribution of Nets Splits Malaria Fighters. *The New York Times,* October 9, 2007.
26. Ibid.
27. Net Benefits. *The Economist,* January 31, 2008.
28. Jessica Cohen and Pascaline Dupas. Free Distribution or Cost-sharing? Evidence from A Randomized Malaria Prevention Experiment. *Quarterly Journal of Economics,* 2010, 125(1): 1–45.
29. Reuben Kyama and Donald McNeil Jr. Distribution of Nets Splits Malaria Fighters. *The New York Times,* October 9, 2007.
30. Net Benefits. *The Economist,* January 31, 2008.
31. *World Malaria Report.* World Health Organization, 2009.
32. An approach that Works. Field Note, Water and Sanitation Program, 2007.
33. Impact Assessment of Nirmal Gram Panchayat Puraskar Awarded Panchayats. UNICEF, August 2008.
34. Available at: http://www.adb.org/Documents/Events/2009/World-Toilet-Summit/default.asp. [Accessed June 25, 2010.]
35. Joseph Hanlon, Armando Barrientos, and David Hulme. *Just Give Money to the Poor.* Kumarian Press, Sterling, Virginia, 2010.
36. Tina Rosenberg. A Payoff Out of Poverty. *The New York Times,* December 21, 2008.
37. Give the Poor Money. *The Economist,* June 29, 2010.
38. Joseph Hanlon, Armando Barrientos, and David Hulme. *Just Give Money to the Poor.* Kumarian Press, Sterling, Virginia, 2010.
39. Alan de Brauw and John Hoddinott. Must Conditional Cash Transfer Programs Be Conditioned to Be Effective? The Impact of Conditioning Transfers on School Enrollment in Mexico. Discussion Paper, International Food Policy Research Institute. 2008. Available at: http://www.ifpri.org/pubs/dp/ifpridp00757.asp. [Accessed June 27, 2010.]
40. Ariel Fiszbein and Norbert Schady. *Conditional Cash Transfers.* The World Bank, Washington DC, 2009.
41. Santiago Levy. *Progress Against Poverty: Sustaining Mexico's PROGRESA-Oportunidades Program.* Brookings Institution Press, Washington DC, 2006.
42. Emmanuel Skoufias. PROGRESA and its Impacts on the Welfare of Rural Households in Mexico. Research Report 139, International

Food Policy Research Institute, Washington DC, 2005. Available at: http://www.ifpri.org/sites/default/files/publications/rr139.pdf. [Accessed June 20, 2010.]

43. Gerardo Esquivel, Nora Lustig, and John Scott. A Decade of Falling Inequality in Mexico: Market Forces or State Action. Discussion Paper, United Nations Development Programme, January 2010.

44. Augustin Lapati and Mercedes de la Rocha. Girls, Mothers, and Poverty Reduction in Mexico: Evaluating PROGRESA-Oportunidades. In *The Gender Impact of Liberalization: Towards Embedded Liberalism*. Edited by Shahra Razavi, Routledge, New York, 2009.

45. Tina Rosenberg. A Payoff Out of Poverty. *The New York Times,* December 21, 2008.

46. C.R. Sukumar. Rural Employment Scheme Leads to Labor Shortages, Higher Wages. liveMint.com, August 4, 2008. Available at: http://www.livemint.com/2008/08/04231517/Rural-employment-scheme-leads.html. [Accessed June 27, 2010.]

47. Some of the literature refers to this as the National Rural Employment Guarantee Act (NREGA).

48. Shamika Ravi and Monika Engler. Workfare in Low Income Countries: An Effective Way to Fight Poverty? The Case of India's NREGS. Working Paper, Indian School of Business, July 2009.

49. Jean Dreze and Sowmya Kidambi. Long Road to Employment Guarantee. *The Hindu,* February 8, 2007. Available at: http://www.thehindu.com/2007/08/02/stories/2007080254241300. htm. [Accessed March 20, 2009.]

50. Jean Dreze and Reetika Khera. The Battle for Employment Guarantee. *Frontline*, 26(1), January 3, 2009. Available at: http://www.hindu.com/fline/fl2601/stories/20090116260100400.htm. [Accessed June 27, 2010.]

51. Jean Dreze, Reetika Khera, and Siddhartha. Corruption in NREGA: Myths and Reality. *The Hindu,* January 22, 2008. Available at: http://www.hindu.com/2008/01/22/stories/2008012254901000. htm. [Accessed June 27, 2010.]

52. Jean Dreze and Reetika Khera. The Battle for Employment Guarantee. *Frontline*, 26(1), January 3, 2009. Available at: http://www.hindu.com/fline/fl2601/stories/20090116260100400.htm. [Accessed June 27, 2010.]

53. Mihir Shah and Pramathesh Ambasta. NREGA: Andhra Pradesh Shows the Way. *The Hindu*, September 8, 2008.
54. Rajeev Bhargava. Indian Democracy and Well-being: Employment as a Right. *Public Culture*, 2006, 18(3), 2006.
55. *NREGA Reforms Building Rural India, First Annual Report of the Consortium of Civil Society Organizations on NREGA. 2008–09,* August, 2009.

8 Civil Society

1. Lester Salamon, S. Wojciech Sokolowski, and Regina L.ist, *Global Civil Society.* Center for Civil Society Studies. The Johns Hopkins University, 2003.
2. Alex Nicholls. "Introduction" in *Social Entrepreneurship.* Edited by Alex Nicholls. Oxford University Press, 2006, pp. 1–35, pages 8–9.
3. Peter Drucker. *Innovation and Entrepreneurship.* Harper & Row, New York, 1985.
4. James A. Phills, K. Deiglmeier, and D.T. Miller. 'Rediscovering Social Innovation. *Stanford Social Innovation Review*, Fall 2008, pp. 34–43, page 36.
5. Center for Advancement of Social Entrepreneurship, *Developing the Field of Social Entrepreneurship.* Duke University, 2008.
6. Lester Salamon, S. Wojciech Sokolowski, and Regina List. *Global Civil Society.* Center for Civil Society Studies, The Johns Hopkins University, 2003.
7. World Development Indicators. The World Bank.
8. International Food Policy Research Institute. *Global Hunger Index,* 2009.
9. David Ruff. India's Malnutrition Dilemma. *The New York Times,* October 8, 2009.
10. See http://www.righttofoodindia.org/. [Accessed February 3. 2010.]
11. Stephanie Strom. As Profit and Charity Mix, Both May Lose. *International Herald Tribune,* October 27, 2010.
12. 'Building a Public-Private Partnership to Transfer Technology to a Life-saving Malaria Prevention Tool in Africa. Case study, World Economic Forum. Available at: http://www.acumenfund.org/

uploads/assets/documents/A%20to%20Z%20Private-Public%20 Partnership%20Study%20-%20Global%20Health%20 Initiative_R1udShKh.pdf [Accessed July 5, 2010.]

13. John Snow. The Main Obstacle to the Eradication of Malaria Lies within Africa Itself. *The Guardian*, January 3, 2006.

14. It is possible to argue that Acumen's funding had a different positive impact of creating jobs in Tanzania. While that might be true, it is useful to separate that discussion from evaluating the impact on eradicating malaria.

15. Julie Thekkudan and Rajesh Tandon, Women's Livelihoods, Global Markets and Citizenship. Working Paper 336, Institute for Development Studies, University of Sussex, October 2009.

16. Mihir Shah. Employment Guarantee, Civil Society, and Indian Democracy. *Economic and Political Weekly*, November 7, 2007.

17. Neera Burra. Transparency and Accountability in Employment Programmes: The Case of NREGA in Andhra Pradesh. Available at: http://www.solutionexchange-un.net.in/NREGA/documents/ Transparency_accountability.doc. [Accessed July 5, 2010.]

18. This case study draws heavily on an earlier paper: Aneel Karnani, Bernard Garrette, Jordan Kassalow and Moses Lee, Better Vision for the Poor. Working Paper, Ross School of Business, University of Michigan, March 2010.

19. Resnikoff, Pascolini, Mariotti, and Pokharel. Global Magnitude of Visual Impairment Caused by Uncorrected Refractive Errors in 2004. Bulletin of the World Health Organization. January 2008; Holden, Frick, et al. Global Vision Impairment Due to Uncorrected Presbyopia. *Ophthalmology*. 2008,. 126(12).

20. See http://www.vdw.ox.ac.uk/index.htm. [Accessed January 23, 2010.]

21. P.K. Nirmalan, S. Krishnaiah, et al. A Population-Based Assessment of Presbyopia in the State of Andhra Pradesh: The Andhra Pradesh Eye Disease Study. *Investigative Ophthalmology & Visual Science*, June 2006.

22. Patel, I. and S. West. Presbyopia: Prevalence, Impact, and Interventions. *Community Eye Health Journal,* 2007, 20(63): 40–41.

23. Patel, I. and S. West. Presbyopia: Prevalence, Impact, and Interventions. *Community Eye Health Journal,* 2007, 20(63): 40–41.

24. Ramke, J., R. du Toil, A. Palagyi, et al. Correction of Refractive Error and Presbyopia in Timor-Leste. *British Journal of Ophthalmology,* 2007, 91(7): 860–866.

25. Lisa Keay, et al. A Randomized Clinical Trial to Evaluate Ready-Made Spectacles in an Adult Population in India. *International Journal of Epidemiology,* 2010, February, 1–12.

26. See http://www.vdw.ox.ac.uk/theneed.htm. [Accessed January 21, 2010.]

27. Katherine Harmon. Designer Focuses on Marketing Adjustable Eyeglasses at $1 a Pair. *Scientific American,* February 24, 2009.

28. VisionSpring: 2008 Growth Capital Offering. VisionSpring. 9 June 2008.

29. Interview with Dr. Michael Lipton, Optometrist and Assistant Professor, the University of Michigan. June 24, 2009 ; R. Maini, J. Keeffe, L.A. Weih, et al. Correction of Refractive Error in the Victoria Population: The Feasibility of "Off the Shelf" Spectacles. *British Journal of Ophthalmology,* 2001, 85, 1283–1286.

30. A drawback of ready-made glasses is that they have the same prescription strength in both lenses.

31. Interview with Dr. Michael Lipton, Optometrist and Assistant Professor, the University of Michigan. June 24, 2009.

32. Lisa Keay, et al. A Randomized Clinical Trial to Evaluate Ready-Made Spectacles in an Adult Population in India. *International Journal of Epidemiology,* 2010, February, 1–12.

33. Yangfa Zeng, et al. A Randomized, Clinical Trial Evaluating Ready-Made and Custom Spectacles Delivered Via a School-based Screening Program in China. *Ophthalmology,* 2009, 116, 1839–1845.

9 *Rage Leading to Action*

1. *The State of the World's Children 2008,* UNICEF, New York, 2007.

2. *The Progress of Nations 2000,* UNICEF, New York, 2000.

Index

CPSIA information can be obtained
at www.ICGtesting.com
Printed in the USA
LVHW08*0342300818
588630LV00011B/201/P

9 780230 105874